LEARN
Adobe Dreamweaver CC
for Web Authoring

SECOND EDITION

Adobe Certified Associate Exam Preparation

Mark DuBois
with Rob Schwartz
and Kim Cavanaugh

Adobe

LEARN ADOBE DREAMWEAVER CC FOR WEB AUTHORING, SECOND EDITION
ADOBE CERTIFIED ASSOCIATE EXAM PREPARATION
Mark DuBois
with Rob Schwartz and Kim Cavanaugh

Copyright © 2019 by Pearson Education, Inc. or its affiliates. All Rights Reserved.

Adobe Press books is an imprint of Pearson Education, Inc.

For the latest on Adobe Press books, go to www.adobepress.com.

To report errors, please send a note to errata@peachpit.com. For information regarding permissions, request forms and the appropriate contacts within the Pearson Education Global Rights & Permissions department, please visit www.pearsoned.com/permissions/.

Adobe Press Editor: Laura Norman
Development Editor: Robyn G Thomas
Technical Reviewer: Candyce Mairs
Senior Production Editor: Tracey Croom
Copyeditor: Scout Festa
Proofreader: Elizabeth Welch
Compositor: Kim Scott, Bumpy Design
Indexer: James Minkin
Cover & Interior Design: Mimi Heft
Cover Illustration: Mrs. Opossum/ShutterStock

ISBN-13: 978-0-13-489265-8
ISBN 10:   0-13-489265-8

1 18

To my wife, Jeri,
you have always been there for me. I could not have
done so many things without your continued help and support.

To Ben and Lindsay,
I am proud of you and all your accomplishments.

And, to Keenan, Gavin, and Owen,
I am glimpsing the future through your eyes.
Never stop following your dreams.

Acknowledgments

Thanks to Rob Schwartz for having the vision and persistence to get this series of books and videos off the ground.

To Chris Flick, for all the tremendous artwork and the flavor that his cartoons brought to the hands-on projects in this book.

To my wife, Jeri, for her help in checking my work and correcting my numerous typos.

To the great team at Adobe Press, Victor Gavenda, Candyce Mairs, Scout Festa, Tracey Croom, Liz Welch, and especially Robyn Thomas, for keeping this complicated project on time and for keeping the author on task.

To all of the awesome educators in the Adobe Education Leaders program. You continue to inspire me with your passion and dedication to your craft. You are making a difference in our world.

About the Authors

Mark DuBois has been developing web pages since 1992 (over a quarter century). He built his first commercial website in 1995. He has been teaching college and adult learners for over two decades and recently retired as a full professor at an Illinois community college. He created the first accredited A.A.S. degree in web systems in the world, along with the first accredited certificate in Rich Internet Application development. Mark is executive director of the World Organization of Webmasters (WebProfessionals.org) and has run an annual national web design competition for the past 15 years (under the auspices of SkillsUSA for both secondary and postsecondary schools [separate contests]). He also helps run international web design and development competitions (most recently in Abu Dhabi, UAE, under the auspices of WorldSkills). Among his many accomplishments, Mark was co-chair of the education task force of the Web Standards Project. He has been an Adobe Education Leader since 2008 (and was one of the first three inducted into this program from higher education). Mark is also a certified Adobe Education Trainer and periodically offers a number of webinars on various topics related to the World Wide Web and eLearning.

Rob Schwartz (author of Chapters 8 and 9) is an award-winning educator with 20 years of experience in technical education classrooms. Rob holds several Adobe Certified Associate certifications, and is also an Adobe Certified Instructor. As an Adobe Education Leader, Rob won the prestigious Impact Award from Adobe, and in 2010 Rob was the first Worldwide winner of the Certiport Adobe Certified Associate Championship. Find out more about Rob at his online curriculum website at brainbuffet.com.

Kim Cavanaugh taught and wrote about web, graphic, and interactive design for over 18 years. With four books, three interactive online courses, and over two hundred tutorials on Adobe Dreamweaver, Fireworks, WordPress, and others to his credit, Kim opened new opportunities to technology newcomers by making his material easy to follow yet technically rich and challenging.

Kim was a founding board member of the Adobe Education Leaders program and a certified Adobe Education Trainer, and he taught classes on programming and design to students at every level from middle school to college. During the day, Kim was the instructional webmaster at one of the largest school districts in the US.

In memoriam: Kim Cavanaugh (d. April, 2018). We are all saddened by the recent death of Kim. He was a respected colleague and friend. Kim touched the lives of many individuals in various ways. He will be missed.

Contents

Getting Started

Book Learning Objectives

- Learn the inner workings of the World Wide Web and how web content is published and delivered.

- Learn the key terms and common language of web developers.

- Learn to use Adobe Dreamweaver to create web pages and websites.

- Understand and write HTML using Dreamweaver's tools to visualize, write, edit, and test your web pages.

- Use modern web standards to lay out web pages and control their appearance with Cascading Style Sheets (CSS) and make them accessible for all visitors to your site.

- Become proficient with the Dreamweaver interface and the tools used to insert and format text, hyperlinks, images, tables, and video files.

- Use Dreamweaver to design web pages that look and work great on computers, tablets, and smartphones and that are accessible to all visitors.

- Publish and update web pages to the World Wide Web.

- Apply principles of design that lead to attractive, engaging, and effective user experiences for all visitors.

- Learn how to work with clients to develop project plans that lead to successful web projects.

Welcome to *Learn Adobe Dreamweaver CC for Web Authoring, Second Edition*! We use a combination of text and video to help you learn the basics of web programming with Adobe Dreamweaver CC along with other skills that you will need to get your first job in web design. Adobe Dreamweaver CC is a powerful program for working with the HTML, CSS, and JavaScript code that make up the modern web experience. Dreamweaver is widely used within the web design industry and by many company web production teams to manage website resources, taking advantage of its dynamic authoring environment to create great user experiences for their customers.

About This Book and Video

Learn Adobe Dreamweaver CC for Web Authoring was created by a team of expert instructors, writers, and editors with decades of experience in helping beginning learners get their start with the cool creative tools from Adobe Systems. Our aim is not only to teach you the basics of the practice of web page design with Dreamweaver, but to give you an introduction to the associated skills (like design principles and project management) that you'll need for your first job.

We've built the training around the objectives for the Web Authoring Using Adobe Dreamweaver CC (2018) Adobe Certified Associate (ACA) Exam, and if you master the topics covered in this book and videos, you'll be in good shape to take the exam. But even if certification isn't your goal, you'll still find that this training will give you an excellent foundation for your future work in web design. To that end, we've structured the material in the order that makes most sense for beginning learners (as determined by experienced classroom teachers), rather than following the more arbitrary grouping of topics in the ACA objectives.

To aid you in your quest, we've created a unique learning system that uses video and text in partnership. You'll experience this partnership in action in the Web Edition, which lives on your Account page at peachpit.com. The Web Edition contains 10 hours of video—the heart of the training—embedded in an online ebook that supports the video training and provides background material. The ebook material is also available separately for offline reading as a printed book or as an ebook in a variety of formats. The Web Edition also includes hundreds of interactive review questions you can use to evaluate your progress. Purchase of the book in any format entitles you to free access to the Web Edition (instructions for accessing it follow later in this section).

Most chapters provide step-by-step instructions for creating a specific project or learning a specific technique. Many chapters include several optional tasks that let you further explore the features you've already learned. Two valuable chapters acquaint you with other skills and concepts that you'll come to depend on as you use the software in your everyday work. Here is where you'll find coverage of Domains 1 and 2 of the ACA objectives, which don't specifically relate to features of Dreamweaver but are important components of the complete skill set that the ACA exam seeks to evaluate. Because these chapters aren't part of the path to learning Dreamweaver itself, they aren't included in the printed book. They're included in the ebook editions and in the online Web Edition (to access the free Web Edition, see pages xii–xiii).

Each chapter opens with two lists of objectives. One list lays out the learning objectives: the specific tasks you'll learn in the chapter. The second list shows the ACA exam objectives that are covered in the chapter. A table at the end of the book guides you to coverage of all the exam objectives in the book or video.

Conventions Used in this Book

This book uses several elements styled in ways to help you as you work through the projects.

▶ **Video 9.5** *About Copyright*

Links to videos that cover the topics in depth appear in the margins.

Text that you should enter appears in bold, such as:

In the Link field in the Property inspector, type **http://www.capesnbabes.com**.

Terms that are defined in the glossary appear in bold and in color, such as:

The web font that's used in the header of the page is just what the client is looking for. That's a great thing.

★ *ACA Objective 2.1*

The ACA objectives covered in the chapters are called out in the margins beside the sections that address them.

Notes give additional information about a topic. The information they contain is not essential to accomplishing a task but provide a more in-depth understanding of the topic:

NOTE

The default behavior for background images is to tile across and down the container where they are set.

Working in Dreamweaver means you'll be working with code. We have used several conventions to make working with the code in this book easier to follow and understand.

In many instructions, you will be required to enter HTML code, CSS rules, and properties and other code-based markup. To distinguish the markup from the instructional text, the entries will be styled with a code font, like this:

Examine the code `<h1>Heading goes here</h1>`.

In instances where you must enter the markup yourself, the entry will be formatted in bold, like this:

Type the following code: **`<h1>Heading goes here</h1>`**.

Within the body of descriptions and exercise instructions, elements may be referenced by name or by class or ID attribute. When an element is identified by its tag name, it will appear as `<h1>` or `h1`. When referenced by its class attribute, the name will appear with a leading period (`.`) in code font, like this: `.content` or `.sidebar1`. References to elements by their ID attribute will appear with a leading hash (#) and in a code font, like this: `#top`. This practice matches the way these elements appear in the Tag selector interface in Dreamweaver.

OPERATING SYSTEM DIFFERENCES

In most cases, Dreamweaver CC works the same in both Windows and macOS. Minor differences exist between the two versions, mostly due to platform-specific issues. Most of these are simply differences in keyboard shortcuts, how dialogs are displayed, and how buttons are named. In most cases, screenshots were made in the Windows version of Dreamweaver and may appear somewhat differently on your own screen.

Where specific commands differ, they are noted within the text. Windows commands are listed first, followed by the macOS equivalent, such as Ctrl+C/ Command+C. In general, the Windows Ctrl key is equivalent to the Command (or Cmd) key in macOS, and the Windows Alt key is equivalent to the Option (or Opt) key in macOS.

As chapters advance, instructions may be truncated or shortened to save space, with the assumption that you picked up the essential concepts earlier in the chapter. For example, at the beginning of a chapter you may be instructed to "press Ctrl+C/ Command+C." Later, you may be told to "copy" text or a code element. These should be considered identical instructions.

If you find you have difficulties in any particular task, review earlier steps or exercises in that chapter. In some cases when an exercise is based on concepts covered earlier, you will be referred back to the specific chapter.

Installing the Software

Before you begin using *Learn Adobe Dreamweaver CC for Web Authoring*, make sure that your system is set up correctly and that you've installed the proper software and hardware. This material is based on the original 2018 release of Adobe Dreamweaver CC (version 18.1) and is designed to cover the objectives of the Adobe Certified Associate Exam for that version of the software.

The Adobe Dreamweaver CC software is not included with this book; it is available only with an Adobe Creative Cloud membership, which you must purchase or which must be supplied by your school or another organization. In addition to Adobe Dreamweaver CC, some lessons in this book have steps that can be performed with Adobe Photoshop. You must install this application from Adobe Creative Cloud onto your computer. Follow the instructions provided at *helpx.adobe.com/creative-cloud/help/download-install-app.html*.

ADOBE CREATIVE CLOUD DESKTOP APP

In addition to Adobe Dreamweaver CC, some extension activities suggested in the text require the Adobe Creative Cloud desktop application, which provides a central location for managing dozens of apps and services that are included in a Creative Cloud membership. Although the central lessons in this book and the videos do not require a Creative Cloud subscription, you should explore the ways the Creative Cloud desktop application can be used to sync and share files, manage fonts, access libraries of stock photography and design assets, and showcase and discover creative work in the design community.

The Creative Cloud desktop application is installed automatically when you download your first Creative Cloud product. If you have Adobe Application Manager installed, it auto-updates to the Creative Cloud desktop application.

If the Creative Cloud desktop application is not installed on your computer, you can download it from the Download Creative Cloud page on the Adobe website (*creative.adobe.com/products/creative-cloud*) or from the Adobe Creative Cloud desktop apps page (*adobe.com/creativecloud/catalog/desktop.html*). If you are using software on classroom machines, be sure to check with your instructor before making any changes to the installed software or system configuration.

CHECKING FOR UPDATES

Adobe periodically provides updates to software. You can easily obtain these updates through Creative Cloud. If these updates include new features that affect the content of this training or the objectives of the ACA exam in any way, we will post updated material to peachpit.com.

Accessing the Free Web Edition and Lesson Files

Your purchase of this book in any format includes access to the corresponding Web Edition hosted on peachpit.com. The Web Edition contains the complete text of the book augmented with hours of video and interactive quizzes.

To work through the projects in this product, you will first need to download the lesson files from peachpit.com. You can download the files for individual lessons or download them all in a single file.

If you purchased an ebook from peachpit.com or adobepress.com, the Web Edition and files will automatically appear on your Account page. The Web Edition will be on the Digital Purchases tab, and the files will be on the Registered Products tab (see step 5 below).

If you purchased an ebook from a different vendor or you bought a print book, you must register your purchase on peachpit.com:

1   Go to *www.peachpit.com/register.*

2   Sign in or create a new account.

3   Enter the ISBN: **9780134892658**.

4   Answer the questions as proof of purchase.

5   The Web Edition will appear under the Digital Purchases tab on your Account page. Click the Launch link to access the product.

    The lesson files can be accessed through the Registered Products tab on your Account page.

6   Click the Access Bonus Content link below the title of your product to proceed to the download page. Click the lesson file links to download them to your computer.

Additional Resources

Learn Adobe Dreamweaver CC for Web Authoring is not meant to replace the documentation that comes with the program or to be a comprehensive reference for every feature. For comprehensive information about program features and tutorials, refer to these resources:

Adobe Dreamweaver Learn & Support: *helpx.adobe.com/dreamweaver* is where you can find and browse Help and Support content on Adobe.com. Adobe Dreamweaver Help and Adobe Dreamweaver Support Center are accessible from the Help menu in Dreamweaver. Help is also available as a printable PDF document. Download the document at *helpx.adobe.com/pdf/dreamweaver_reference.pdf.*

Adobe Forums: *forums.adobe.com/community/dreamweaver* lets you tap into peer-to-peer discussions, questions, and answers on Adobe products.

Adobe Dreamweaver CC product home page: *adobe.com/products/dreamweaver* provides information about new features and intuitive ways to create responsive web page layouts that display beautifully on any screen.

Adobe Add-ons: *creative.adobe.com/addons* is a central resource for finding tools, services, extensions, code samples, and more to supplement and extend your Adobe products.

Resources for educators: *adobe.com/education* and *edex.adobe.com* offer a treasure trove of information for instructors who teach classes on Adobe software at all levels.

Adobe Certification

The Adobe training and certification programs are designed to help designers and other creative professionals improve and promote their product-proficiency skills. Adobe Certified Associate (ACA) is an industry-recognized credential that demonstrates proficiency in Adobe digital skills. Whether you're just starting out in your career, looking to switch jobs, or interested in preparing for success in the job market, the Adobe Certified Associate program is for you! For more information, visit *edex.adobe.com/aca*.

Resetting the Preferences to Their Default Settings

Dreamweaver lets you determine how the program looks and behaves (like tool settings and the default unit of measurement) using the extensive options in Edit > Preferences (Windows) or Dreamweaver CC > Preferences (macOS). To ensure that the preferences and default settings of your Adobe Dreamweaver CC program match those used in this book, you can reset your preference settings to their defaults. If you are using software installed on computers in a classroom, don't make any changes to the system configuration without first checking with your instructor.

To reset your preferences to their default settings, follow these steps:

1 Quit Adobe Dreamweaver.

2 Hold down the key combination Windows key+Alt+Shift (Windows) or Command+Option+Shift (macOS), and launch Dreamweaver.

3 Continue to hold down the keys until the Reset Preferences dialog appears.

4 In the Reset Preferences dialog, click Yes.

The file containing your preferences will be deleted.

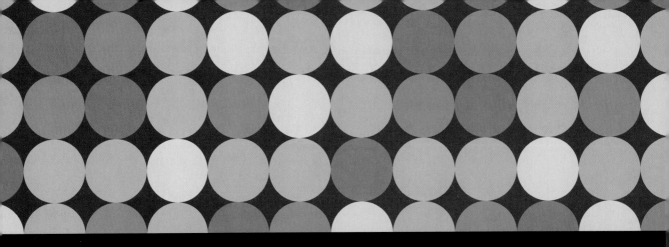

CHAPTER OBJECTIVES

Chapter Learning Objectives

- Understand basic terminology of the World Wide Web and how web pages are delivered.

- Learn how HTML, Cascading Style Sheets (CSS), media, and other technologies are used for creating modern web pages.

- Understand the basic structure of web pages and how content is contained in HTML tags, and understand the common tags found within a web page.

- Learn how web designers use Dreamweaver to visualize and modify their designs.

- Define a new Dreamweaver website.

- Use Dreamweaver to modify basic elements of a web page, such as text, links, images, and page title.

Chapter ACA Objectives

For full descriptions of objectives, see the table on pages 258–264.

DOMAIN 1.0
WORKING IN THE WEB INDUSTRY
1.4

DOMAIN 4.0
WORKING WITH CODE TO CREATE AND MODIFY CONTENT
4.1, 4.2, 4.3

CHAPTER 1

Welcome to the World Wide Web

Chances are pretty good that before you ever got to school or work this morning you were already using the Internet. And why not! Whether it is using social media, playing games, or checking the weather (or our home devices connecting on our behalf), we have come to rely on the Internet as a core infrastructure. It's estimated that over *four billion* people use the Internet in some way every day. In the United States, roughly 95 percent of people have some access to the Internet.

Behind the scenes, millions of individuals are making it possible for us to stay connected, find information, or be entertained and educated through the magic of the Internet. But of course, it isn't all magic and cat videos. The modern Internet experience is built on a vast complex of specialized computers, an incredible number of cables, and a vast number of data packets flying through the air from cellphone towers and Wi-Fi hotspots.

Now you're about to learn how to *become* one of those people. Looking ahead, you are going to learn how to use Adobe Dreamweaver CC to design, publish, and maintain web pages and web applications so you can become one of the creators of today's Internet experience through the code you write and the user experiences you design. The skills you'll develop and the tools you'll learn to use will put you in the elite company of the webmasters, code warriors, and creative professionals who make the Internet what it is today, and what it just might become in the future.

How awesome is that?

World Wide What?

If you were born after 1994 you've never known a world without the Internet. It was in that year that the very first computer program appeared that allowed the average person to read text *and* view images at the same time. Amazing, right?

The term *browser* was coined to describe a program that allowed one computer to view specially coded documents that could be found on the worldwide *inter-*connected *network* of computers. The network had already been around for nearly 25 years, but the difference was that instead of using that network just for sharing scientific data and reference materials, these new programs gave the average person access to information and entertainment that was as close as the new computers that were making their way into their homes. Once it became easy for consumers to discover what was possible on this network, the Internet became part of our shared culture and our daily lives.

The Internet of All Things

As you become a web designer and not just a web consumer, you'll need to know what's happening behind the scenes when you're checking out the latest viral video or searching for some information. That means knowing some of the basic terms that describe how the Internet works.

Most people use the terms Internet and World Wide Web (aka the web) as if they were the same thing, but in fact there is a difference. The Internet includes *all* the ways that computers can communicate with each other. That includes email, the ability to transfer files from one computer to another, message boards, online games, cloud storage, and file sharing programs (among other technologies). The Internet also allows you to view documents that are written especially for view-ing by humans on your desktop computers, tablets, and smartphones. That part of the Internet that lets you view those pages and navigate from one page to another using hyperlinks is known as the World Wide Web.

Now before we get too far, you should always keep in mind that computers are fun-damentally just machines. Computers can perform calculations and comparisons at blistering speeds. That speed may make them look "smart," but they do only what they are told. Telling a computer to do something involves code (instructions) at almost every level. From the moment the computer is switched on to the moment it's actually doing something useful, some sort of code is involved.

Not only is there code, but when it comes to having one computer connect and communicate with another there also has to be an agreement on the language that will be spoken. Without an agreement on the protocol that will be used to exchange information, your computer would be just as lost as you would be if you were dropped into an alien world where no one spoke your language. In fact, it was the invention of standard methods for one computer to send and receive information that really made the Internet and the web possible.

YOUR FIRST STEPS ON AN ALIEN PLANET

Imagine you've been dropped onto an alien planet (**Figure 1.1**) and you're all set to meet up with the local population of friendly creatures. How will you communicate with them? Maybe they don't even use a spoken language, and you have to learn to talk with them by combining clicks and whistles and hand gestures—except they have four hands and a tail!

The first steps in learning to code are a lot like that.

Figure 1.1 You have to learn how to communicate before you can begin to share information in an alien language.

MAKING CONNECTIONS

You might say that the invention of Hypertext Transfer Protocol (HTTP) truly marked the beginning of the web as we know it. You've no doubt seen a web address written like this: *http://www.adobe.com*. Back in the olden days you would actually have to *tell* someone to visit a website by sounding it all out to them. "Go to aich tee tee pea colon slash slash dubyou dubyou dubyou dot adobe dot com." Seems ridiculous now, right?

But those letters and symbols are really important to the computers on the network. When someone types that into the address bar of their web browser or clicks a link, it's like saying, "Hey, I'd like to see a document that you have on your computer over here on my computer please." Since your web browser is in agreement on the

▶ Video 1.1 *How the World Wide Web Works*

language that will be used for the connection to a remote computer, the two can begin to communicate as your computer (the client) receives information from a computer on the network (the server).

In order for these handshakes to take place between client and server, the client must identify itself and special devices must know how to route your request to the right server that houses the web page you want to see. The Internet Protocol (IP) was established to get that done. Each and every computer on the web is identified with an IP address—a combination of numerals that is unique to every single desktop, tablet, or phone that wishes to use the network. An IP address looks like this: 2601:242:8200:72:19dc:1052:3cdc:61d (in older books, you may see addresses like 192.0.2.0, but that numbering scheme allowed for only 4,294,967,296 possible addresses, and we have now exhausted those; an alternate numbering scheme has been adopted). This current numbering scheme allows for up to 340,282,366,920,938,463,463,374,607,431,768,211,456 possible addresses (so we should have enough for quite some time).

TIP

If you ever do plan to use an address like http:// [2601:242:8200:72:19dc: 1052:3cdc:61d] in your browser, make certain you enclose it in square brackets—that is the standard.

As you can imagine, it would be pretty hard to remember that your favorite website could be found at http://[2601:242:8200:72:19dc:1052:3cdc:61d], so a system was created that allowed for different *names* to be assigned to computers that were serving up web pages to clients. This system of domain names is what makes it possible for individuals, companies, and government agencies to register a particular name for their exclusive use. And so, when you visit *Adobe.com* or *Microsoft.com* or any other website, the name that is used in your request is translated by a domain name server, a special computer on the network that works like a traffic cop, directing the client's request to the correct IP address (**Figure 1.2**).

Figure 1.2 Diagram of Internet connections

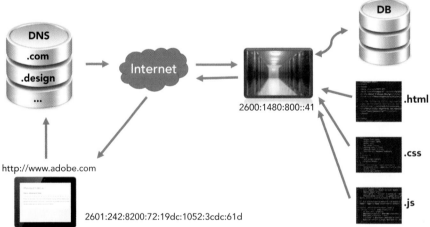

Whew! And all *that* happens before you ever see anything on your computer screen or phone!

Video 1.2 How the Internet works

LEVEL UP!

How amazing is the system that connects computers and delivers web pages? Check out this video to learn more about this network of networks.

SERVING UP THE GOODIES

Now that you understand the importance of having a common language so computers can speak to each other and make network connections, let's take a look at the second set of standards that allow web pages to be delivered and displayed.

ACA Objective 4.1

Learning to write in code is just like learning a foreign language. You have to understand the rules that have been established that let web browsers communicate with servers to display the text and images and links that make up a web page. These rules are known as the syntax of the coding language you're using.

No doubt you've heard the term HTML tossed around, and you probably have a basic understanding that it has something to do with web pages. And you'd be right! Hypertext Markup Language (HTML) is the basic language that web servers and web browsers use to describe how a web page should be delivered, how the content is structured, and how it should behave.

But HTML is far from the only player needed on the team of technologies that make web pages possible. Although HTML provides the order and structure to a page, the styling of the page—the colors that are used, the position of HTML blocks on the page, the size of text and images, and much more—are controlled by another kind of code, known as Cascading Style Sheets (CSS). Modern web pages use CSS to determine just how the structured elements found in the HTML are displayed by the browser. This combination of structure (HTML) and style (CSS) is what makes it possible for web pages to have almost limitless designs.

The third and final set of code that gets poured into many (if not most) web pages is JavaScript. JavaScript is the programming language of the web that adds interactivity to web pages and turns them into more than just a lifeless document. For example, when you click the Like or Share button on a social networking site, it's JavaScript that allows your browser to transmit back to the network just how much you love the latest video your friend has shared. Some animations and sounds, the opening of new windows, and resizing a web page from full screen to phone size are handled by JavaScript.

Think of it this way:

- HTML is used to structure the content on a web page.
- CSS is used to control how the content is displayed by the browser.
- JavaScript is used to control most behaviors the visitor experiences on a web page.

Whoa! That's a lot of stuff to know, right? Two different languages *plus* scripting? But that's where Dreamweaver is going to come to the rescue. Dreamweaver is a visual editor that allows you to write the code that displays your page with the right styling and interactive elements and provides all the tools you need to create entire websites, full of beautifully styled pages that are responsive to the people who view them.

TAG: YOU'RE IT

▶ *Video 1.3*
Tag: You're It

So. You've cranked up your favorite web browser. Whether you're using Chrome, Safari, Edge, or Firefox—or even if you opened a web-enabled app on your phone—you know that a transaction is taking place across the web. Your request is being routed to the right web server that contains a web page written in HTML. Now what?

Your browser begins receiving the content of the web page in a very particular way. Web pages are organized using the Document Object Model, or DOM. This is how your computer and browser interact with a web page. The DOM is just a programmer's way of saying that there should be a standard order to the parts that make up a web page. In fact, we validate our pages using this standard model. Web pages need

- A document type. This should be the first line of content in the web page. For HTML5 documents, it is simply coded as `<!doctype html>`.
- An area of the page where special instructions for the browser are located but are not displayed on the page.
- Content of the page that can be viewed by humans.

Each area of a web page is described using HTML tags. Tags are the special descriptors that tell the browser how to decipher what's inside them. Tags are enclosed in angle brackets, such as `<thetagname>`, and are (almost always) written in pairs.

The very first tag that a web browser needs to see (after the DOCTYPE mentioned above) to display a web page is the HTML tag, written like this:

```
<html> </html>
```

Notice that the second tag has an added forward slash (/) character. This tells the browser that this is the end of the HTML container. Seeing the `</html>` tag tells the browser that it has reached the end of the code for the page.

Now let's see the combination of the DOM and tags in action. Here is all the code a browser needs to display a web page with the text "Hey! How are you doing?"

```
<!doctype html>
<html>
<head>
<title>How are you doing?</title>
</head>
<body>
<h1>Hey!</h1>
<p>How are you doing?</p>
</body>
</html>
```

LEVEL UP!

You can make your very own web page using the example HTML code.

1 Open a text editor (such as Notepad on Windows or TextWrangler on a Mac—*do not* use a tool such as Microsoft Word, which introduces too much hidden code).

2 Type the code that you see in the example.

3 Save the file to your computer with the file extension set to **.html**, and then open the file in your browser.

Voilà! Your first web page! I named mine **hey.html** and then pressed Ctrl+O (Command+O) in a browser window and navigated to the page to open it.

When you look back at the essential building blocks of every web page, you can see how HTML tags are used to describe them.

This really simple web page includes

- The document type defined followed with the `<html> </html>` tags. These tags enclose the entire page. They also indicate the primary language of the page with the `lang` attribute (for example `lang="en"`).

- The hidden area of the page—the head—where instructions to the browser are hidden. The head of the page is enclosed in `<head> </head>` tags.

  Inside the `<head>` tags, you see the `<title>` tag with the title of the web page that appears in the tab at the top of the browser (assuming you have multiple tabs open). The title doesn't actually show *on* the page, but it's what you would see in a Google search or if you were to bookmark the page.

- The contents of the page that can be viewed by humans. The visible parts of a web page are enclosed in the `<body> </body>` tags.

But what about the tags and content *inside* the body tags? What's with the `<h1>` and `<p>` tags?

Did you guess that the `<h1>` is a heading? And that the `<p>` tag defines the content of a paragraph? Pat yourself on the back if you did!

HTML is intended to be *pretty* easy to understand with tags that make sense to both the humans who write them and the programs (browsers) that interpret them. As you begin using Dreamweaver, you'll see how changes you make visually are written into the instructions that the computer will read.

For now, what you should take away from this overview is the understanding of how web pages are structured and coded at the basic level. Now let's see how to make them pretty!

LEVEL UP: HTML

The World Wide Web Consortium (W3C) is the international authority on web standards, and it is the organization that maintains all references on how HTML and CSS should be used by web browsers and web designers. You can find an A to Z listing of all HTML tags that are currently in use on the Mozilla Developer Network HTML Reference Page at *developer.mozilla.org/en-US/docs/Web/HTML/Element*.

This reference also includes a description of how the tags are used and whether they are currently approved, and it lists those that are no longer recommended (the technical term for these is deprecated).

TIME TO DRESS THINGS UP

When you look at **Figure 1.3** (which is the result of the HTML code you saw earlier), you see a web page that has just the very basics in place. A heading and a little text. You've probably not seen a page like that in the real world, and if you did you probably didn't look at it for long!

 **Video 1.4** *Let's Get Stylish*

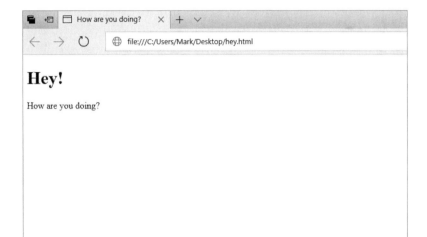

Figure 1.3 Simple web pages can be created with very little HTML.

Real web pages are made up of many more tags that contain all *kinds* of information. Some of them are pretty easy to figure out. The `<img>` tag, for instance, is for inserting an image. Need a table for tabular data? The `<table>` tag will see to that. In the latest version of the HTML specifications, known as HTML5, there are even more tags that provide new methods for putting content on the page. Tags like `<section>` and `<article>` and `<summary>` make sense to humans and browsers alike.

Some tags are a little more obscure. For example, when you want to write a hyperlink you enclose it in an `<a>` tag. One of the most common tags you'll learn to use is the `<div>` tag, used to divide the page into different blocks that can be positioned and styled as needed.

HTML tags aren't limited to simply telling a browser that "This is a paragraph" or "This is an image." Good thing! Without the ability to specify more information within a tag, web pages would look just like the boring example you saw in Figure 1.3.

Tags are modified by adding an attribute. This is done by including extra instructions right within the angle brackets of the first tag in a pair.

TIP

If you're writing this in another language, change the `lang` *attribute on the HTML tag to indicate your language (for example* `lang="es"` *for Spanish or* `lang="fr"` *for French).*

It is likely that pages we write will be viewed by others throughout the world. Therefore, one of the common attributes we should include is the language the page has been written in. Assuming you live in the United States, you likely use English. Therefore, we code the language as an attribute for the HTML tag:

```
<html lang="en">
```

The following code block tells the browser that the text within the paragraph has been assigned a class named `mission`:

```
<p class="mission">Our mission is to provide you with
→ excellent service. </p>
```

In this case, the `class` attribute allows the page's designer to include styling information using a style that is written to describe how the text should look. More on styling in a minute. Patience, grasshopper!

Some attributes are optional, as in the example above, and some are mandatory. The `<a>` tag that defines a link, for instance, isn't much good without the attribute that tells the browser the address of the link. Similarly, an image tag needs the location where the image can be found in order for the browser to get the image and display it in the page. Notice how the attributes are written in the following examples:

```
<a href="http://adobe.com">Visit Adobe!</a>
<img src="myphoto.jpg" alt="Photo of me at the beach"
→ style="width:250px; height:300px;">
```

As you'll learn, attributes are essential to how web pages are designed and styled. And very often they are used in combination with CSS to define the way this content is displayed in your browser.

LET'S GET STYLISH

★ *ACA Objective 4.3*

The final elements of modern web design are the styling rules that are written into the HTML for the browser to interpret. Styles are designed using CSS, and once again, there is a particular way that the rules must be written. Remember! Computers are dumb, and they require precise instructions in order to do their jobs. There is a syntax to CSS styling rules just as there is for writing HTML.

Let's look at the example from the simple web page that you saw in Figure 1.3. To style the text in the (only) paragraph on that page, a class attribute might be added that assigns the class named **"highlight"**.

```
<p class="highlight"> How are you doing?</p>
```

To apply a style to the paragraph, a CSS rule is written that alters the appearance of the text. A CSS rule contains a selector and a declaration block, as you see in **Figure 1.4**.

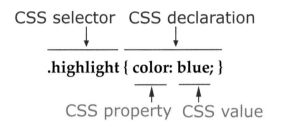

Figure 1.4 CSS styling rules follow a standard convention for the selector name (in this case, `.highlight`), property and value used to define the style.

In this example, text with the class `highlight` (the selector) will be colored blue and will be bold (the styling declaration).

```
.highlight {
   color: blue;
   font-weight: bold;
}
```

When you look at what's been added to the HTML, you see that the styling rule has been added to the head, or hidden area of the page.

```
<!doctype html>
<html lang="en">
<head>
<title>How are you doing?</title>
<style>
.highlight {
   color: blue;
   font-weight: bold;
}
</style>
```

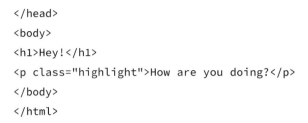
```
</head>
<body>
<h1>Hey!</h1>
<p class="highlight">How are you doing?</p>
</body>
</html>
```

Dreamweaver allows you to see both the code and how the page looks when it's displayed in a browser. As you see in **Figure 1.5**, the addition of the styling rule results in text that is indeed blue and bold. Hooray for styles! Hooray for a visual editor like Dreamweaver that lets you work in both worlds at once—the alien world of HTML and the visual world that humans are comfortable in.

Figure 1.5 CSS styling rules allow the designer to modify the appearance of HTML tags found in the document.

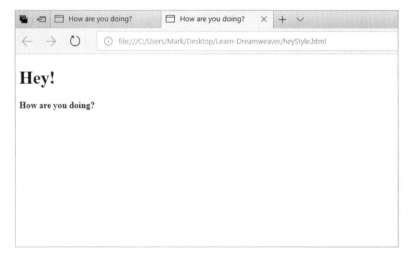

Once More. With Feeling.

That's a lot of information to take in at one time. But think of the power that you have in your hands. A web designer can write in a language that allows your ideas—expressed in words and colors and images and things that move and make sounds—to be transmitted instantly around the world. You're well on the way to doing amazing things now that you have these basics under your belt:

- The Internet is the global collection of computers that are joined together using standard methods of communicating known as protocols.

- The World Wide Web is that part of the Internet that allows web pages to be viewed using Hypertext Transfer Protocol (HTTP), which allows remote computers (servers) to talk with other computers on the network (clients).

- Web browsers are used to connect to the World Wide Web and get the information found on servers to our computers, smartphones, and tablets.

- Web pages are written in a language that browsers understand, known as HTML.

- Browsers are able to display information efficiently because there are standard ways for web pages to be built (the DOM).

- Web pages contain tags—the keywords that wrap around the content of a web page so that the browser knows how and where to display the information.

- Tags can be assigned additional qualities by adding descriptors known as attributes.

- CSS rules are used to provide styling information to the browser so that the information enclosed in tags can be displayed in the way that the designer wishes.

- Coding for the web is powerful and awesome! Stay tuned—we are just getting started.

Working in the Web Design World

All this talk of code and different languages can be a bit scary at the start. Really? Web pages are created by typing all these complicated text commands in a whole new language?

Yet that is exactly what the early pioneers of the World Wide Web were doing—creating web pages and entire websites with little more than a text editor, a web browser, and a program that let them copy files from their computer onto a web server somewhere. How very geeky.

But a funny thing happened on the way to providing access to all this information stored on those web servers. As the average, less geeky people of the world began discovering the web, the expectations of what they could *do with* web pages changed. The web became as much about the *experience* as it was about the data, and a whole new industry grew up around the work of designing websites that were attractive, informative, and highly interactive.

The Rise of the Machines

With all this new work to be done, it wasn't long before some *extremely* geeky people decided that some people had lots of great ideas about how they wanted their web pages to look and act, but they didn't have a lot of experience in writing code. What they needed was a *visual* editor that would let them create web pages without having to dig too deep into the code behind their designs. One of the earliest web design software programs to really get this right was Adobe Dreamweaver. Released in March 1998 by a company named Macromedia (the company was purchased by Adobe in 2005), Dreamweaver has continued to this day to be one of the most popular What You See Is What You Get (WYSIWYG) web editors. Dreamweaver is a great tool to learn the fundamentals of web design (and understand how this code actually appears in the browser).

With Dreamweaver, it's possible to view the results of the code that you write into a web page *and* write the HTML and CSS when you use its built-in visual editing tools. Dreamweaver also lets you manage the files and folders that make up a website, transfer those files back and forth between your computer and a web server, and automate the common work that web designers need to do. Dreamweaver provides a much easier design environment for creating, testing, and ultimately publishing a website from the designer's computer to a web server so it can be viewed online.

You've seen a preview of how the code inside a web page determines how things on that document *look*, but (surprise!) there's still a little more you need to know about how websites are put together. Dreamweaver helps you keep all this straight by providing file management tools that work the way that web servers expect, and make it possible for you to keep everything in proper working order.

★ *ACA Objective 4.1*

▶ **Video 1.5**
Understanding the Structure of Websites

THE STRUCTURE OF WEBSITES

Earlier you saw a very simple page in action with nothing but the HTML tags and a few CSS styling rules that modified the way the text on the page was displayed. But a web page that consists of *nothing* but text is a rare thing to find these days. Even a very simple web page is made up of more than an HTML file.

Modern web pages consist of HTML, Cascading Style Sheets stored in separate files, images, JavaScript files that create interaction, and even embedded content that is stored on another web server such as YouTube computers. A web page is hammered together by the browser by drawing from the HTML file and all the other resources that make up the page. This sort of website is considered a **static website** because it primarily draws from copies of files stored on a web server.

A second kind of website is one that draws from a database of information that can be updated on the fly, allowing for live updates. When you post a picture to Facebook or Instagram and a friend of yours "likes" it, information is written to a database and then republished to the viewer. This kind of site is considered a dynamic website.

Dreamweaver is capable of operating in both worlds, and in fact many websites feature a mixture of dynamic and static elements. For instance, the data displayed in a table might be drawn from a database, while the styling rules that control its appearance are in a static file stored on the web server. Dreamweaver allows web designers to write the styling rules and view how they will appear even when the source of the data is on a remote file server.

All of this functions the way we expect because the system behind the World Wide Web is predictable to the computers, devices, and browsers we use to access web pages. You've already seen how web pages are delivered. Now let's look at how *websites* are organized in predictable ways. And—you guessed it—there are some rules that web developers need to follow so that the required patterns are maintained in your work.

HOW FILES AND FOLDERS DEFINE A WEBSITE

In this book, you'll primarily be working with a static site—a common development environment where designers work on the files for a website on their own computer and then publish them by copying the files to a remote server.

When you visit any web page, you are literally looking at a document that contains a specific filename. Throughout the web, when you land on the home page of a website you are looking at a file usually named either `index` or `default`. Even though the file extension might be different, so that some home pages are named `index.html` while others are `index.htm` or `index.php`, the key predictable pattern is that the name of the web page at the top level of any given domain will be named either `index` or `default`, with `index` being far more common.

The name of the home page depends on the type of server you deploy the site on: `index` is used on servers running either Apache or Nginx web server software (usually a Linux operating system); `default` is commonly used on servers running IIS web server software (usually a Windows Server operating system).

The folder where all the files, subfolders, and resources for the entire site are located is known as the root folder for the site. Web servers and Dreamweaver both operate with the understanding that for a given website, *all* the files and subfolders for the site will be inside the root folder.

Figure 1.6 shows how a typical website is structured and how the HTML files within the site are usually named.

Path to File

Figure 1.6 Websites are organized into folders to allow for easy navigation and the organization of resources.

Notice how the root folder has a home page and each subfolder also has a home page. There can be many more HTML files within each folder, but this predictable pattern means that when you visit a site that has content in subfolders—such as *www.adobe.com/education*—what you see is the index page of the subfolder. In this case the name of the folder is **education**.

In addition to segmenting a site into the subjects that the owner of the site wants visitors to see, there are usually additional folders where assets for the site are stored. These files and resources are used to feed content onto the pages within the site and are not viewed by the public. Typical folders for a website might be named `images`, `styles`, `videos`, `scripts`, or other names that define the content stored within them. **Figure 1.7** shows how these folders might be added as a way to organize a site and work more efficiently.

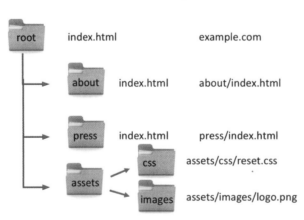

Figure 1.7 Special folders within a website are used to store the assets that are included in documents on the site.

The folder structure of a website also determines another important predictable pattern: the path that is taken by the web browser to a given file within the site. Servers need to know both the *name* of the file and its *location* in order to retrieve and send the document to the browser. For example, if you reference the corporate logo image, which is named logo.png, and place it in a folder named `images` within a folder named `assets`, the path to the file will be written as follows:

```
root-folder-name/assets/images/logo.png
```

You'll find that all of this makes more sense as you dig in and start looking at the code in the web pages you create, as you'll begin doing in **Project 1.1**. But first, here's one more set of rules to follow.

THE GROUND RULES FOR NAMING FILES AND FOLDERS

You need to be aware of some hard-and-fast rules before you begin creating files and folders and writing content to your new website. There's nothing too earth-shattering here. Just some simple standards that all web servers and web designers need to follow:

- Filenames and folder names cannot contain spaces.
- In place of spaces, use the two allowed symbols: a dash (-) or an underscore (_). The dash (hyphen) symbol is preferred by search engines.
- No symbols other than a dash or an underscore may be used in a file or folder name.
- Never start a filename or folder name with a symbol.
- Use all lowercase letters when naming files or folders. Some web servers might consider a file named `AboutMe.html` to be different from one named `aboutme.html`. It's easier to remove any possibility of confusing the server by simply sticking to all lowercase. Remember that if the server can't find the file, it sends that dreaded 404 (file not found) error.
- Keep your folder names and filenames short but understandable by humans.
- Browsers are able to display information efficiently because there are standard ways for web pages to be built (the DOM).

Let's Review!

We've covered a lot of ground so far in this chapter, and you've learned lots of new terms and been introduced to some new concepts. If your head is spinning just a little bit, not to worry. As you begin working with your own web pages things will become clearer.

Your key takeaway at this point should be that computers and computer networks like the World Wide Web depend on patterns, predictability, and processes that are well established and agreed upon by all the parties involved. From the methods that allow your desktop computer, tablet, or phone to connect to the web right down to the nitty-gritty of how the code in a web page is named and styled, the work of creating great websites depends on your understanding of what is expected by web browsers and the technologies that make this amazing network possible.

Create Your First Dreamweaver Website

No matter how good the visual editor in Dreamweaver may be, to accomplish the mission of learning to *design* for the web, you still have to know how to *code* for the web.

Just like there's no better way to learn a foreign language than to visit another country, there's no better way to get started with coding than to dive in and start making web pages. Let's do that now with your first hands-on project.

Get Your Files Here

To jump-start your work in Dreamweaver, a sample website has been created for you so you can examine the HTML and CSS in the page and see for yourself how a simple web page is constructed using tags, attributes, and styling rules, and how the site is organized.

BRUSH UP ON YOUR SKILLS

This project and others that you'll encounter as you go forward assume that you know how to work with files and folders on your Windows or Macintosh computer. If you need to brush up on these skills, the two videos linked below cover the basics of working with files and folders on your operating system.

- **Video 1.6** How to Use File Explorer on a Windows 10 Computer
- **Video 1.7** How to Use Finder on macOS

You can watch the following two videos to review how zipped project files can be unzipped:

- **Video 1.8** How to Unzip and Zip Files on Windows
- **Video 1.9** How to Unzip and Zip Files on macOS

▶ **Video 1.6** *How to Use File Explorer on a Windows 10 Computer*

▶ **Video 1.7** *How to Use Finder on macOS*

▶ **Video 1.8** *How to Unzip and Zip Files on Windows*

▶ **Video 1.9** *How to Unzip and Zip Files on osMac*

Download the project files for this lesson, named `chapter-01.zip`, from the Lesson & Update Files tab on your Account page at *www.peachpit.com*, and store them on your computer in a convenient location.

Define a New Dreamweaver Site

You'll remember from the introduction of this chapter that a website is defined as a collection of all the files and folders that are found at a particular domain. You won't actually be publishing any of the work that you do here to a live website that the world can see, but Dreamweaver assumes that you'll *eventually* publish your work, so right from the start your site will be structured just as it would if it were located on a web server. Having a site properly defined is also essential for previewing your work in Dreamweaver's Live view environment and in web browsers installed on your computer. So the first step is to create the root folder for your site. This one operation has to be done outside Dreamweaver, using either Windows Explorer or, if you are using a Macintosh, the Finder.

COPYING PROJECT FILES

For this book and all the exercises you'll do in upcoming chapters, you'll want to create a master project folder where all your projects will be located. On my computer, I am using the Desktop as the location for a folder named `Learn-Dreamweaver`, as you see in **Figure 1.8**.

1 Create a folder on your computer named **Learn-Dreamweaver**.

2 Unzip the `chapter-01.zip` files that you downloaded.

> **TIP**
> *If you're working in a classroom setting, your instructor may have a specific location where your project files are to be stored.*

Folder location

Figure 1.8 Create a project folder on your computer where all your websites for this book will be located.

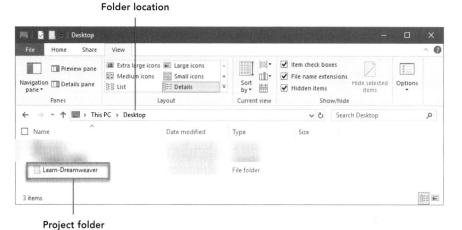

Project folder

3 Copy the unzipped Chapter 1 project files—folder and all—and paste them into the **Learn-Dreamweaver** folder. **Figure 1.9** shows how your folder should look once you've copied the resources into place.

Folder location

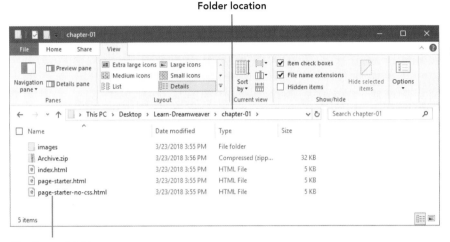

Figure 1.9 Once your project files are in place, you're ready to begin working on your first website.

Site files and folder

CREATING A DREAMWEAVER SITE DEFINITION

Now let's get started with Dreamweaver!

When you open Dreamweaver for the first time, you'll encounter the Welcome screen. There are all sorts of goodies tucked away on this screen, but for now you'll get right to work creating the Dreamweaver site. First, click Next to move past the initial "Welcome to Dreamweaver" message (**Figure 1.10**).

Figure 1.10 Click Next to move past the welcome message.

1 Click the Site Setup tab under the Quick Start options (you may need to scroll down a bit to locate this option) (**Figure 1.11**).

Figure 1.11 Select the Site Setup tab to start the process of defining a new website.

Select the Quick Start tab

Choose Site Setup

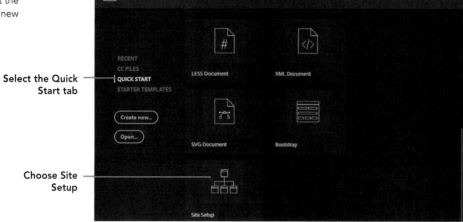

When you make this selection, Dreamweaver will open the Site Setup dialog window. The steps you'll need to take to define the site have been labeled for you in **Figure 1.12**.

Figure 1.12 Defining a simple Dreamweaver website requires only that you name the site and point to the location of the site (root) folder.

Type chapter 1 in the site name file

Click to browse to your chapter-01 project folder

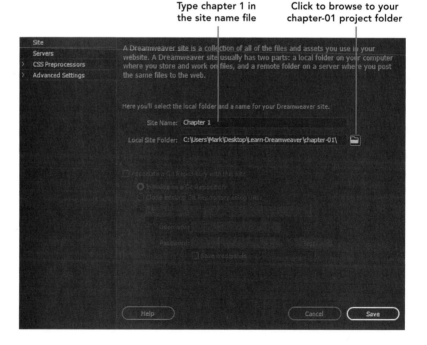

2 Name your site by entering **Chapter 1** in the Site Name field.

The site name is used so that you can move between one site and another in Dreamweaver and doesn't need to follow file-naming rules. Site names are used only when you are working in Dreamweaver and are never posted to the web.

3 Click the folder icon next to the location of the site folder, browse to the `Learn-Dreamweaver` folder, and select the `chapter-01` folder.

4 Click the Select Folder button (click Choose on a Mac).

5 Click Save to finish up and return to Dreamweaver.

Set Up Your Work Environment

Congratulations! You've defined your first website, and you can now start working with Dreamweaver. So that we are all on the same page for this first exercise, let's set the workspace layout in Dreamweaver so that your view matches what you'll see here.

The Standard layout is a logical way to start, so confirm your workspace by selecting **Window > Workspace Layout > Standard**, as you see in **Figure 1.13**.

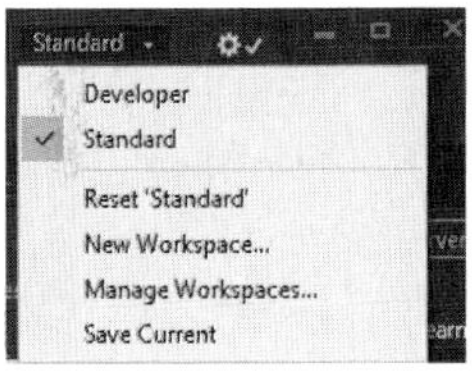

Figure 1.13 The workspace layout in Dreamweaver determines how the various panels and inspectors display.

Let's Review Project 1.1

You'll be learning a lot more about how to navigate the Dreamweaver workspace as you move through this book, but for now take a look at the Files panel, located on the right side of the screen, as you see in **Figure 1.14**. If the Files panel doesn't display for you, just click the tab labeled **Files** to see the panel. With the Files panel open, you'll see the name of the site you just created and a listing of the files and folders it includes.

Now you're ready to get to work.

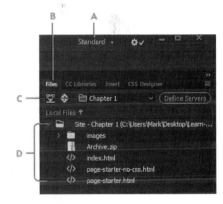

Figure 1.14 After you define your website, the Files panel appears as you see here.

▶ **Video 1.11**
*Under the Hood—
Examining Code in
a Web Page*

PROJECT 1.2

Under the Hood—Examining Code in a Web Page

Congratulations on your new website. Now let's get started on understanding how a web page is created using HTML tags and CSS styling rules.

The goal of this project is for you to look under the hood at how a simple web page is constructed of HTML tags, the styling "hooks" that are created by assigning classes and IDs, and the styling rules that govern how the contents of the page are displayed.

The downloaded files for this project include two starter pages. We will be looking at one that uses CSS to style the pages.

1 Click the Files tab to view the files and folders for this site, and then double-click the filename **page-starter.html** to open the file.

Dreamweaver opens your beautiful page in Split view, as you see in **Figure 1.15**.

Figure 1.15 The
page-starter.html file
opened in Dreamweaver

TIP

If you wish to compare this document to a version in which the CSS has been disabled, open **page-starter-no-css.html**. *The CSS rules in this document have been disabled by enclosing the styling rules in a comment so that Dreamweaver will ignore their properties.*

To view the code that creates this page, you'll need to change your view of the Dreamweaver workspace so you can see both the code and how that code will be interpreted by a web browser at the same time. Dreamweaver calls this view Split view mode. This should be your current view of the document.

2 If that is not the case, click the word Split in the top center of the Document window. Make certain you are in Split view.

If you click your mouse in front of the first word in the center of the page (Welcome), you'll see that a cursor appears in both Live view (above) and Code view (below). In both places (as well as the DOM Inspector panel), you are positioned on the first h1 tag.

It's possible to have this window split in different ways by clicking the View menu at the top of the screen and switching between a horizontal and vertical layout of the Document window (**Figure 1.16**).

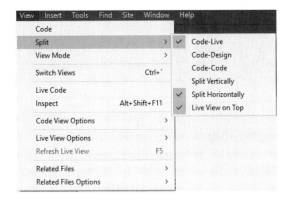

Figure 1.16 You can change from vertical to horizontal layout in Split view in Dreamweaver.

For the purposes of this project you should leave your view set to the default, with Live view on top and Code view on the bottom, as you see in **Figure 1.17**. You see the h1 tag in Design view and Code view and the DOM inspector panel. You may need to click the + in front of the body tag to see all of the DOM.

Figure 1.17 The Dreamweaver workspace with the cursor positioned on the first **h1** tag in both Design view and code view

If your view of the workspace doesn't match the one you see in Figure 1.17, you can change the view by selecting View from the menu bar and looking for check marks next to the options you see in **Figure 1.18**.

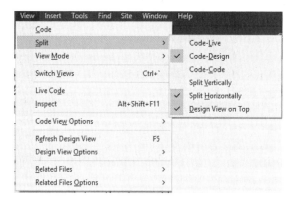

Figure 1.18 The View menu shows how your workspace is configured. You should see check marks next to Code-Design, Split Horizontally, and Design View on Top.

Examining the Properties of a Web Page

You'll recall from earlier in this chapter that there are certain patterns to how web pages are constructed. Let's look at each of those principles and see how they are applied in a real web page and how Dreamweaver allows you to access and modify the properties of the page.

- Web pages are written in a language that browsers understand, known as HTML. A file type is declared at the very top of the document in the very first line of code. When you scroll up in the Code window, the first line in the document declares it to be a web page.

    ```
    <!doctype html>
    ```

- Information that is hidden from the visitors' view of the page but is still critical to how the page displays in the browser is contained within the `<head>` tag. In this document, you see that the `<head>` tag includes the title of the page (My First Web Page), which is enclosed in the `<title>` tags, and the styling rules, which begin immediately following the `<style>` tag.

    ```
    <head>
    <meta charset="utf-8">
    <title>My First Web page</title>
    <style type="text/css">
    ```

- The visible elements of the page are contained within the `<body>` tags.
- Browsers are able to display information efficiently because there are standard ways for web pages to be built using the DOM.

    Dreamweaver allows you to view how the content in the page is organized in the DOM panel, located right under the panel group that contains the Files panel. You can navigate within the content of the page by clicking a tag that is listed in the DOM panel, and Dreamweaver will jump to that part of the page in both Design (or Live) and Code views. In **Figure 1.19**, you see how the DOM panel was used to select the `<h1>` tag at the top of the document tree and how Dreamweaver highlights that tag.

- Web pages contain *tags*—the keywords that wrap around the content of a web page so that the browser knows how and where to display the information. In this document you can see instances of the `<div>` tag (used to divide the page into different containers), heading tags, and

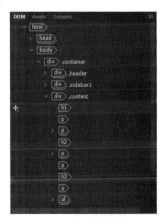

Figure 1.19 The DOM panel displays the structure of the page and allows you to select tags within the document.

paragraph tags, as well as unordered lists (and other tags). These tags contain the content of the page.

Tags can be assigned additional qualities by adding descriptors known as *attributes*. When you look at the opening `<body>` tag, you'll see several tags that have had attributes assigned to them by providing a class. Classes can be assigned multiple times within a document and are the most flexible styling hook that can be applied to a tag. Here you see how classes are applied to the tags that come right after the opening `<body>` tag. You'll also see attributes that have been assigned to the image tag (`<img>`) and hyperlink tag (`<a>`), which assign particular attributes to provide additional information. For the `<img>` tag, those attributes include the width and height of the image measured in pixels. For the `<a>` tag, a pound sign (#)—also known as an octothorpe and not to be confused with the British pound sign (£)—has been used to assign a temporary link for that tag.

```
<div class="container">
<div class="header">
<a href="#"><img src="images/web-design-banner.gif"
 → alt="Awesome Web Designer logo" id="logo" width="960"
 → height="110" /></a> </div>
<div class="sidebar1">
```

- CSS rules are used to provide styling information to the browser so that the information enclosed in tags can be displayed the way the designer wishes. Even in a simple web page such as this one, the CSS styling rules can become quite extensive. In this document all the styling information is contained right within the web page itself. This kind of style sheet is called an internal style sheet.

- To make the styles in this document easier for you to read, the styles have been organized into four different sections based on how they are used. First, you see the element styles, which apply to every instance of a particular tag found within the page. For instance, in the following code block you can see how all of the heading tags (h1, h2, h3, h4, h5, h6) have been grouped together so that every time the browser encounters tags from `<h1>` to `<h6>` the text will be displayed with the top margin set to 0 pixels, and with a bit of padding to the right and left of the content enclosed in the tag. The `<p>` tag is also included in this group of selectors so that content within paragraphs is given that styling information.

```
h1, h2, h3, h4, h5, h6, p {
    margin-top: 0;
    padding-right: 15px;
    padding-left: 15px;
}
```

- The styling rules that are applied to tags that contain a class attribute are defined in the next block of CSS. Here you see how the container division (`<div class="content">`) has been styled so that it includes a width, a bit of padding, and a border that extends down the left side of the main content section of the page. Class selectors are the most common method for styling content in a web page.

```
.content {
    padding: 10px 0;
    width: 778px;
    float: left;
    border-left: 1px solid #000000;
}
```

- Styling rules can be combined in different ways to make your coding more efficient and specific. For instance, in this document the navigation buttons on the left side of the page are contained in an unordered list using the `<ul>` tag. This rule tells the browser that when it encounters an element with the class nav assigned to it *and* that element is enclosed in the `<ul>` tag, the normal bullet should be removed (`list-style: none;`) and border and margin properties assigned as indicated. Notice that the tag name (`<ul>`) is followed by the dot symbol and the name of the class, with no space between the two. This kind of rule combines an element selector with a class selector to provide more specific information.

```
ul.nav {
    list-style: none;
    border-top: 1px solid #666;
    margin-bottom: 15px;
    margin-top: -21px;
}
```

- Styling rules can also feature what are known as descendent selectors. With these styling rules, the browser can be directed to treat the content within a tag in a particular way with even more specificity. In this case the browser is being told that when an unordered list with the class of name of nav is encountered (`<ul class="nav">`), all the individual items that make up the list (`<li>`) should be styled with a solid border.

```
ul.nav li {
    border-bottom: 1px solid #666;
}
```

- The final set of styling rules in this document is used for floating elements within the page. The image that you see on the right side of the page has a class of `.fltrt` assigned to it, which allows the image to be placed on the right side of its container so that the text flows around it to the left with a little bit of padding to hold the text away from the image.

```
.fltrt {
    float: right;
    margin-left: 8px;
}
```

- Dreamweaver features code coloring that allows you to see the different kinds of code that exist in your document. Not only does code coloring allow you to clearly see the difference between the different kinds of code in your document, it also helps you see when you've made a mistake. Notice in **Figure 1.20** that the different kinds of code within the page have their own colors assigned.

TIP

Most visitors to your page don't see the contents; they are search engine bots. The more meaningful text you provide, the higher your page will rank in search engine query results.

- Dreamweaver gives the designer several ways to modify the properties of elements within the page. The Property inspector, located at the bottom of the workspace, provides quick access to the attributes assigned to a selected tag. For instance, when you click the photo embedded in the page, you can see the path to the source of the image (`src`), along with its filename, the class that has been assigned to the tag, and the alternate attribute (`alt`) of the image. You'll be getting lots of practice in using the Property inspector as you move through the projects in this book, but for now you should become comfortable with the Property inspector contents, as shown in **Figure 1.21**. If you don't see the Property inspector, on the menu choose **Window > Properties**.

```
page-starter.html  ×
114 ▼ .fltrt {
115       float: right;
116       margin-left: 8px;
117 }
118 ▼ .fltlft {
119       float: left;
120       margin-right: 8px;
121 }
122 ▼ .clearfloat {
123       clear: both;
124       height: 0;
125       font-size: 1px;
126       line-height: 0px;
127 }
128 </style>
129 </head>
130
131 ▼ <body>
132 ▼ <div class="container">
133      <div class="header"><a href="#"><img src="images/web-design-banner.gif" alt="Awesome Web
          Designer logo" width="960" height="110" id="logo"/></a> </div>
134 ▼   <div class="sidebar1">
135        <p class="linklist">My List of Links</p>
136 ▼      <ul class="nav">
137          <li><a href="#">Link one</a></li>
138          <li><a href="#">Link two</a></li>
139          <li><a href="#">Link three</a></li>
140          <li><a href="#">Link four</a></li>
141        </ul>
142        <p>This sidebar navigation is very common in modern web design. Notice that it is just an
          unordered (bulleted) list that has special properties assigned using CSS. </p>
143        <p>You can change the links above to web pages that you like to visit or to topics that
          interest you. </p>

body    div .container   div .content   h1                          ⊘   HTML  ∨   INS  147:9   🔲
```

Figure 1.20 Dreamweaver uses code coloring to make it easier for designers to view the different kinds of code within a page.

Figure 1.21 The Property inspector displays the properties assigned to a selected tag in the page.

Note that when you are examining images, you should always provide meaningful alternate text for assistive devices. "My photo" doesn't convey nearly as much information as "Photo of me on the beach watching the waves roll in." What information do you want to convey to visitors who can't see the image?

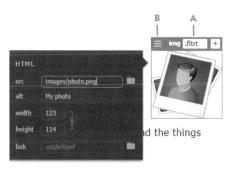

Figure 1.22 You can quickly select properties when working in Live view.

TIP

*If you are working in Live view, you can quickly select the properties associated with an image (and modify them). You may recall that we could change this in the View menu (Figure 1.16). A quick example is shown in **Figure 1.22**. You should switch to Live view to modify the selectors.*

Current tab is for those styles applied to the current selector.

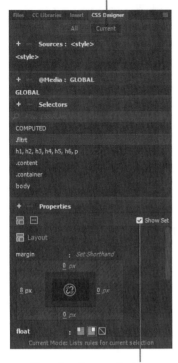

Show Set shows only those declarations which have been set.

Figure 1.23 The CSS Designer panel allows you to see the styling rules applied to an element.

Figure 1.24 You can switch from Design view to Live view quickly.

Figure 1.25 You can view your web page in various browsers (and we recommend you do so). There may be subtle differences in how the page appears.

The CSS Designer panel displays the styling rules applied to a specific selector. For example, you can see all the rules that define the links in the navigation section of the page by selecting the ul.nav a, ul.nav a:visited styling rule, selecting the Show Set option in the panel to view the properties that have been set, and then viewing the styling rules that have been applied for that rule, as you see in **Figure 1.23**. You can view either the rules for a specific HTML tag or all the rules for the document. Make certain the image is still selected, click the CSS Designer tab (to the right of the Files tab), and click Current.

- You can preview how your page will look in a web browser by switching Dreamweaver to its Live view mode. To do this, click the drop-down arrow next to the Live view or Design view option at the top of the Document window, as you see in **Figure 1.24**.

- You can also preview your design in the default web browser on your computer by pressing the F12 key (Option+F12). The page will open in your browser, and you'll be able to see your design in all its glory. If you have multiple browsers installed (and I recommend testing in multiple), you can preview the page in several. From the menu, select **File > Real-time Preview**, as shown in **Figure 1.25**. If you encounter any difficulty with this approach, you can also right-click the HTML file in the File Explorer and choose Open in Browser (and then select a browser).

If you plan to make enhancements to your first page, we recommend that you make a copy and modify that copy. From the menu, select **File > Save As** (and give your file a new name; just make certain it ends in .html) (**Figure 1.26**).

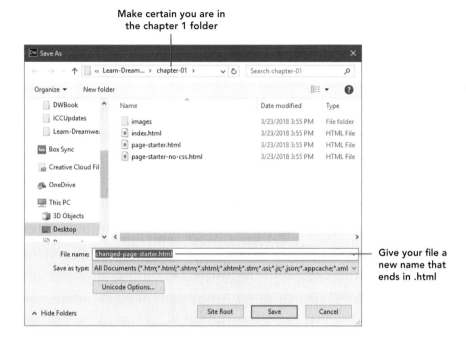

Make certain you are in the chapter 1 folder

Figure 1.26 You can make a copy of the starter page by using the Save As dialog.

Give your file a new name that ends in .html

Project 1.2 Wrap Up

That's a fair amount of information for you to understand all at once, but remember that the goal here is not for you to understand *everything* that Dreamweaver does, but rather for you to dip your toes into how web pages are made up of tags and CSS styling rules, and how Dreamweaver's workspace displays this information to the web designer. In the Challenge portion of this chapter, you'll have a chance to experiment with Dreamweaver as you take this starter page and make it your own creation.

But before we move on, how do you know that you "properly" coded your web page? How do you know that your coding follows DOM standards? This is where validation of your HTML comes into play. If you have access to the Internet, you can visit validator.w3.org and directly validate your code (by placing a copy of it on the Validate by Direct Input tab). Alternatively, you can use the built-in capability in Dreamweaver. From the main Dreamweaver menu, select **File > Validate > Current Document (W3C)**. You may see a prompt indicating that the document is about to be sent to the W3C validator via the Internet (**Figure 1.27**). No worries—nothing is stored on the validator; it just checks the document against the DOM and informs you of errors. If you entered the code correctly, you should see the validation panel appear with zero HTML errors, as you see in **Figure 1.28**.

Figure 1.27 You will be reminded the code is going to be sent to the W3C validator. This will work only if you have an Internet connection.

Figure 1.28 You should see no HTML errors in the validation panel for your web page.

Challenge! Customize the Starter Page and Make It Your Own

★ ACA Objective 4.1

★ ACA Objective 4.2

★ ACA Objective 4.3

▶ **Video 1.12**
Challenge! Customize the Starter Page and Make It Your Own

Now that you've worked in Dreamweaver just a little bit, you can take things to the next level by using your own content and making the starter page your very own. Here are the objectives for this challenge and some tips on getting things done.

GOAL 1

Change the Name of the File and Create a Home Page for Your Site

Before you can start making your own page, you'll want to give the starter page a new filename and make sure it is located within the website you just defined. In these first few steps you'll do just that.

1   Make a copy of the `page-stater.html` file by opening that page (if it's not already open) and choosing **File > Save As**.

2   In the Save As dialog box, name the file **index-*xx*.html** (where *xx* represents your initials), as you see in **Figure 1.29**, and be certain it's saved within the root folder for this site: `chapter-01`.

3   Click the Save button to save the file with this new name.

    You now have another page for your site!

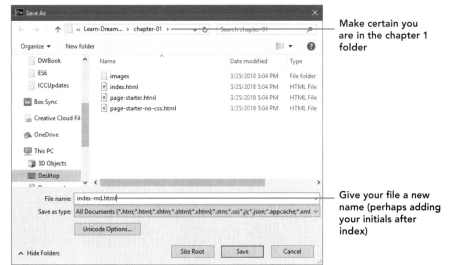

Make certain you are in the chapter 1 folder

Give your file a new name (perhaps adding your initials after index)

Figure 1.29 You can make a copy of the starter page by using the Save As dialog. I used my initials (md) when I saved the file.

Change the Title of the Page

From the menu, select **File** > **Page Properties** to change the title of the page so that it uses your name and some awesome new name for the page. For example, you might name the page **Emily's Amazing First Web Page** (assuming your name is Emily!). **Figure 1.30** shows the location on the Page Properties panel where you can change the document title.

Choose the Title/ Encoding tab   **Give your page a title**

Figure 1.30 You can change the title of a document directly in the Page Properties panel.

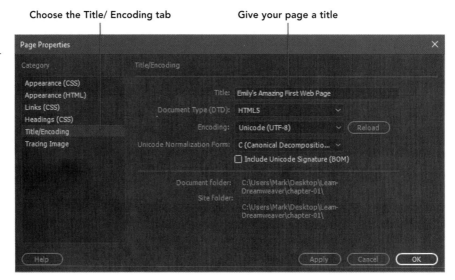

Change the Navigation Links

The navigation area on the left side of the page contains temporary dummy links that let you see how the design looks when you place your mouse over the links. Use the following steps to change these links. Make certain you are in Design view, not Live view, before completing this goal.

1   Click inside each button, and change the name of the link to the name of a website you enjoy visiting. Just type over the text with your preferred text.

2   Visit the web page, copy the URL from the address bar of your browser, and paste the link into the Link field of the Property inspector, as you see in **Figure 1.31**.

Figure 1.31 Select the link you wish to change, and paste the web address (URL) into the Link field of the Property inspector.

In this example, the name of the link has been changed to **Adobe Education Exchange** and the URL has been inserted into the Property inspector. Note that the full URL—including the protocol—must be included when you link to a web page. For this example, the entire correct link is **http://edex.adobe.com/**. Of course, you can link to a page of your own choosing.

GOAL 4
Write Your Own Story

The body of this page has text that won't have much meaning after you start working on the document. But now it's time to tell your own story. Change the text to tell the world (or at least anyone who sees this page on your computer) a little more about yourself.

You can use the My Achievements section to list some of the things you've done that make you proud. Then scroll down a bit and modify the list of goals that you've set for yourself.

Once you have made these changes, don't forget to validate your page again. If you do encounter errors, review the code and correct it. You will learn why this is so important when we discuss making our web pages accessible to everyone.

ADVANCED GOAL

Replace the Images on the Page

If you have images of your own that you'd like to use in this design, you can certainly do so, but you'll need to do a few things first so that the new images will work with this design. First, switch to Live view so what you see will match the screen capture below.

1 Check the size of the images in this design so that the new images you create are the same size as the ones you see in the starter pages. If you want to replace the header image, it will need to be exactly **960** pixels wide by **110** pixels high.

The placeholder photo that is embedded in the page is currently set to be 123 pixels wide by 114 pixels high. In the case of this image, you can use a photo that is a little bigger if you'd like, but make sure it's not too big or the page might blow up (look funny, not really explode).

2 Copy any image files you want to use in your design into the root folder for this site (`chapter-01`), and place them inside the `images` subfolder.

3 Once you have the files in place, click the Browse for File button next to the image source (src) field in Live view to locate your image, and replace the image that was included on the starter page. **Figure 1.32** shows where to locate the Browse for File button in Live view.

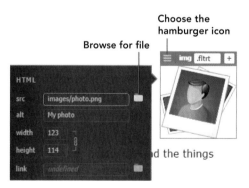

Figure 1.32 Use the Browse for File button (while in Live view) to locate the image you saved into your project folder.

Conclusion

In this chapter, you've learned about the standard language of the Internet and how the communication system known as the World Wide Web functions using a system of connected computers to deliver information to people all over our planet. You've seen that this system depends on the predicable patterns found in the coding languages of HTML and CSS, which are used to create web pages.

You've also taken a short journey into the inner workings of Dreamweaver by defining your first website and examining how the software displays the code that underlies a web page while simultaneously showing you how the page will look when it is rendered by a browser. You have also learned how to make certain your web page does not contain coding errors by validating it through Dreamweaver.

Along the way you've been introduced to the terms and technologies that web designers need to understand so they can be successful in their work. There's still much to learn, but as you wrap up this introduction, you should feel confident that you'll soon make your mark on the web by using Dreamweaver to design and code attractive, functional, and interactive web pages of your very own.

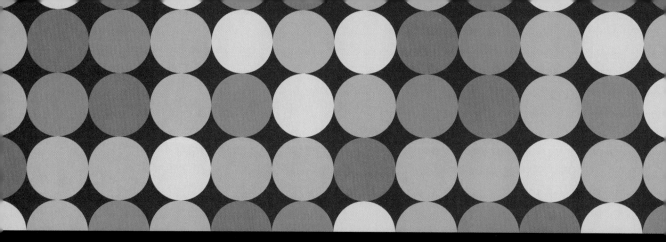

CHAPTER OBJECTIVES

Chapter Learning Objectives

- Identify the primary elements of the Dreamweaver CC user interface and understand how they are used.

- Learn the different ways that you can display web pages in the Document window.

- Define the functions of the panels contained in Dreamweaver CC and how they are used.

- Understand the functions of the Property inspector for working with content in a web page.

- Learn how the Files and Favorites panels are used to display files and resources located within a website.

- Employ different methods for displaying styling information using the CSS Designer panel.

- Learn the location and purpose of Dreamweaver interface elements in preparation for the ACA exam.

Chapter ACA Objectives

For full descriptions of objectives, see the table on pages 258–264.

DOMAIN 2.0
PROJECT SETUP AND INTERFACE
2.1, 2.2, 2.3, 2.4

DOMAIN 3.0
ORGANIZING CONTENT ON A PAGE
3.1

DOMAIN 4.0
WORKING WITH CODE TO CREATE AND MODIFY CONTENT
4.1, 4.3

DOMAIN 5.0
PUBLISHING DIGITAL MEDIA
5.1, 5.2

CHAPTER 2

Dreamweaver CC 2018 Essentials

Imagine that your word processing program—say, Microsoft Word—had to display a document in all sorts of different sizes. Of course, there's the standard 8.5" x 11" format, which is used most often, but what if Word also had to generate another view of the page so that the document could be printed on 3" x 5" and 5" x 7" index cards (and you had no idea whether the individual would choose to view the 8.5" x 11" document or one of the other formats)? Your work in that program would probably be way more complicated than it is now and would look a whole lot different.

But that is what a web design program like Adobe Dreamweaver CC has to be able to do, especially now that everyone wants to view web content on their smartphones, tablets, and desktop computers. The complexity of web pages and web design is the reason that Dreamweaver doesn't look like other computer programs you've used. Although there are common design elements in Dreamweaver that you'll see in other Adobe programs, such as Photoshop, Dreamweaver can be a bit intimidating when you first open it and see how the user interface is arranged.

Not to worry! Dreamweaver is a full-featured program chock-full of all the tools that a web designer needs to create and publish to the web.

In this chapter, you'll learn about the essential elements of the Dreamweaver working environment. The goal is for you to get past that uncomfortable feeling you get when you open a computer program for the first time—especially one as different as Dreamweaver.

How Does Dreamweaver Help?

Adobe created Dreamweaver with the ability to allow designers to work the way that is most efficient for them. It is highly customizable. Among its unique features, Dreamweaver does the following:

- Allows you, as a web designer, to work in a completely visual environment where you work directly on the page much as you would in a word processing program.

- Lets you simultaneously see the code behind the page and work on both the code and the page at once.

- Gives you a live design environment that shows you how your page will appear in a modern web browser.

- Provides tools that let you display your page at different sizes so you can see how the design will appear on iPhones and iPads, Android phones, and tablets, as well as on full-size monitors on a laptop or desktop computer.

- Provides visualization tools for writing, organizing, and managing the CSS styling rules that determine how your design looks.

- Allows code warriors to work entirely in the HTML code that makes up their web pages and includes all sorts of tools to assist in visualizing HTML and CSS, as well as tools that help you write code more quickly and efficiently.

- Provides a resource management panel so you can track and organize the assets within your site, including images, links, colors, and more.

- Includes a file management program that lets you publish to a live web server and make sure your files are correctly synchronized. You can also check out files from a web server for subsequent modification on your local computer.

Accomplishing all that is a pretty tall order, but Dreamweaver has been doing all this and more for a long time. Along the way, Adobe updated and tweaked Dreamweaver as new technologies and methods became prominent across the web and web designers needed tools that let them accomplish the very cool work of designing for an interactive environment.

Get Your Files Here

To follow along with your tour of the Dreamweaver workspace, I've created a sample website for you so you can see how different files and resources are displayed in Dreamweaver. Your first task is to copy the folder that contains these files to your computer and define a website in Dreamweaver.

1 Download the project files for this lesson, named `chapter-02.zip`, from the Lesson & Update Files tab on your Account page at *www.peachpit.com*, and store them on your computer in a convenient location.

2 Unzip the files, and copy the `chapter-02` folder to the `Learn-Dreamweaver` folder you created in Chapter 1.

The `Learn-Dreamweaver` folder where you have saved your files should appear as you see in **Figure 2.1**.

Figure 2.1 Copy the `chapter-02` folder to the `Learn-Dreamweaver` project folder you created in Chapter 1.

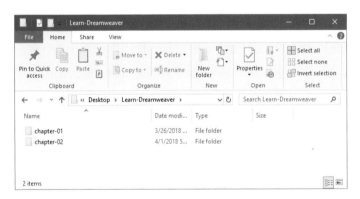

Windows

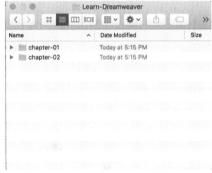

Mac

Define the Chapter 2 Website

You need a website to experiment with. Use the following steps to define the Chapter 2 website.

★ *ACA Objective 2.1*

1 From the application bar at the top of Dreamweaver, select Site > New Site, as you see in **Figure 2.2**.

Figure 2.2 Use the Site menu in the application bar to open the Site Setup dialog.

2   In the Name field in the Site Setup dialog, name the site **Chapter 2**.

3   Use the folder icon to the right of the Local Site Folder field to browse to the `chapter-02` folder in your project folder.

Your Site Setup window should look like the one in **Figure 2.3**. Of course, your local root folder is on your own computer, so the path will be different than the one shown here. Just make certain that chapter-02 is listed at the end of the Local Site Folder path.

4   Click the Save button.

Figure 2.3 The Chapter 2 site is ready to go when your settings match the ones you see here.

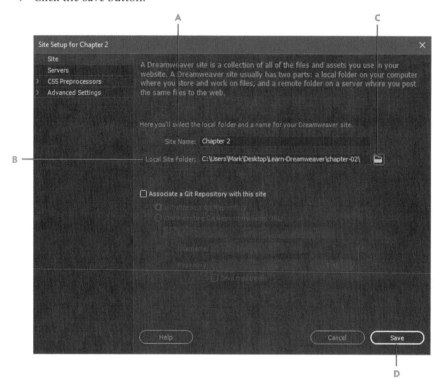

Dreamweaver Workspace Overview

Writing code for the web or working on websites is quite a bit different from editing a photograph in Photoshop or designing an illustration in Illustrator. The interface in Dreamweaver has all sorts of panels, inspectors, and visualization tools that help you do the work of coding for the web.

So let's start out with a quick guided tour of the entire Dreamweaver workspace before we look at each element in more detail.

Open the files named `page-starter.html` and `responsive-sample.html` from the Files panel by double-clicking their filenames.

The Dreamweaver interface (**Figure 2.4**) has four primary elements:

A **The Document window** is where all the action takes place in your design. It's the place where your web page visually comes to life, as well as the location where you can simultaneously view the code of your page and the web page itself (Split view). Alternatively, you could work entirely in the code for the page by switching to Code view. You can choose to view your page in Design view, where you'll have complete freedom to enter text, format text, and drop objects onto the page. Or you can switch to Live view and see interactive elements, such as rollovers and videos, in a view that more closely mimics how a web browser will display a design.

The Document window also contains tools that allow you to change the layout of the page and a button that lets you preview pages in a web browser. You can even select tags directly on the page and in your code by using the tag selector.

Figure 2.4 The four primary elements of the Dreamweaver workspace

B **The panel groups** are located on the right side of the Standard workspace (the one we will use). This area displays panels that have specific functions. The most commonly used panels include the Files panel, CSS Designer panel, DOM panel, and Assets panel.

C **The Property inspector**, which floats in the Dreamweaver workspace by default, is the command center for each page. Using the Property inspector, you can inspect items within the page to see what properties have been applied to them, but you can also make significant changes to the code in your page in this area. This includes inserting hyperlinks, styling text, and creating bulleted and numbered lists, as well as assigning styling properties when you switch over to CSS mode within this panel.

D **The application bar** is the area of the Dreamweaver workspace that runs across the top of the window, as is common for most computer applications.

★ *ACA Objective 2.2*

★ *ACA Objective 2.3*

▶ **Video 2.2** *The Dreamweaver Document Window*

The Document Window

Let's look a bit closer at the Document window. This is where your design comes to life. In Split view (in either Live view or Design view), you can view the code in the page along with the visual design, or you can work with the code in Code view.

Wrapped around these views of your design are a number of additional tools and inspectors that allow you to work on your design. Let's take these one by one as we review all the features in the Document window. Refer to **Figure 2.5** and follow along as each element of the Document window is described.

TIP

If you make a mistake, you can easily revert to the last saved version (another reason to save frequently) by selecting File > Revert.

A **Document tabs** appear at the top of the Document window for every file that is open in Dreamweaver. You can use these tabs to switch between open documents, and you can close an open file by clicking the little x that appears next to the filename. One important visual aid on the document tabs is the asterisk that appears when you've made a change to the file but you haven't saved it yet. Keep an eye out for that little star that appears next to the filename, and save often! Remember that Dreamweaver does not have an auto-save feature built in. Save frequently.

B **The view switcher** contains three buttons that allow you to switch between the different ways you can examine and edit your page. You can see only the code that describes the page for a browser when you are in Code view, you can work in the code and in the visual design while in Split view, or you can see only the visual elements when you are in Design or Live view. To switch between these views, click the name (for example, Live); you can then select the alternate view (Design, in this example).

Figure 2.5 The Dreamweaver Document windows

As you begin working in your documents, you'll quickly learn to switch between the two visual displays of your design. Which one is right?

Design view is the easier setting when you need to work with lots of text, insert images, and work with the content that's in your page. Design view lets you insert various objects into the page and edit their properties.

Live view, on the other hand, shows a much more accurate view of the page (as it would be viewed when someone visits your page using a web browser). You can work with most of the content in your design, but many find that it takes a little more effort to get that done. This is particularly true when your

continues on next page

continued from previous page

pages are more complex (and include JavaScript, which may change what is visible on the page).

In the end, it's up to you to determine your favorite method of working in Dreamweaver. At the very least, you'll likely find yourself switching between the two visual versions of your page—to enter and edit content in Design view, and then check to see how it would really look by switching over to Live view.

As you see in **Figure 2.6**, Live view shows a font (letter style) that is actually stored on the Adobe Edge Web Fonts service. Dreamweaver connects to the service, pulls down the font just as a web browser would do, and then displays this live element in the Document window. If you switch to Design view, you see the same text, but it's displayed in a font that is on your computer. You also see how the CSS positioning rules that are used in the design place content in a different location in Live view. Live view accounts for the CSS selector rules; Design view focuses more on the content (with less styling applied).

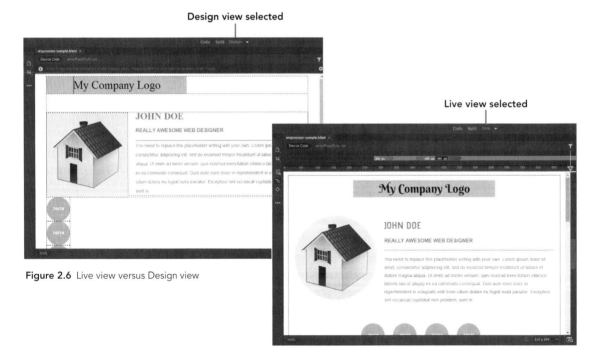

Figure 2.6 Live view versus Design view

One final element in this area of the Document window is the related files that appear when there is a link from the page you're working on to another file that the browser is instructed to use. In the case of responsive-sample.html, an external CSS file has been linked to the page and all the styling rules that the browser uses are actually in that file. You'll soon learn that this is the preferred method for maintaining the styles for a website because it allows you to keep a master styling document that has to be changed only one time to update all the web pages that use the CSS document. In **Figure 2.7**, you can see how Dreamweaver shows these related files in the area right underneath the tabs that show the filename; the file named aboutPageStyle.css has been linked to the page. You will see additional files only if they are referenced in the page (for example, if all the CSS rules are in the <style> tag on that page, there will not be a reference to an external CSS, and no separate CSS file would appear as a related file).

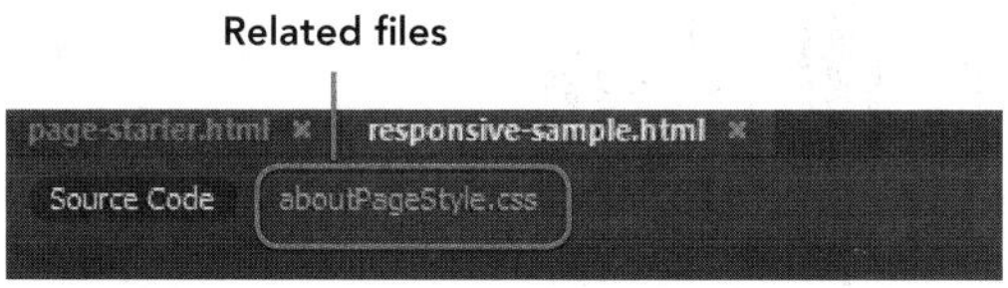

Related files

page-starter.html ×   **responsive-sample.html** ×

Source Code   aboutPageStyle.css

Figure 2.7 Dreamweaver shows you all the files related to your web page file.

The next icons you see at the left of the Document window are located in the Document toolbar. If you switch to Live view, the following items show:

C **Inspect mode** ⊕ does pretty much what you think: It allows you to inspect elements on your page. When you click the Inspect mode button and float your mouse over the page, Dreamweaver shows you how CSS properties are set to position elements on the page. Inspect mode allows you to see how the CSS box model has been used to place different content boxes on your page relative to each other, and it uses color coding to show how margin and padding properties are applied to the element. **Figure 2.8** shows Inspect mode in action; the mouse is floated over the header text at the top of the page.

Inspect mode selected   Layout properties displayed

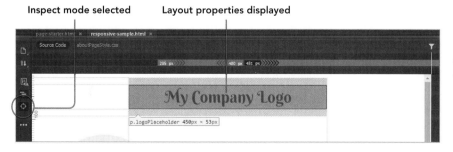

Figure 2.8 Use Inspect mode to visualize the content containers on a page.

D **Live view options** are available for how Live view will display the contents of your page.

E **Media Queries** is a button that displays the Media Queries bar below the Document toolbar, as you see in **Figure 2.9**. This will be shown by default. CSS media queries are styles that are written so that the page responds to a change in the size of the window or viewport. You can click directly on one of the colored blocks to show how the page would appear when it is viewed at a particular size. This is a valuable tool to have at your disposal when you are designing pages that respond to a change in the viewer's screen size, as they do in `responsive-sample.html`.

Figure 2.9 The Media Queries bar

Media Queries button selected

Media Queries bar

F **File management** is a button that displays options that are available to you when you interact with a live web server. For example, you can use this button to copy files from your computer to a web server (Put) or to download a copy of a file from the server to your computer (Get).

G **Open Documents** shows you the current file being edited (designated with a check mark) and other open files. It displays the fully qualified path to each file on your computer.

That concludes our look at the items that are located on the left side of the Document window in the Document toolbar. The following elements in the Dreamweaver interface are located at the bottom of the window, as shown in Figure 2.5.

H **Real-time Preview** pops up a list of web browsers installed on your computer; choose one to open the current page and see that page as it would appear if it were opened on the web. These previews give you the most accurate view of a web page and are an important part of testing your page designs. It is imperative to test in multiple browsers because some use rendering engines that may display your HTML and CSS a bit differently. Windows computers automatically display the option to view the page in Edge, whereas Mac computers will automatically have their Safari browser listed. You should add other browsers, such as Google Chrome and Mozilla Firefox, to this area as well. Simply click the icon and then choose Edit List (and add more browsers).

Preview on Device is also included with Real-time Preview (**Figure 2.10**). This includes a QR (Quick Response) code that you can scan with your phone or tablet. As long as the page is open, you'll see a real-time display of the page you're working on right on your device. How cool is that!

Real-time Preview macOS

Real-time Preview Windows

Error appears when devices are on different networks (or your computer is not connected to the Internet).

Figure 2.10 Real-time Preview with Preview on Device included. Both macOS and Windows are depicted.

Figure 2.11 Real-time display on an iPhone

NOTE

For Preview on Device to work, you must be connected to the Internet and both the computer with Dreamweaver and the smartphone or tablet must be on the same network. The result of such a scan (for a connected iPhone) is shown in **Figure 2.11***.*

I This indicates the row and column `INS` `27:3` where you are presently working in the document.

J **Window size** allows you to switch the size of the display to view your page as it would appear in different devices, such as the iPad, different iPhone models, and popular Android devices.

K **Dreamweaver** HTML ⌄ indicates the type of document you are presently editing. You can click this to see the wide variety of document types that Dreamweaver can edit.

L **Error checker**, as the name implies, gives you instant feedback on whether there's a problem in the code on the page. A green check mark indicates that your code is good to go, whereas a yellow warning sign indicates there is a recommended change that you should be aware of. A red X means that there is a serious problem you need to fix or your page might not display correctly.

M **The tag selector** body p shows you the actual tags within the page and the structure of the page in a left-to-right arrangement. You can use the tag selector to quickly select a tag within a document so that the tag can be removed or changed.

Wow! The Document window sure has a lot of tools and inspectors. This window is by far the most important element of the Dreamweaver design environment. Now let's turn our attention to the Property inspector.

★ *ACA Objective 2.1*

★ *ACA Objective 2.2*

▶ **Video 2.3** *The Property Inspector*

The Property Inspector

The Property inspector is the command center for working with your web pages and is probably the second most important element of the Dreamweaver work environment.

The Property inspector displays information about an item you have selected on the page, and it is also the place you go when you need to perform common operations such as inserting links, assigning attributes (such as a CSS class), and making other changes to elements of your designs.

The Property Inspector for Text in HTML Mode

With `responsive-sample.html` open, you can examine the different ways that the Property inspector appears based on the kind of object that you have selected in the Document window. While in Live view, click in front of the first line of text

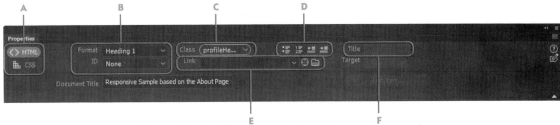

in the page (John Doe) and have a look at **Figure 2.12**, where the various areas of the Property inspector are labeled.

Figure 2.12 The Property inspector as it appears when text is selected on the page in HTML view

A **Switch views** of the inspector, depending on the properties that you wish to view or edit. When you select HTML mode, as you see in Figure 2.12, the Property inspector displays attributes that have been applied to the selected HTML tag. When you switch to CSS mode, you'll be able to see the styling properties that have been applied to the selection and make changes to the CSS.

B **Format and ID settings** give you additional control. You can change the kind of tag format that is applied to text, including setting a line of text as a paragraph or heading tag. The ID refers to the identification, or ID, attribute that is applied to a selected tag.

C **The CSS Class rule setting** allows you to add a new class to a selected tag or object on the page.

D **List and Indent settings** allow you to assign and remove various tags for text that you have selected: the `<ul>` tag for an unordered list, the `<ol>` tag for an ordered list, and the `<blockquote>` tag to indent. As you assign these properties, the appropriate tag will be inserted into the code on your page by the Property inspector.

E **The Link field and linking tools** allow you to assign or edit a link that is attached to text or an image. You can add a link to a selected image. You use the small icon (looks like cross-hairs) to the right of the Link field to drag a link to a file in the Files panel, or use the folder icon to open your system viewer and browse to find the file.

F **The Title field** lets you assign a title to the link. This creates a tool tip when you hover over the link in many browsers. It can help in making a page more accessible.

TIP

Each ID must be unique on a web page. You can use the ID attribute to assign styling properties to an item using CSS, and the Property inspector is where you can see what ID has been applied or add a new ID to a selected tag.

The Property Inspector for Text in CSS Mode

When you change the view of the Property inspector from HTML to CSS using the buttons on the upper left, a different set of options and buttons appear (**Figure 2.13**).

Figure 2.13 The Property inspector as it appears in CSS view

A **CSS view** of the Property inspector provides different tools and options than the HTML version.

B **Targeted Rule** is the CSS rule that is applied to the currently selected text or tag on the page. You can hover over the rule to see which .css file contains the rule.

C **CSS styling properties** allow you to choose a font for the selected text or tag; assign a font style, such as italic or oblique; set the font weight; align the text; set a font size; and set a font color. If you make changes to settings in this area, the CSS that defines the style will automatically be updated no matter where those rules are located.

D **CSS properties** (**Edit Rule** and **CSS Designer** buttons) allow you to open two separate locations in Dreamweaver where you can edit a styling rule. If you click the **Edit Rule** button (in the Property inspector), Dreamweaver's CSS Rule Definition dialog pops up. Refer to **Figure 2.14** to see the contents of this dialog.

If you click the CSS Designer button, that panel will open in the panel group area on the right side of the screen and the currently selected rule will automatically be selected (**Figure 2.15**).

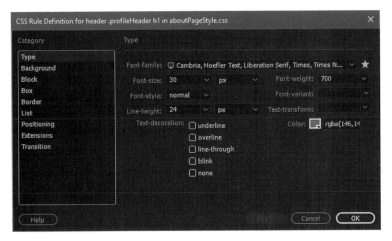

Figure 2.14 Dreamweaver's CSS Rule Definition dialog allows you to change `font-family`, `font-size`, `font-weight`, and many more attributes.

Figure 2.15 ▶ Dreamweaver's CSS Designer panel allows you much greater flexibility in making changes to your CSS than does the CSS Rule Definition dialog.

CAUTION! HERE BE MONSTERS!

Well, maybe not monsters, but you can write some monstrously sloppy code by using the Property inspector. Sure, this is probably the easiest way to select a block of text or a tag and make all sorts of changes to how it looks, just as you would in a word processor, by creating an inline style.

But don't go there! Inline styles should be avoided whenever possible because they are much harder to maintain when you have more than one web page. It's much better to use CSS classes that are consistent across all your web pages by creating style sheets in the head of the page or, even better, in an external style sheet.

THE PROPERTY INSPECTOR FOR IMAGES

The second most common element that you'll likely work with using the Property inspector is images. Open the file **page-starter.html** (and make certain you are in Design view), select the image (which looks like a snapshot) on the right side of the HTML document (near the heading "Make It Your Own"), and refer to **Figure 2.16** for this review of the options you see when an image is selected.

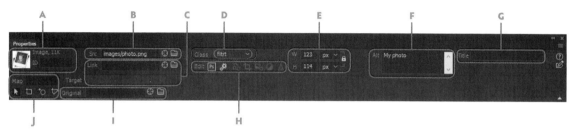

Figure 2.16 The Property inspector as it appears when images are selected in Design view

A   **The image thumbnail and ID** are displayed here. You can assign the image an ID for use in styling rules. Remember that each ID name must be unique on a web page.

B   **Path to image** lists the location of the file (its path) and the name of the file. The buttons to the right of this field let you drag a pointer to an image listed in the Files panel, or you can use the folder icon to browse to the image using Windows Explorer or the Mac Finder window.

C   **Link applied to image** is displayed here. You can set the properties for how the link should open using the Target drop-down area below the Link field. Be careful when using **target="_blank"** because people suffering short-term memory impairments may not realize that a new window has been opened in the browser.

D   **CSS class style** is the name of the currently assigned CSS class style. You can use the drop-down area to the right to change to different styling rules that exist in your document.

TIP

Use an image editing program (such as Photoshop) to change the dimensions of an image.

E   **Width and height** for the image, measured in either pixels or percentage, can be changed here. With the lock icon active to the right of these settings, your image keeps the proper proportions if you change either of these values.

F   **Alt text** must be provided to meet international standards regarding the accessibility of web pages for disabled persons. Alternative text provides a short description of the image in case the image doesn't load properly in the browser. Alternative text is also used by those with vision problems who might use a software program that reads the text on the page to them. Make certain you use meaningful and descriptive alternative text. What is important in the image that you want to convey to visitors who cannot see it?

G **The title attribute** appears as a pop-up when a visitor moves a cursor over an image. Screen reader software can be configured to read this information and inform the person using an assistive device.

H **Image editing tools** provide quick access to Adobe Photoshop. Clicking the program icon opens the image so that you can make and save changes. This allows you to **round-trip** your edits using the source, updating the image on the page when it is saved. This assumes you have Photoshop installed on your computer.

For much greater control, use a photo editing software (such as Photoshop) to make changes to your image.

You'll also find buttons that allow you to adjust the optimization settings for the image, edit the brightness and contrast of the image, and even crop or sharpen the image. Although these tools are fine for making very tiny corrections to an image you're using, you should keep in mind that any changes you make become permanent as soon as they are applied.

I **Original image** is the path and name of the source image that you have used to create the image on the page. This is commonly done if you compose your image in Photoshop and then export the image to a format that can be used on the web.

Avoid using image maps unless there is an overriding business need. They are considered antiquated, although most modern browsers still support them.

J **Image map tools** allow you to visually draw a hotspot in different shapes and assign its link properties. Image maps are clickable hot spots that can be placed above an image. This is achieved when Dreamweaver writes the code that maps out the location of the clickable region relative to the image.

ADDITIONAL PROPERTY INSPECTOR VIEWS

As you continue to work in Dreamweaver, you'll come across a number of ways that the options on the Property inspector are contextually presented. Tables and the tags that make up tables—such as `<th>`, `<tr>`, and `<td>`—all have specific options that are available for your use in viewing and modifying your code. You'll see those tools in action when you complete the hands-on exercises that are coming up. Remember that table tags should be used only to mark up tabular data. Table tags should never be used to design your page layout.

The Property inspector also displays specific properties for multimedia objects, such as movie files. You'll be using the Property inspector often as you view and edit your work.

Panels and Panel Groups

The third and final prominent elements of the Dreamweaver user interface are the panels and panel groups that you'll find on the right side of the window (in the Standard workspace). Each panel in this area is designed to give you access to common actions you'll need to take when working on single documents or an entire website. The panels and panel groups are arranged based on their function.

Preparing the Workspace

You can customize the Dreamweaver workspace to fit the style of the work you are doing. And no wonder! Dreamweaver is used by many people around the world, and they use many different kinds of technologies to create content for the web. Dreamweaver needs to be flexible to meet the requirements of its many customers and how they prefer to work.

For this overview of the behavior of the Dreamweaver work environment for panels and panel groups, open the `page-starter.html` file you've been working with from the Chapter 2 site in the Files panel. Then refer to **Figure 2.17** for an overview of the ways you can customize the appearance of the workspace.

A **Workspace Layout settings** allow you to quickly customize how panels and other areas of the user interface are displayed by choosing one of the workspace layouts that Dreamweaver provides (Standard or Developer).

B **Collapse or Expand Panel Groups** is a tiny icon at the upper right of the Panel Groups area that allows you to collapse or expand the entire column of panels. The collapsed view gives you more real estate in the Document window.

C **Panel options** ▤ are available for every individual panel through a button in the upper-right corner. At the very least, you have the option to close the panel. Some panels, such as the Files panel, provide several settings and operations. You should know that these options are context sensitive (depending on the particular panel).

Figure 2.17 Customization options in the Panel Groups area

D **Panel tab** displays the name of the panel. You can click the top of the Panel tab and drag it to pull the panel away from the column, or you can drag it to place the panel anywhere inside the Panel Groups area. If you double-click the top of a panel tab, the panel will collapse. A single click on a panel tab will open the panel again.

Using the CSS Designer Panel

★ *ACA Objective 4.3*

▶ *Video 2.5 The CSS Designer Panel*

The **CSS Designer panel** provides a location where designers can create, investigate, and modify the styling properties assigned to a page. Taming the many styling rules that make up an average web page is a tall order. But once you begin working with your own designs, you'll find that the layout and functions of the CSS Designer panel make sense.

For this look at the CSS Designer panel, open both `responsive-sample.html` and `page-starter.html` from the Files panel. You'll find the major functional areas of the panel labeled for you in **Figure 2.18**.

A Switch between **All and Current** view in the panel to change the appearance of the items shown in the CSS Designer panel. When All is selected, you see all the available sources, media queries, selectors, and properties.

If you select Current, only the properties for an object selected in the Document window appear, along with the name of the selector, its source, and any applied media queries.

B **CSS Sources** are the locations of the CSS styles for the open document. If the style is located in the head of the document, you'll see the `<style>` tag. If an external style sheet is in use, as you see in `responsive-sample.html`, the name of the CSS file will be listed. You can add or remove style sheets by clicking the + or – button, respectively, in the upper-left corner.

C **Media queries** are those special CSS position and styling rules that transform a page based on the size of the screen. You'll see the kind of media that is modified in this area and the screen size that has been defined.

Figure 2.18 The functional areas of the CSS Designer panel

D Selectors show all the tags, classes, and ID styling rules that exist in this document or in any style sheet attached to the page. The list of the selectors allows you to choose a selector by its name and then view and edit the properties of the selector in the Properties area of the panel.

E The Properties section contains the many different CSS styling values that can be applied to a selector. This visual editor allows you to view only the properties and values that are in use for the current item selected in the Document window when the Show Set check box is selected, or lets you see every possible value when that check box is deselected.

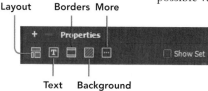

Layout Borders More

Text Background

Figure 2.19 Use the categories in the Properties section to filter the available options.

The available values that you can set in the Properties section are organized using five buttons that appear at the top of the panel (when Show Set is not selected). These buttons appear as you see in **Figure 2.19**. You can use these buttons to filter the values that appear in Layout, Text, Border, Background, and More so that only the values in each category are shown.

F The Show Set check box either shows the properties applied to a selected object or shows all the available properties.

Using the Files Panel

★ ACA Objective 2.3

★ ACA Objective 5.1

★ ACA Objective 5.2

▶ Video 2.6 The Files Panel

Dreamweaver provides many ways for web developers or even teams of developers to manage all the files and resources for a site. The Files panel makes all this possible with tools that let you manage, edit, and duplicate, and it provides a built-in File Transfer Protocol (FTP) program that allows you to work with files on a live web server.

You have already viewed the Files panel after defining two websites so far (in the New Site dialog), and you know how to open a file within the Files panel by double-clicking it. Let's take a deeper dive now as you refer to **Figure 2.20**. Open both `page-starter.html` and `responsive-sample.html` for this review. I have opened all folders by twirling down the > symbol on the left of the folder. If you want your view to be the same, you will need to do the same.

A Site name displays the name of the site you are currently working on. You can switch to other sites you've defined by clicking the drop-down arrow on the right and choosing a different site from the list.

B Local files allows you to right-click and choose additional file properties (such as the date the file was last modified).

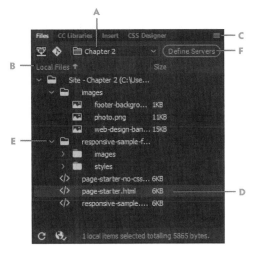

Figure 2.20 The functional areas of the Files panel

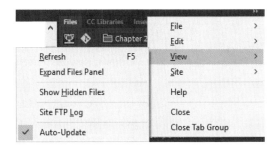

Figure 2.21 Additional options in the Files panel, including the ability to expand the view to full screen

C The "hamburger" icon  provides the ability to see many additional options (**Figure 2.21**). This includes the ability to expand the Files panel to full screen.

D **Filenames** in the Files panel allow you to right-click them (or the empty space near a file) to display a menu with numerous options for managing your files. You can make a duplicate copy of a file, copy or paste a file into a new location, or use other operations for working with the files in your site. Accessing menus by right-clicking will save you lots of time as your site becomes more complex.

Among these many options, you can copy files from a server (Get) or publish files to a server (Put). In **Figure 2.22**, you can see these links and others that are typically used when multiple people are collaborating on a website. The Check In and Check Out links allow different people to work on a single website without worrying about one person overwriting someone else's file. If you are not working with a server, these options will be grayed out.

E **Expand/collapse folder views** displays a "tree structure" to visually represent the files and folders within your site. Clicking the > icon expands or collapses the contents of the folder.

F **Define servers** allows you define a web server associated with your site. This may be a testing server (a quality assurance region) or a production server.

Figure 2.22 Additional options in the Files panel when you right-click a file

★ *ACA Objective 2.4*

▶ **Video 2.7** *The Assets Panel*

Using the Assets Panel

The Assets panel gives Dreamweaver users a central location where they have access to the various images, colors, links, movies, and other resources found within the site.

The Assets panel appears in the lower right of the Standard workspace layout that you've been using. You can double-click it to expand it; you can also expand the Assets panel by selecting Window > Assets. The Assets panel will appear beside the DOM Inspector panel in that panel group (by default).

Continuing on with your tour of the Dreamweaver workspace, refer to **Figure 2.23** and note the location of the primary tools in the Assets panel.

Figure 2.23 The functional areas of the Assets panel

A **Site or Favorites view** allows you to toggle to see either all the assets for a site (Site) or those assets you've set as a favorite so they can be accessed more easily (Favorites).

B **Images**, when selected, allows you to see a listing of all the images within a site, no matter what folder they are stored in. A thumbnail version of the image appears in the preview area, making it easy to check that you have the right image before you insert it into the page.

C **Colors** shows all the color values that have been specified in any styling rules. You'll see the color values written in both hexadecimal and RGB code, along with a preview of the color in the preview area.

D **URLs**, which are the links to external websites, display in this area.

E **Media** shows any media files, such as movies, that are used in the site.

F **Insert** is a button at the bottom of the Assets panel that allows you to insert a selected asset into a page. This button is used for inserting images and media files. When you're working with text, the button name will change to Apply.

G **Asset preview** displays image thumbnails, colors, and other information about assets that are cataloged in a site.

If you are working in Design view, the view of the Assets panel is different. There are additional options available. Refer to **Figure 2.24** and note the location of these added tools in the Assets panel.

H **Scripts** shows the JavaScript files used in the site.

I **Templates** shows any Dreamweaver template files used in the site.

J **Library** shows Library assets used in the site. A Library item is reusable code that can be used throughout a website. When the code in a Library item is changed, all the pages that use the item can be easily updated.

Figure 2.24 Additional functional areas of the Assets panel when working in Live view

Coding Tools in Dreamweaver CC

Dreamweaver has a whole set of features that help you visualize and work with code more efficiently. You can view the code that makes up a web page in the Document window by using Split or Code view. Or you can open a separate code window from the Window menu on the application bar. No matter how you access the code in your page, Dreamweaver will continuously update the visual display of your work.

★ *ACA Objective 4.1*

When you're working in code, Dreamweaver provides code coloring so you can clearly see the distinction between tags, attributes, and values. You can also take advantage of the code hinting feature, which lets you write and modify your code more quickly. Refer to **Figure 2.25** for a run-through of the coding tools in Dreamweaver.

▶ *Video 2.8*
Coding Tools in Dreamweaver CC

A **The Document toolbar** contains buttons that let you collapse and expand code blocks, insert comments, and perform other functions that help modify and clean up code in a document.

B **Syntax coloring** is a Dreamweaver feature that colors the HTML tags and CSS rules in your code and then displays the attributes, values, and content within the tag in different colors. If you see all one color for tags and attributes, Dreamweaver is telling you there is a problem with your code syntax.

C **Code hints** appear as you type within any code window, displaying and filtering the available tags, CSS selectors, and properties. To accept a suggested value from the list, just highlight the value and press Enter/Return on the keyboard.

Figure 2.25 Dreamweaver
coding tools

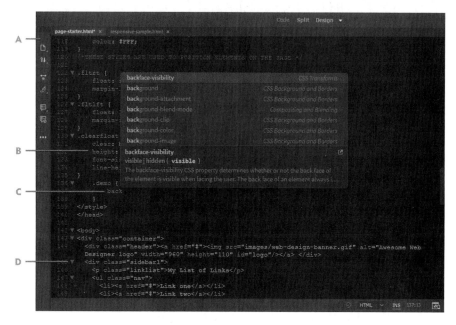

D **Code collapse** allows you to hide or display a block of code. As you hover your mouse over the line numbers in a block of code, small triangles appear next to the line numbers. The same button allows you to expand the selection when you're ready to see more of your code. There is also an Expand All icon in the Document toolbar.

Figure 2.26 Code Navigator

When you are working in Design view, you will also see the Code Navigator. This icon appears next to your content. Refer to **Figure 2.26** for an overview of this feature.

A The Code Navigator icon allows you to see a thumbnail version of all the CSS settings that are applied to a tag. This "floating" icon appears when you are in Design view and you select a new area of the page.

B **CSS settings** appear when you click the Code Navigator icon. As you hover your mouse over the list of selectors, the properties that have been applied to the selector are displayed. If you click a selector name, you will jump to the CSS settings in your code.

Conclusion

Wow. We just covered a massive number of windows, panels, inspectors, buttons, and options that are packed into Dreamweaver. Remember that web design can become pretty complicated. Not because writing good, valid code is so difficult, but because the medium of the web—with its unique ability to display documents at all sorts of sizes and on many different devices—requires a lot from the web designer. Dreamweaver helps you meet those requirements by giving you many ways to visualize, modify, and manage the pages and documents that make up a website.

As you move onward and upward in learning how to use Dreamweaver—and to study for the Adobe Certified Associate exam—return to this chapter to review the user interface features in Dreamweaver and the methods used to create awesome content for the web.

CHAPTER OBJECTIVES

Chapter Learning Objectives

- Learn project planning techniques to determine the structure of a website and create the folders and files that support the client's requirements.

- Add content into web pages using both Live view and Code view.

- Modify the basic properties of a web page.

- Modify the text elements of a design, including formatting and links.

- Examine wireframe documents and translate the specifications into page design.

- Understand how content containers are created using <div> tags and segment a web page into separate containers.

- Complete the layout of a page by assigning CSS styling and positioning properties to page containers.

- Employ various methods for visualizing, editing, managing, and creating styling rules.

Chapter ACA Objectives

For full descriptions of objectives, see the table on pages 258–264.

DOMAIN 1.0
WORKING IN THE WEB INDUSTRY
1.1, 1.2, 1.3, 1.4, 1.5

DOMAIN 2.0
PROJECT SETUP AND INTERFACE
2.1, 2.2, 2.3, 2.4

DOMAIN 4.0
WORKING WITH CODE TO CREATE AND MODIFY CONTENT
4.1, 4.2, 4.3

DOMAIN 5.0
PUBLISHING DIGITAL MEDIA
5.1, 5.2

CHAPTER 3

Building Your First Website

If you've worked through all the lessons in the first two chapters, you should have a solid understanding of how web pages are created using coded instructions. You should also know how Adobe Dreamweaver allows you to visualize, modify, and manage all the web pages that you'll create for a typical website. Well done!

Now that the basics are under your belt, it's time to dig in and make some real live web pages. In this chapter, you will learn about the process of working with a customer by creating an entire website from scratch. From there, you'll begin making your first web pages come to life with text, styles, and images. Let's get started on your next mission by meeting your new client.

Your First Client—
Chris the Cartoonist

Over the course of the next three chapters, you'll be working with Chris (**Figure 3.1**), a cartoonist friend who is launching a new comic strip and needs your help. Chris's comics will be based on a world he's creating in which a group of werewolves, zombies, vampires, and other monstrous creatures operate a company that provides security services. Kind of goofy, but that's Chris for you.

Chris is hard at work on the storyline and artwork for his new comic strip, but he's asked if you can get a website together for him, just like a company in the real world might have. Of course, knowing what you know now about writing code for the web and working in Dreamweaver, you're ready to dive right in.

Figure 3.1 Meet Chris, your first customer.

You have only a little bit of information that Chris has provided in an instructions file that is included in the site files for Chapter 3. Chris is working on a deadline, so you'll be getting information from Chris as you move along. Just like in the real world of web design.

MEET THE ARTIST

Chris the cartoonist is the alter ego of Chris Flick (**Figure 3.2**), a real live person (or so he claims) who works by day as a professional user experience designer in the Washington, DC, area. Chris also has a passion for cartooning, and he operates the *Capes & Babes* online comic at *www.capesnbabes.com*. You can find Chris at comic conventions on many weekends all over the United States and especially in the Northeast.

Chris has been kind enough to provide the cartoon artwork for this book, and you have his explicit permission to use the images that come with this chapter's project files as you wish.

Figure 3.2 Chris Flick

If you're interested in cartooning, you should also check out the *Webcomic Alliance* podcast (*webcomicalliance.com*), where Chris hangs out with his comic artist buddies as they discuss what it takes to be a working creative artist.

Get Your Files Here

To get started on your mission to build a website for Chris, you'll need to get the initial files that he's provided. As you did in Chapters 1 and 2, copy the folder that contains these files to your computer and define a website in Dreamweaver.

1. Download the project files for this lesson, named `chapter-03.zip`, from the Lesson & Update Files tab on your Account page at *www.peachpit.com*, and store them on your computer in a convenient location.

2. Unzip the files and copy the `chapter-03` folder to the `Learn-Dreamweaver` folder you created in Chapter 1.

Define the Chapter 3 Website

This is now the third time that you've defined a website in Dreamweaver, and you should be getting pretty good at it. Remember the process. You first get your files into the proper location on your computer, and then you set up the site in Dreamweaver by giving it a name and pointing to the project folder for this chapter. Ready? Let's go!

★ *ACA Objective 2.1*

1. From the application bar at the top of Dreamweaver, select Site > New Site.

2. In the Site Setup dialog's Site Name field, name the site **Chapter 3**.

3. Use the folder icon to the right of the Local Site Folder field to browse to the `chapter-03` folder in your `Learn-Dreamweaver` project folder.

4. Click the Save button to save these settings.

5. Check the site name at the top of the Files panel. With your site properly defined, it should appear as you see in **Figure 3.3**.

> **NOTE**
> *Refer to Video 1.10, "Defining a Site," if you want a quick demo of how the site definition process works.*

Chapter 3 site name ⎯⎯⎯⎯⎯

Chapter 3 root folder ⎯⎯⎯⎯⎯

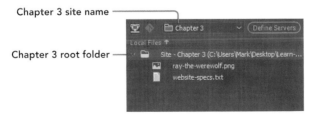

Figure 3.3 The Chapter 3 website as it appears in the Files panel

▶ *Video 3.1*
Translating
Requirements
into Structure

PROJECT 3.1

Translating Client Project Requirements

Chapter 9 of this book has a comprehensive guide to working with clients, and it outlines the steps that a typical web design project follows. But guess what? In the real world of working with clients, things don't always follow the optimal path to get to where your client wants to go. You'll often be faced with a task like the one you'll tackle here: Take the rough ideas and base information that a client has provided and then translate it into a functional website. Even with a lot of information missing, you can still do some of the first steps needed to create a new website.

For this project you'll do the following:

- Identify the purpose of and audience for the website.
- Work with the client and create a plan for the site.
- Structure the site following the standard methods used for creating websites.

You'll do that now by reviewing the list of requirements that Chris has provided, and then you'll build out the structure of his new site in Dreamweaver.

Think Like a Boss

Starting a new design project is an exciting time. It doesn't matter whether the idea is one of your own or you've been asked (or hired) to design a new website. Getting to see something new and original come to life before your eyes is pretty cool.

But before you get to all that coolness, you need a plan. If you follow the planning process outlined in Chapter 9, you'll see that the first step in the planning process is to learn what the goals are.

The problem for most design projects is to figure out how you can help your clients share their goals with the people they want to reach—their target audience. The biggest challenge as a designer is really understanding the client's goals and message and identifying the target audience. Often, even the client won't clearly know what to communicate.

To begin understanding where your client is and what he wants, you need to view the project specification file.

Open the file named `website-specs.txt` from the `chapter-03` project folder. Dreamweaver will open this file in Code view if you double-click the file in the Files panel, but it might be easier to read in a word processing program such as Microsoft Word or a text editor of your choice.

As you read the file, consider some common questions that are typically asked during a client interview process. It's important that you learn as much as possible about the goals your client has at this point.

- What is the purpose of the website?
- What are your goals for this website?
- What key information do you want visitors to see?
- Who is the audience for this website?
- What key adjectives (goofy, modern, dark, light, serious, friendly, and so on) would you use to describe the look and feel of the site?
- What is the title of the site?
- What topics are covered in your site?
- Are there particular colors or fonts that you like?
- Do you have existing artwork, such as a logo, pictures, or other media, you want on your website?
- Do you have examples of other websites that you like?
- What is the domain name?

In the case of this project, where you can't really interview your client, you have to rely on the instructions in the specifications file. From the specifications, you can determine the following about the work that Chris wants:

- **Site title:** Werewolves UnLimited Valuables Security Services, Inc. (WULVS).
- **Domain name:** *wulvs.info*.
- **Key information:** The website supports a fictional company run by cartoon werewolves, zombies, and other creatures.
- **Look and feel:** Kind of goofy, but looking like a "real" company website.
- **Topics and pages:** Home, About, Services, Rates, Contact.
- **Colors and fonts:** The client doesn't really know.

That might not seem like a lot, but in the real world the instructions you've been provided are better than most. In fact, with just that bit you can move to the next phase of making this site—creating the file and folder structure that will support the client's requirements.

Finally, the client also provided some sample artwork that helps to determine the look and feel of this site. If you open `ray-the-werewolf.png` in Photoshop (or another image editing program), you'll see that the style of the featured cartoons is meant to be fun and a little goofy. This will help establish the look and feel for the site as you begin your design work.

Creating the Site Structure

Recall from Chapter 1 that most websites follow a standard folder structure and file-naming convention. It's essential that you tend to the **information architecture** of a website right from the start. Having a site that is properly organized will make things far easier to maintain as time goes on. But perhaps more importantly, the structure of the site helps with the **usability** of the site. In other words, a well-structured website should make it easy for visitors to find their way around and determine where they are at any given moment.

The site structure also allows the client to easily tell visitors how to navigate to content within the site. If, for instance, Chris wanted to tell someone how to navigate to his contact page, it's easy to say, "Just go to wulvs.info/contact." Compare that address to one you might find in a poorly designed structure, where files are assigned without any thought to how they'll be available to visitors. In that case, poor Chris might have to tell someone "Go to wulvs.info/pages/contact-us.html to get in touch with us." Try comparing those two by saying them out loud, and you can tell the difference right away.

One method for sketching out how a website should be organized is the **sitemap**— a visual representation of how the content of the site is arranged. You learned about how websites are organized using folders in Chapter 1. Having examined the instructions that you've been provided, you should already have a good idea that this site will be organized as you see in **Figure 3.4**.

At this point, a completed sitemap is all you need to jump over to Dreamweaver and use the Files panel to start creating the files and folders for this site.

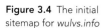

Figure 3.4 The initial sitemap for *wulvs.info*

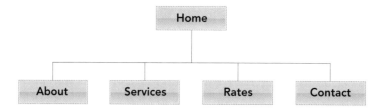

Creating the Site Structure in Dreamweaver

The process of creating the files and folders for this site is pretty straightforward. Use the Files panel in Dreamweaver and the following steps to build out the site. Refer to **Figure 3.5** to complete these steps.

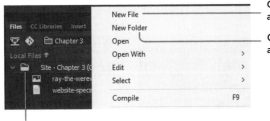

Choose New File to create a file in the selected folder.

Choose New Folder to create a folder in the selected folder.

Right-click the root folder.

Figure 3.5 When you right-click a folder in the Files panel, a context menu appears.

1   Right-click the site (root) folder at the top of the Files panel.

2   From the context menu, select New File.

3   Change the name of the file from `untitled.html` to **index.html**. Don't forget to press Enter/Return after you have typed the name to save the new name.

    You now have a home page for the site.

4   Right-click the root folder, and choose New Folder.

5   Name the new folder **assets**.

6   Right-click the `assets` folder and choose New Folder.

7   Name the new folder **images**.

    You now have a location in which to store the images that will be used in the site (`assets/images`).

8   In the Files panel, drag the `ray-the-werewolf.png` file into the `images` folder you just created.

    You now have a location in which to store the images that will be used in the site.

9   Create four new folders in the root folder. Name these folders **about**, **contact**, **rates**, and **services**.

    You now have locations in which to store the home pages for each area of the site.

10 Right-click each of the folders you just created, and then select New File from the menu. Name each new file **index.html**.

You now have a home page for each topic area of the site.

With all those actions complete, your Files panel should appear as you see in **Figure 3.6**.

You're now ready to move along to the next project.

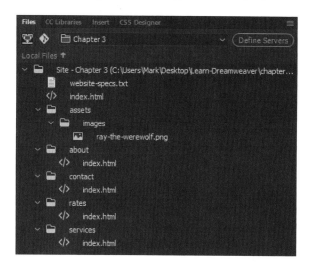

Figure 3.6 The initial site structure for Project 3.1 as seen in the Files panel

---

LEVEL UP: GRAPHIC DESIGN

The next steps in the design process for a project like this would typically be to start getting ideas onto paper and, ultimately, create sketches in your favorite graphic design program. Of course, Adobe makes it easy to work between Dreamweaver and Photoshop.

Creating mock-ups of how the pages in the site should look usually begins right about now. With the information this client has provided, you can draw how you think the site should look. Image editors don't have all the technical challenges that web pages have, where code has to be written to define how things look, so you can let your imagination have free rein. Now is an excellent time to work on your own unique design for *wulvs.info*, or think about how you would design a site of your own with a structure similar to the one you see coming together here.

PROJECT 3.2

Modifying Page Properties

Now that the structure of the site has been prepared, it's time to turn your attention to the initial work that can be done in formatting and styling the pages. Even though the client hasn't provided all the information that's needed for this site to come together, there's still a lot that you do know based on the specifications you've been provided.

For this project, you'll complete the following tasks:

- Review the requirements of the site based on the client's instructions.
- Think about the look and feel that the client wants to achieve with the site.
- Determine how the content of the page should be organized.
- Add content onto the home page so you have material to work with as you continue to build out the design.
- Use the Page Properties dialog to assign values to the working document in the site.
- Copy and paste critical information from the client's specifications onto the working web page.

★ ACA Objective 1.2

★ ACA Objective 1.5

★ ACA Objective 2.4

★ ACA Objective 4.1

★ ACA Objective 4.2

▶ Video 3.2
Modifying Page
Properties

Taking the Next Step in the Design Process

In Project 3.1, you started reviewing the client's requirements for the new website, and you determined some critical information about the structure of the site.

Now it's time to move along to the next logical step in the design process—to learn more about what the client hopes to achieve, and think about how you as the designer can meet those needs.

Many times this involves a second interview or an exchange of emails and phone calls with the client to get a feel for exactly what they're looking for. It's also common at this stage to be thinking about the look and feel for the customer's website. There's still plenty of work to do before the real visual design can begin, but having a general idea of what the client wants will help get things started out right.

Although the visual design process has not yet begun, this is a good time to find out how your client envisions the visuals for the new page. You might want to ask your client to send you links to sites that he likes and to describe what he likes about them. Your client might also have an existing logo or artwork that will help

Figure 3.7 Ray the hipster werewolf

you pick up color schemes and that all-important "feel" that the client is after. Your cartoonist client, Chris, has provided you with a sample of his work, Ray the hipster (**Figure 3.7**). Judging by the appearance of this werewolf character, you can tell that this site is meant to be fun and a bit goofy. Imagine if Ray were instead a scary, snapping, dangerous-looking creature. The site would have an entirely different feel, and the design process would be heading off in a whole different direction.

Keep in mind that the experience of the visitor to the site is of the utmost importance. User experience relates to the emotions and attitudes of those using the website. If the client knows actual individuals who would use the site, now is the time to involve them in the review process. Of course, for our fictional client, this is not possible. We could create personas (fictional characters) that represent how certain types of individuals would use the site. Practicing professionals typically create half a dozen personas and document how they would experience the site. In our case, we are focusing on learning how to build a site with Dreamweaver. Be aware that there is much more to the initial development of a website by practicing professionals than we are covering in this book. As your knowledge grows, you will also want to think in terms of user experience design. For now, let's concentrate on building our first website.

Examining Client Resources

As you read through the client's specifications, you'll see that he has provided a fair amount of information. You'll use this information right within Dreamweaver as content is added to the home page of the site. The home page will become your working document, and you'll be adding content and styling to this page as the design comes together. From what the client has already said that he wants, you can determine the following crucial information:

- **Site name:** Werewolves UnLimited Security Services Inc.
- **Header text:** Werewolves UnLimited Security Services Inc.
- **Tagline:** Let us protect your stuff with a snarling pack of crazed creatures! (Maybe)
- **Navigation:** Links to the pages within the site
- **Content:** The text beginning with "Welcome to Werewolves UnLimited Valuables Security Services Inc.!"

Double-click the `website-specs.txt` file that was initially provided to you. Also double-click the `index.html` file you created. Double-clicking opens the files in Code view, making it easy to copy and paste between files.

Be sure that you open the correct `index.html` file. You can click the text Local Files in the Files panel (shown in **Figure 3.8**) to sort the files and folders (if they are in descending order, click again to see them in ascending order). You can collapse the subfolders in the site so you don't confuse those home pages in the Files panel, as you see in Figure 3.8, with the primary home page of the site.

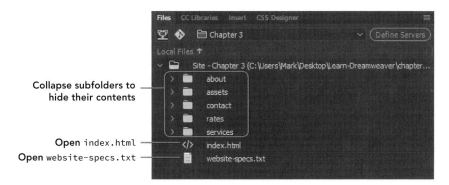

Figure 3.8 Open the documents for this project from the Files panel.

Adding Content to a Web Page and Setting Basic Properties

With both the `index.html` and `website-spec.txt` documents open, you'll be able to switch from one file to another by clicking the file tab at the top of the Document window. This will be helpful as you follow along with these steps and put content onto the page. From the menu, select File > Page Properties. Make sure you have the `index.html` file open. Refer to **Figure 3.9** to complete the first part of this project.

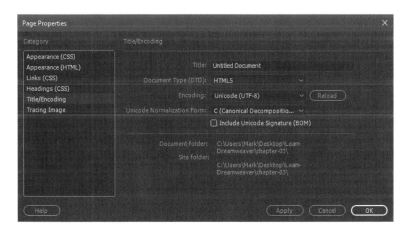

Figure 3.9 The Page Properties dialog provides a location where properties for an entire document can be set based on different categories.

The first thing you need to set is the page title. Titles are the names that humans read when they see a page name listed in the title bar of their browser or when they save the page as a favorite or bookmark. Page titles also appear in a browser's history listing and appear when the page is found by a search engine. This differs from the filename (`index.html` in this case), which is what servers need when a request to open the page is sent to a web server.

Within the Page Properties panel, confirm that the Title/Encoding category is selected (on the left). The title of new web pages created in Dreamweaver is Untitled Document (which is not overly descriptive).

1 Open the `website-specs.txt` file and highlight the block of text that contains the name of the company: Werewolves UnLimited Valuables Security Services. Copy (Ctrl+C/Command+C) the highlighted text.

2 Click the tab `index.html` at the top of the Document window to switch to that file. In the application menu at the top of the screen, choose File > Page Properties. This opens the Page Properties dialog you see in Figure 3.9.

3 Select the Title/Encoding category on the left side of the window.

4 Click in the Title field, highlight and delete the existing text (Untitled Document), and replace it by pasting in the company name you copied in step 1. You can use the standard keyboard shortcut Ctrl+V/Command+V to paste in the text, or right-click and choose Paste.

5 Type the word **Home** after the company name. Your completed page title now reads Werewolves UnLimited Valuables Security Services, Inc. Home.

   For new documents you create for entirely new websites, you should stay with the most current HTML specification: HTML5. You would change this setting only if you were working on an existing website where older pages are in use and you needed to match the existing encoding.

6 Leave the Document Type field set to HTML5 and click OK. Your page now has a title.

   To get the rest of the content onto the page, you'll return to the text file and copy and paste the essential elements that the client has provided.

7 From `website-specs.txt`, scroll to line 32 and copy the company name, tagline, and introduction to the company that the client has provided and paste them into `index.html`. You want to paste the contents from line 32 through line 44. Make certain you are in Design view when pasting into the white Document window.

8 Don't forget to save your work. From the menu, select File > Save.

Your completed document (in Design view) should appear as you see in **Figure 3.10**.

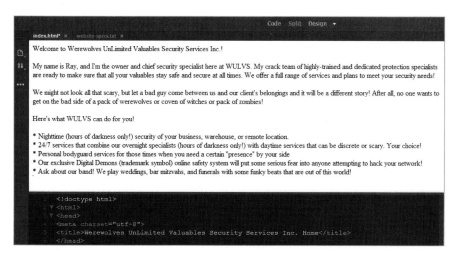

Figure 3.10 Plain text can be copied directly into the Document window to add content to a page.

ADDING ELEMENTAL CSS PROPERTIES

The final few steps for this project include setting some basic styling properties for the page. One of the little things that drive web designers crazy is how page margins change based on which browser is being used. This is because different browsers (such as Chrome and Firefox) use different layout engines. Chrome uses Blink and Firefox uses Gecko. These rendering engines interpret the HTML specification a bit differently. One browser might add five pixels to the left and top of the page window, and another might make that setting three pixels. To take control of this little discrepancy between browsers, it's standard practice to "zero out" the page margins by adding some CSS. While you're at it, also set a default font that you want to use in this design. Both of these actions take place in the Page Properties dialog. Refer to **Figure 3.11** as you complete the final steps in this project.

1 In `index.html`, choose File > Page Properties. Click the Appearance (CSS) category on the left.

2 In the margins area at the bottom of the window, enter **0** for each of the four margin properties.

Figure 3.11 The Appearance (CSS) category of the Page Properties dialog

Appearance (CSS) category selected

Page font settings

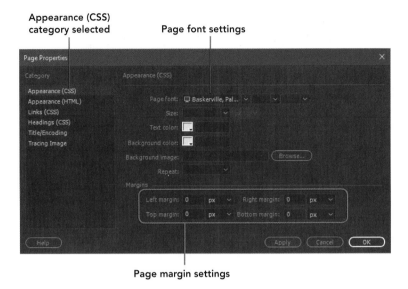

Page margin settings

3   At the top of the window, use the dropdown menu to set the default font for this page from the available fonts. This example uses Baskerville, Palatino.

4   Click OK.

5   Review the changes that have been made to the head of the document. Make certain you are in Split view in the Document window. Scroll to the top of the HTML. You'll see these two styling declarations listed because Dreamweaver (and you) wrote the code to set the margin properties of the page and to set the font to be used in the document.

Take note of one little thing in the CSS. Notice how the first rule combines three tag selectors so that the font used within the page (`<body>`) is the same font used in table cells (`<td>`) and table headers (`<th>`). This takes care of the places where most text might appear; using the kind of selector that styles more than one tag with a single set of properties and values is a very efficient way to write your code.

These kinds of style rules, which define how a tag should appear at a very elemental level, are known as **element selectors**. With these rules in place, every time the tag is encountered the browser will apply these styling rules.

```
<style type="text/css">
body,td,th {
font-family: Baskerville, "Palatino Linotype", Palatino,
→"Century Schoolbook L", "Times New Roman", serif;
}
body {
  margin-left: 0px;
  margin-top: 0px;
  margin-right: 0px;
  margin-bottom: 0px;
}
</style>
```

That takes care of adding content to the page and setting some basic styling properties. Now, be sure you saved your work, and get ready for the next project.

Setting Font Formats and Links

★ ACA Objective 2.2

★ ACA Objective 4.1

★ ACA Objective 4.2

★ ACA Objective 4.3

▶ **Video 3.3** *Setting Font Formats and Links*

Now that the structure of the site has been prepared and some basic content is in place, it's time to turn your attention to the initial work that you can do in formatting and styling the pages. In this project, you'll add some additional text to the page and prepare the content on the page for further production by creating links to files that are internal to the client's website.

Here's what you'll get done in this project:

- Type directly into a document.
- Learn about the difference between paragraph (`<p>`) tags and break tags (`<br>`).
- Use the Property inspector to convert the format of text.
- Add links to your document using three common methods that Dreamweaver provides: directly entering the URL in the Property inspector, dropping a link onto the page, and browsing to a file location on your computer.

Working with Text and Text Formats

Text formatting in a web page is a lot like the styling rules that you'll find in a word processing program—word processors can do way more than just setting the size and color of text on the page. During the creation of this book, for example, particular styles are being used so that the many people who work on the document can track what's going on and convert the Word document into the layout you see on this page.

When text is marked up in the HTML document, fundamental changes happen to how browsers and even search engines interpret the content of tags. For example, if text is marked up with an `<h1>` tag, a search engine considers that element to be the most important one on the page (the main heading). In the same way that you might outline a topic for a school report, heading tags assist the search engine (such as Google or Bing) to find content on the page based on how important its meaning is. Creating semantic structure in a web page is one of the many ways you can help your clients achieve their goals—because everyone wants to rank high in search engine results.

Text format is also used to define lists on a page. In modern web pages, the unordered list (`<ul>`) in particular gets used a lot. The `<ul>` tag and the items that are listed inside the unordered list using the `<li>` tag are flexible containers for styling elements on the page, and are probably used more for page navigation than they are for making lists. Dreamweaver has numerous ways for you to mark up text in a document, with most of the action taking place in the Property inspector.

HOW YOU LOOK ISN'T WHO YOU ARE

How you're *marking up* text is very different from how you're *styling* text. The markup of the text determines its purpose within the document and doesn't really have much to do with how it looks. Sure, heading tags have some default sizes, but for the most part, the format of text is used to give it meaning, not to change its appearance.

Styling text is an entirely different thing. Just as you can dress based on what you're doing—going to school, going to work, heading out to the movies, or playing a sport—you can dress up text in a web page just about any way you want. The tag (purpose) of the text doesn't change when you apply a style any more than you change into a different person when you put on different clothes or change your hairstyle.

Let's return to the home page for your site, where you're doing the initial development work using the specifications that the client has provided. Your first task is to create the text block that will be used for page navigation as the site is built out.

1 Open `website-specs.txt` and `index.html`, if they are not already open. Set the view of the page to Split Code and Design.

2 Select the tagline from the `website-specs.txt` file (line 14) and copy it. Paste the tagline on a new line directly beneath the Werewolves UnLimited Security Services paragraph. Position your cursor at the end of the above line. Press Enter/Return.

3 Right-click, and paste the tagline you copied.

4 From `website-specs.txt`, copy the block of text that describes the pages that the client wants to have in his site. You'll find this block of text on lines 22 through 28.

5 Switch to `index.html`, and place your cursor right after the exclamation point at the end of the tagline text. Press Enter/Return.

6 Right-click and select Paste to paste the text into the document. The text at the top of the page should appear as follows:

```
Werewolves UnLimited Security Services
Let us protect your stuff with a snarling pack of crazed
→ creatures!
Pages:
* Home page (With Ray's introduction)
* About Our Team (With pictures and "bios" of the company
→ employees)
* Services (With a list of the work the company will do)
* Rates (I'll need a table with prices)
* Contact (A way to send the fake company fake e-mail)
```

7 Delete the asterisk at the beginning of the lines, and delete the parentheses and all the words inside the parentheses.

8 Change the word **Pages** to **Navigation**.

You now have the basic site navigation content created.

Next, let's set the markup for this text. In the code for this text block, all the names are contained in a single paragraph tag (`<p>`) with a break tag (`<br>`) following each name. You should see this in Code view.

```
<p> Home page<br>
    About Our Team <br>
    Services <br>
    Rates <br>
    Contact <br>
</p>
```

Break tags drop a line of text down a line, but they don't have any other inherent purpose. It's pretty common to get a lot of break tags when you copy and paste from a source other than Dreamweaver. With just a little bit of keyboard work, this can be quickly corrected.

9 In Design view, place your cursor in front of the letter A in `About Our Team`. Press the Backspace/Delete key to remove the break tag, and then press the Enter/Return key.

Visually, you'll now see the text drop down two lines. But most importantly, the first word (Home) in the list is now enclosed in a `<p>` tag.

10 To complete the conversion of this code block, place your cursor in front of each line, press Backspace/Delete to delete the break, and then press Enter/Return to generate the `<p>` tag. Your code should appear as follows:

```
<p>Home page</p>
<p>About Our Team</p>
<p>Services</p>
<p>Rates </p>
<p>Contact </p>
```

Good job! You've added some needed markup to this text. Now you need to convert the text into an unordered list that can be used for navigation. You'll use the Property inspector to do all the work for the next part of this project. If it is not visible, from the menu select Window > Property Inspector. Refer to **Figure 3.12** to complete these next tasks.

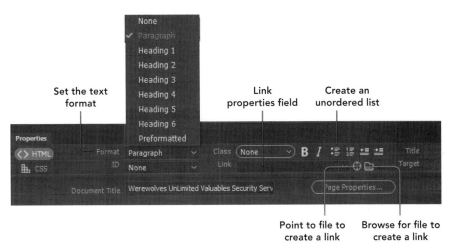

Figure 3.12 The Property inspector with text selected

11 The first element to format on the page is the text that begins with the word *Welcome*. Select this entire line, and then use the Format field in the Property inspector to change the formatting of this line of text to Heading 1.

12 Highlight the names of the pages in the navigation text block that were just converted to paragraphs. In the Property inspector, click the Unordered List button to convert the entire block to an unordered list, with each word contained in a list item tag (`<li>`). Your HTML should look like the following in Code view:

```
<ul>
  <li>Home page</li>
  <li>About Our Team</li>
  <li>Services</li>
  <li>Rates </li>
  <li>Contact </li>
</ul>
```

Don't worry about the bullets that appear next to the names of these pages. This is the default appearance for list items. Those bullets can be hidden or styled in different ways using CSS. You'll take that step when you start writing styles.

Now that you know how to convert a block of text into an unordered list, you can turn to the final block of text on the page.

13 Following the procedure in the previous steps, convert the text marked with asterisks at the very bottom of the page into an unordered list. Your HTML should look like the following in Code view:

```
<ul>
  <li>Nighttime (hours of darkness only!) security of your
  ⟶ business, warehouse, or remote location.
  </li>
  <li>24/7 services that combine our overnight specialists
  ⟶ (hours of darkness only!) with daytime services that
  ⟶ can be discrete or scary. Your choice!
  </li>
  <li>Personal bodyguard services for those times when you
  ⟶ need a certain "presence" by your side
  </li>
  <li>Our exclusive Digital Demons (trademark symbol)
  ⟶ online safety system will put some serious fear into
  ⟶ anyone attempting to hack your network! </li>
  <li>Ask about our band! We play weddings, bar mitzvahs,
  ⟶ and funerals with some funky beats that are out of
  ⟶ this world! </li>
</ul>
```

Creating Hyperlinks

The last stop in this project is to create the hyperlinks that will allow a visitor to navigate within the site. The text is now ready, and all you need to do is attach the link property to the names that are in the list. Refer to Figure 3.12 and locate the area of the Property inspector where links are listed and created. You'll start by creating the link to the home page of this site. Your view should be set to Split Code and Design.

1   Highlight the words *Home page*, and then turn to the Property inspector. Type **index.html** in the Link field and press Enter/Return.

    Inserting the URL or filename and path in this area by typing or copying and pasting is one way you can create a link in Dreamweaver.

2   Highlight *About Our Team* in the next line.

3   In the Files panel, expand the `about` folder so you can view the `index.html` page located in that folder.

4   Click the Point to File icon in the Property inspector, drag the marker onto the `index.html` file in the `about` folder Files panel, and release the mouse.

    You've now used the second method for creating a link.

5   Highlight *Services* and click the Browse for File icon in the Property inspector.

6   When Windows Explorer or the Mac Finder opens, browse to the `index.html` file that's inside the `services` folder.

7   Select the file and click OK/Open.

    You have now used the third method for inserting a link in Dreamweaver.

8   Continue linking all the text in the navigation area using one of the three methods to create a link.

9   Save your work.

    The code block for this area of the page will appear as follows:

```
<ul>
   <li> <a href="index.html">Home page</a></li>
   <li><a href="about/index.html">About Our Team</a></li>
   <li><a href="services/index.html">Services</a></li>
   <li><a href="rates/index.html">Rates </a></li>
   <li><a href="contact/index.html">Contact </a></li>
</ul>
```

FOLLOW THAT FILE!

When you look at the links you created in Project 3.3, you'll notice that the `href` value inside the quotation marks is written differently for the link to the home page versus the links to the pages inside folders.

When a link is made to a file within the same folder as the document, the path to the file is simply written with the filename. Since the home page is in the root folder for this site, a link to a page that's also in that folder will be written as `index.html`.

When a link points to a file inside a folder one level *down*, the path to the folder has to be spelled out, then a slash character, and *then* the filename. And so, a file inside the `about` folder is written as `about/index.html`. For a link that points *up*, the path is written with two dots and then a slash, like this: `../index.html`.

One of the great things that Dreamweaver does is maintain the correct file path for you, even when you move things around in the Files panel.

In this project, you've learned more about the purpose of text formatting and how text formats are set in Dreamweaver. Remember that text markup has a purpose, and it isn't to determine how text looks. You've also used three methods for inserting a hyperlink in Dreamweaver.

Adding Content Containers and Attributes

The first web page in the site is starting to shape up. So far, you've added the text that the client has provided and set the formatting for the text so that the page has some structure. Now you'll continue with another common way that web designers get their web pages ready to be styled and laid out. In this project you're going to add the containers for this page and the "hooks" for the CSS styling rules that are yet to come. In essence, you'll be assembling the building blocks of the page design.

To create these building blocks, you'll use named `<div>` tags and tag attributes that are a snap to put into place. Your client has given you a mockup of how he wants the web page to look—or at least the beginnings of a design. From the client's initial ideas, you'll be able to determine how the containers of the page need to be built so that in the final construction process the design of the page can be set into place.

You have these tasks ahead of you to complete this project:

- Understand how **wireframe** diagrams are created based on client requirements.
- Learn how to break down the different content containers that are required for a typical web page.
- Wrap the existing content on the page in `<div>` tag containers.
- Understand the difference between ID and class attributes.
- Examine your code to be certain that the content on the page is properly placed in the correct container.

Working with Wireframes

Since your client gave you a design composition (or **design comp**, as it's frequently called), you can now examine the design and prepare a wireframe diagram to show the building blocks that you'll need to lay out the page. Sure, this comp isn't all that close to how the final design should look, but at this point in the design process, knowing how the page needs to be structured takes you farther down the path of getting a final design done. You can see the client-supplied design for the site in **Figure 3.13**.

★ *ACA Objective 2.3*

★ *ACA Objective 2.4*

★ *ACA Objective 4.1*

★ *ACA Objective 4.2*

★ *ACA Objective 5.1*

▶ *Video **3.4** Adding Content Containers and Attributes*

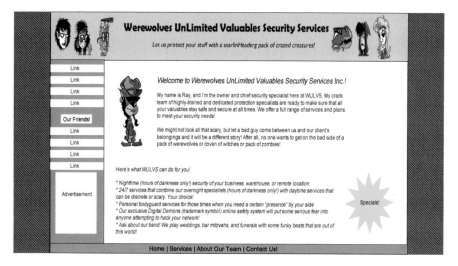

Figure 3.13 An initial design comp for the cartoonist's website shows how the page might be constructed.

Wireframe diagrams are intended to show the architecture behind a design and are often simply sketched out freehand on a piece of paper. Wireframes usually go through many versions as the designer and the client nail down what's possible, what's in the budget, and how well your ideas match up to the client's expectations.

In the case of this design, if you translate the comp into the different boxes of content that will appear, you can see that the client's requirements can be turned into the wireframe pretty easily. This design requires

- Content that "floats" over the top of a background
- The entire page centered on the screen, with margins on the left and right
- A header across the top of the page for the page name and some artwork
- A sidebar down the left side for navigation and advertising
- The main content area of the page with some images and the text for each page
- A footer where links and other information can be listed

Once those ideas are translated visually, you end up with a wireframe that might look like the one you see in **Figure 3.14**. You can even label the different containers to get an idea of how things are positioned on the page.

With the content containers identified, the next step for this project is to insert the named `<div>` tags that will be used for the final layout.

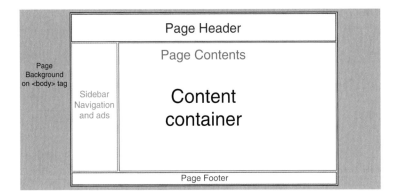

Figure 3.14 Wireframe diagrams break down a design into the essential containers in which the page contents will be located.

Inserting <div> Tags in Dreamweaver

Dreamweaver makes inserting `<div>` tags a snap. Using the Insert panel, you can easily wrap the content that's already on the page in the building blocks that are needed to construct the page layout.

1 Open the `index.html` file that you've been working on in Dreamweaver. When you compare the wireframe to the content that's already on the page, you'll see that the footer area of the page hasn't been included yet. Client change!

The footer for this design is just a copy of the same links that are over in the Navigation area, so you can easily duplicate the links.

2 Copy the list of links from the Navigation area, and then paste them under the last item on the page. Type **Footer** as the name above the list of links (replacing *Navigation*), as you see in **Figure 3.15**.

Figure 3.15 Copy and paste the unordered list of links to the bottom of the document to create the Footer area.

TIP

If you don't see the Insert panel in the group, as shown in *Figure 3.16*, you can open the panel by selecting Window > Insert.

To complete the next steps, you'll use Dreamweaver's Insert panel. This panel is grouped at the top of the right column, next to the Files and CSS Designer panel.

3   Click anywhere within the Document window, and press Ctrl+A/ Command+A. This will select all the content in the visible area of the page.

4   Click the Div button in the Insert panel (Figure 3.16). The Insert Div dialog will appear.

5   Set the Insert field at the top of the Insert Div dialog to "Wrap around selection."

6   Click in the ID field, and enter **container** as the name of this div. Click OK when your settings match the ones you see in Figure 3.16. The `<div>` tag will be inserted into your code.

Dreamweaver has all sorts of ways to check your code to make sure the action you took wrote the code correctly. Remember that the goal for this `<div>` is to create a container that will appear inside the `<body>` tag.

Figure 3.16 When the Insert panel is set to the HTML category, the Div button appears at the top of the list of items you can insert. Additional Insert categories are available from the category drop-down arrow.

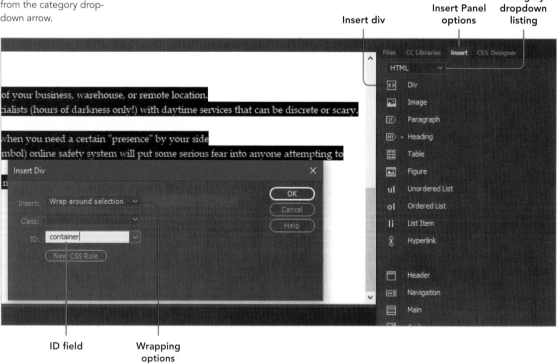

7   In Code view, place your pointer next to the line where the `<div>` is located and click the code collapse arrow (**Figure 3.17**).

Figure 3.17 Collapsing and expanding code

It's easy to see that the container `<div>` is completely within the `<body>` tag. Nesting code like this allows for styling rules to be written that take advantage of the order of the tags in the document. Well done!

Now you're going to repeat this process of selecting text on the page and inserting a `<div>` tag to wrap around each selection. Ready? Set... Go...

8   Select the company name and the tagline at the top of the page. Insert a `<div>` tag that wraps those two lines of text and set the ID to "header."

9   Select the navigation text and the list of links. Insert a `<div>` and set the ID to "sidebar."

10 Select the Heading 1 text (starting with company name) and all the text below it until you get to the end of the list of services. Insert a `<div>` that contains this area and set the ID to "content."

11 Select the footer area. Insert a `<div>` and set the ID to "footer."

Before you finish things up, this is a good time to carefully check your code using some of Dreamweaver's visualization tools. The DOM panel, for instance, is a great way to see how the containers you just inserted are nested within each other and to check for problems such as stray paragraphs and other code that doesn't belong. In the Design window, you'll see dotted lines around the `<div>` tags in the document, and if you select one of the dotted lines, Dreamweaver will place a blue border around the selected tag. You'll even be able to use the Code Navigator to have a look at any styling rules that apply to the selection.

12 Review your document and compare it to the screen capture you see in **Figure 3.18**. Take care of any cleanup that's needed then save your file.

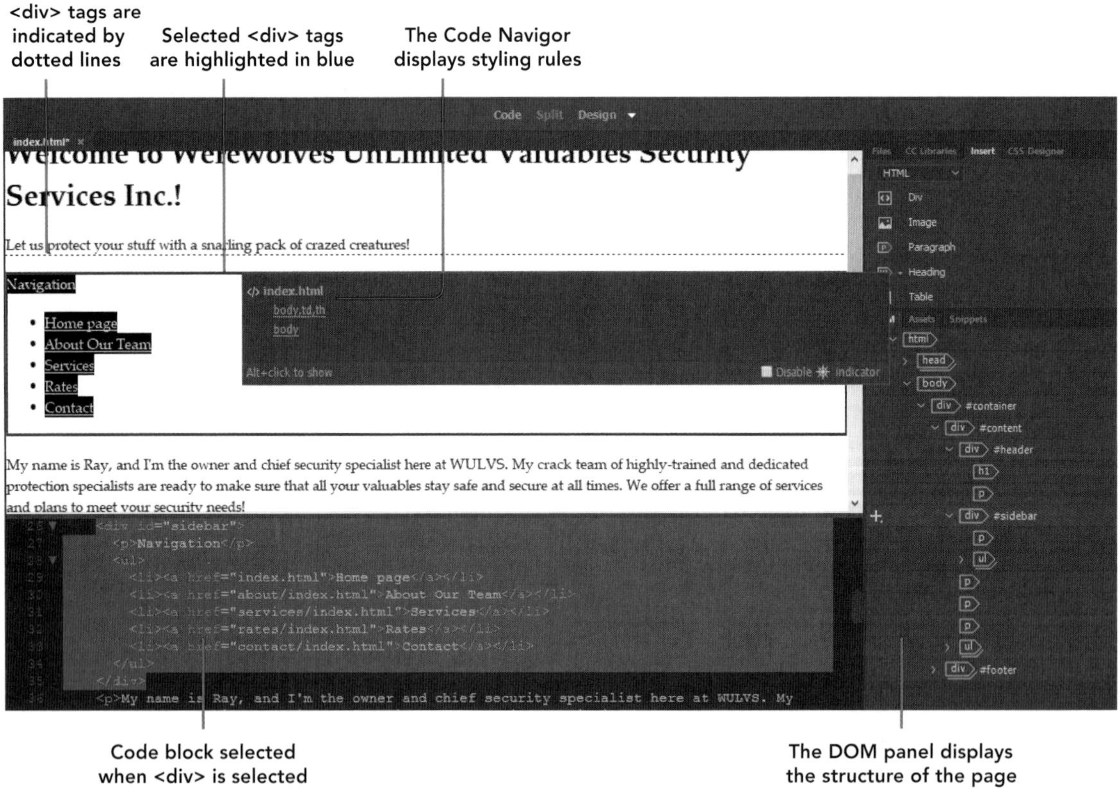

Figure 3.18 Dreamweaver provides multiple ways for you to visualize the contents of a page and check for errors.

Congratulations! You've gotten the building blocks for this page all set. In the next project, all this groundwork will finally come together as your design begins to take shape.

`<div>` tags are indicated by dotted lines

Selected `<div>` tags are highlighted in blue

The Code Navigor displays styling rules

Code block selected when `<div>` is selected

The DOM panel displays the structure of the page

From Blueprint to Assembly: Positioning Page Elements with CSS

The wulvs.info design shop has lots of excitement today. All the blueprints have been completed in the wireframe, Chris the Cartoonist has given you a better idea of how he wants the design to look, and most importantly, all the elements are baked into your code for the page using named content containers. Now it's time to experience the joy and wonder of laying out a modern web page using CSS positioning techniques. In this project, you'll complete the following tasks:

- Understand how the CSS box model is applied to elements within a design.
- Use the CSS Designer panel to add selectors to the style sheet.
- Apply margin and padding properties to selected content containers and selected elements on the page.
- Understand how float properties are applied to content containers to position elements.
- Convert an unordered list into a horizontal menu.
- Use Dreamweaver's tools to examine and modify styling rules in your document.

To begin, let's look at the CSS box model and how it affects positioned objects in an HTML document.

★ *ACA Objective 4.3*

★ *ACA Objective 5.1*

▶ *Video 3.5 From Blueprint to Assembly: Positioning Page Elements with CSS*

DO NOT MISS THIS MOVIE!

More than any other project in this book, this project really needs to be done after watching Video 3.5, "From Blueprint to Assembly: Positioning Page Elements with CSS."

Lots of the visualization tools that Dreamweaver provides are interactive, and you'll get a better feel for how they work if you see them in full-motion action. The video also gets you right down into the action as the layout of the page moves along.

The CSS Box Model

Elements within a content container in a web page have certain values applied to them by default. Values for the margin, border, and padding wrap around the content within a container and have width values that you can apply to all four sides of the box.

You should always keep in mind that every element within a web page lives within a box, and every one of those boxes contains values that might be hidden from plain view. Content inside a container is wrapped by invisible padding and margin properties. In between those two invisible elements lies the border, which may be styled with a color value and even a border style. Visually represented, the box model appears as you see in **Figure 3.19**.

CSS Box Model

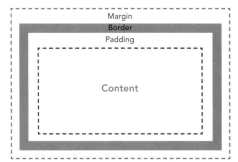

Figure 3.19 The CSS box model refers to the way that content in a web page is wrapped by padding, borders, and margins.

You'll witness some of the gotchas that the CSS box model can create when you lay out this page. With that in the back of your mind, press ahead and start putting the building blocks for this design into position.

Positioning Elements with CSS

You'll be using the CSS Designer panel to complete the steps that follow, but before starting you may wish to drag the left edge of the panel even farther left so that you see two columns displayed. You'll see this configuration in the screen captures that follow.

SETTING SOME BACKGROUND COLOR

It's helpful to visualize the layout of the page by assigning temporary background colors to the different containers. This will allow you to see any gaps that might appear and to check the position of the content blocks.

1 In the CSS Designer panel, click the **body** selector, as shown in **Figure 3.20**. You may have to drag the left side of the panel farther to the left so your display matches that shown in the figure. Note that the view at the top of the panel is set to All and that the **<style>** tag is highlighted in the Sources area. The Show Set check box should be unselected.

2 Click the Background category at the top of the Properties section, as shown in Figure 3.20. Drag the color selector to the position you see indicated, and set the background of the **<body>** tag to a light gray. Alternatively, you can type the hexadecimal value highlighted in the image, #D7D7D7.

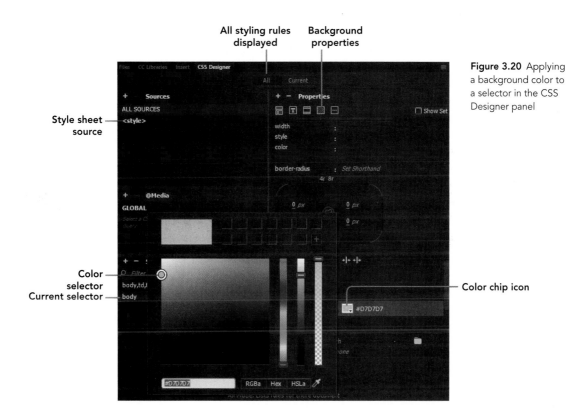

Figure 3.20 Applying a background color to a selector in the CSS Designer panel

STYLING THE OUTERMOST <DIV>

Now you can begin to style the outermost <div> in this design—the
#container div.

1　In the Code window, select <div id="container"> in the Code window.

2　In the CSS Designer panel, click the + next to the word Selectors to create
a selector.

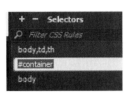

Figure 3.21 Dreamweaver
automatically names the
new selector.

Dreamweaver will identify the selection on the page and automatically name
the selector based on its attribute, as you see in **Figure 3.21**. How slick is that?

This container needs to "float" on top of the <body> tag and needs margins
applied left and right. One way to achieve this is to set a width for the container and apply an auto value to the margins of the container.

3　In the CSS Designer panel, select the Layout category, and set the width value
to **960 px**. Then set the left and right margins to **auto** in the margin section.
Set the top and bottom margins to **0 px**. Use **Figure 3.22** as a guide.

Figure 3.22 Use the CSS
Designer panel to apply
width and margin proper-
ties to the container <div>.

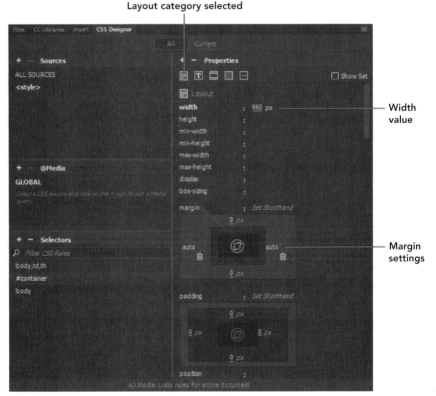

4   Switch to the Background category and set the Color value to white using the same process you followed in step 2 of the previous exercise.

5   Preview this page using the Preview in Browser button located in the lower-right corner of the Document window. If you have unsaved changes, you'll be prompted to save the file before you preview.

You'll see that the container `<div>` is floating above the page and that margins appear to the left and right (**Figure 3.23**). Great job!

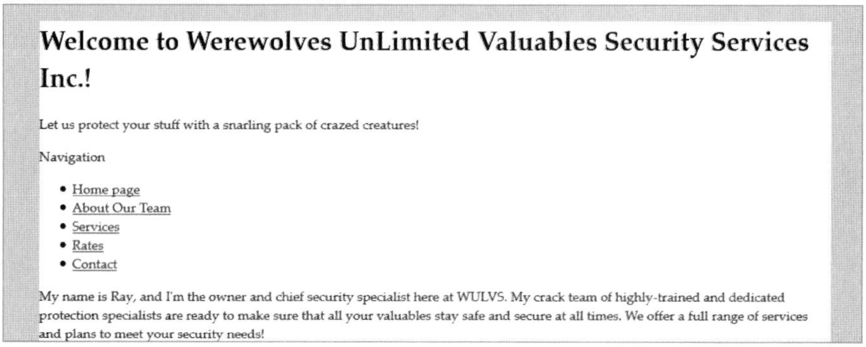

Figure 3.23 The preview shows the container `<div>` styled with a white background and gray margins.

STYLING THE HEADER <DIV>

The next `<div>` to style is the header.

1   Select `<div id="header">` in the Code window, and then click the + in the Selectors section to create a selector for the header. If your code is still collapsed from your previous exploration, you may need to expand the code to see this tag.

You'll see that in this case Dreamweaver creates a *descendent* selector by putting the `#container` selector in front of the `#header` selector. You can make these settings more or less specific by pressing the Up Arrow key on your keyboard. The only selector you need in this case is `#header`.

2   Press the Up Arrow key until only the `#header` value remains, and press Enter/Return.

3   Switch to the Text category in the CSS Designer panel, and set the `text-align` value to "center" using the button located next to the name of the property.

4   Select `<div id="sidebar">` in the Code window.

5   Click the + to create a selector. Press the Up Arrow key on your keyboard to change the value of the selector until only the `#sidebar` name remains, and accept the name.

6   In the Layout category, apply the following values to the `#sidebar` styling rule to set the width of the box and move it to the left side of the screen:

    Width: **180 px** Float: **left**

7   Select the line of code containing the `<div>` named `content` and create a new selector with the name set to **#content**.

    The goal here is to set the width of this container so that it snugs up against the sidebar. Since you have a 960 px container `<div>` and the sidebar `<div>` is 180 px, the content `<div>` *should* be 780 px, right? But not when a little padding is added to the left side of the container. When that happens, the CSS box model comes into play, so the content actually slides underneath the sidebar. But you can adjust that easily enough by subtracting the 10 px of padding from the formula to get a width value of 770 px.

8   Apply the following values to the `#content` styling rule in the Layout category:

    Width: **770 px** Float: **left** Padding-left: **10 px**

    When you finish creating that styling rule, the content `<div>` will float up against the sidebar, and you'll be good to go.

STYLING THE FOOTER <DIV>

The final content container to address is the footer `<div>`. This container needs to have a special float property applied to it so that the sidebar and content containers stay put and aren't allowed to move next to the footer.

1   Select `<div id="footer">` in the Code window, and create a selector named **#footer**.

2   Apply the following values to the `#footer` styling rule in the Layout category to clear out the previous floats in the page and make the text center aligned:

    Text-align: **center** Clear: **both**

    Now is a good time to temporarily assign background color values to the containers on the page so you can see how things lay out and see if there are any gaps that need to be addressed.

3 Return to the selectors for the #header, #sidebar, and #footer, and set a background color of your choice in the Background category.

FIXING THE GAPS

If you preview your design in a browser now, you'll see that there are indeed two issues with this page. There's a margin at the top of the page and a margin below the header.

These gaps (**Figure 3.24**) are caused by the default margin properties that the paragraph tags in the header contain. A great way to see these hidden margins is by switching to Dreamweaver's Live view and turning on Inspect mode. With that little button selected, Dreamweaver will display hidden margin and padding properties as you float your mouse over the different containers on the page. To correct those margins, you'll need to add some new attributes to the paragraphs within the header.

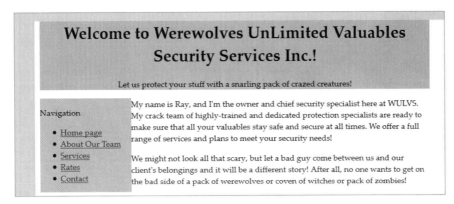

Figure 3.24 Dreamweaver provides multiple ways for you to visualize the contents of a page and check for errors.

1 Select the line of text that contains the company name, at the very top of the document. In the Property inspector's ID field, type **header-name**.

2 Create a selector for #header-name and set the margin-top value to **0px**.

3 Select the next paragraph in the header area—the tagline—and set the ID of the paragraph to **header-tagline**.

4 Create a selector for #header-tagline and set the margin-bottom value to **0px**.

Once this action is complete, you'll find that the margins that were at the top of the page have disappeared, as you see in **Figure 3.25**. Great work.

Figure 3.25 Gaps have been eliminated with a little CSS.

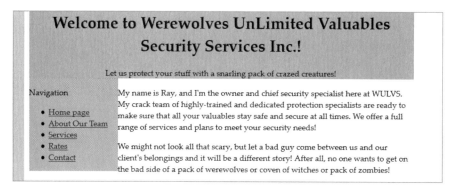

STYLING THE LINKS IN THE FOOTER

The final bit of work that needs to be done is in the footer area. The list of links in this part of the page need to be displayed side by side, and you certainly don't want those bullets to appear. Let's take care of those things with a few more styling rules.

1   Locate and select the `<ul>` tag that's inside the footer container. Add a selector using the descendent selector. Dreamweaver suggests names for selectors based on the element that's selected. For this selector, set the name to #footer ul.

2   In the Text category, set list-style-type to **none** as the value for the text in this list.

The bullets magically disappear.

3   Click the first `<li>` tag in the list, and click the + in the Selectors area. Accept the suggested new selector name: `#footer ul li`.

4   In the Layout category, set the display value to **inline** to have the text appear side by side.

More magic! The list of links shrinks down to a single line, and the footer area now appears as it was envisioned. Once again—well done.

Hooray! You made it!

5 Save your work, preview your design in a browser, and make note of any issues that appear. After you compare your design to the one you see in **Figure** 3.26, save your file and take a well-deserved break.

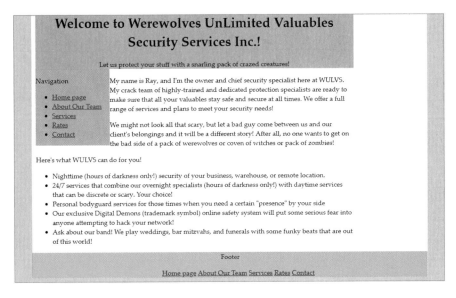

Figure 3.26 The final page layout as viewed in a browser window

Challenge! Create Your Own Page Comps

You've learned a lot about page layouts and the building blocks of HTML in this chapter. Now it's time to think about how you might go about creating your own designs. What you know about web design and how pages are constructed should give you an appreciation of how to go about creating (in your favorite graphics editor) new designs that can be translated into HTML and CSS.

Whether you use Adobe XD, Photoshop, or Illustrator for designing your page comps, keep in mind a few things that have to do with the available canvas sizes and other measurements that you'll want to use.

If you design for a default monitor resolution of 1024 x 768 pixels, when you subtract for scroll bars along the sides and browser buttons across the top, the actual viewable area is approximately 1000 x 475 pixels. That's all the space you have to work with before the viewer starts needing to scroll to see additional content. Of course, there are high-resolution monitors (4K, for example).

Where you want to have margins on the page, you'll need to reduce the area of the page where the content sits to an even smaller size. The size that was used in the final project here (980 pixels) is a good one to begin with.

Keep in mind that it's awfully common these days for page comps to be designed for multiple screen sizes. In fact, there is a push to design for mobile first. You might have one design for the page as it will be seen on a desktop computer, another comp for a tablet view, and a third comp for the design as it would appear on a phone. Online, you can find free blank templates that show the various sizes that are used in design comps, and you can use those templates when you open Photoshop and get to work on your own unique creation. As your knowledge of web design increases, you will learn to set media queries to adjust the content to the available screen real estate. You will also learn to make your pages responsive so that the content adjusts depending on the device resolution.

Conclusion

When you think back on all you've done in this chapter, you have to be feeling pretty good about what you can now do with Dreamweaver. Along the way you learned how text is formatted on the page. You saw how links are inserted. You also learned how a page layout is designed using named content containers with CSS styling. You have used many of Dreamweaver's tools for visualizing and modifying the code that makes up your new web pages. In one (kind of) short chapter, you've built out a complete website. You created the folders and files that are needed for the site to function and be easy to use. You've even done some detective work in figuring out what a client wants and translated those clues into code. You are well on your way to getting a handle on the amazing things you can do when code comes under your command.

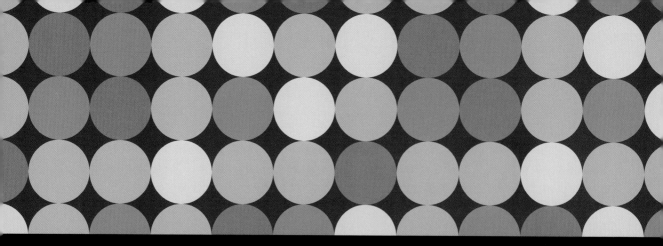

CHAPTER OBJECTIVES

Chapter Learning Objectives

- Understand how the client-to-design process works for creating page prototypes that meet the customer's requirements.

- Create CSS styling rules that make use of background images.

- Use round-trip editing to insert a source Photoshop image file and edit the file from within Adobe Dreamweaver.

- Insert images on a web page and position them using CSS floats.

- Learn the location and purpose of Dreamweaver's image editing tools and the recommended methods for their use.

- Use Dreamweaver's visualization tools to troubleshoot designs and align elements on the page.

Chapter ACA Objectives

For full descriptions of objectives, see the table on pages 258–264.

DOMAIN 1.0
WORKING IN THE WEB INDUSTRY
1.1, 1.2, 1.3, 1.5

DOMAIN 2.0
PROJECT SETUP AND INTERFACE
2.1, 2.3, 2.4

DOMAIN 4.0
WORKING WITH CODE TO CREATE AND MODIFY CONTENT
4.1, 4.2, 4.3

CHAPTER 4

Getting the Big Picture

Human beings are incredibly visual creatures. Our brains can process more information when we view a picture or illustration than we can by reading a long passage of text. The old saying "a picture is worth a thousand words" is certainly true.

Images and visuals are a huge part of the modern web experience, and in a world in which you can snap a photo on your phone and instantly publish it online, visitors to a web page expect to see lots of images. And just like graphics, images can be used to define the layout of web pages and assist in the usability of the site, making it easier for visitors to find their way around and get to the information they're after. Don't forget to make your images accessible for visitors who cannot physically see your site.

In this chapter, you'll take a look at how to use images to further define the look and feel of a design, how to insert and position images, and the tools that Dreamweaver provides to help you get those jobs done.

Bring On the Art!

Figure 4.1 Chris

Great news! Your client Chris the Cartoonist (**Figure 4.1**) has provided a *ton* of artwork for the *WULVS.info* website, and he's also given you excellent guidance on how he wants the design to proceed.

From Chris:

I really like the layout of the page! Those colors are kind of weird, but I know that's just temporary, right? Let me tell you a little more about the storyline and the characters in my made-up world.

WULVS is a comic strip built around a security service run by Ray the Werewolf.

In Ray's world, he works with a group of vampires, zombies, witches, mummies, aliens, and other characters who work as guards for hire by the "regular" humans of the world.

Part of the fun of the comic strip is how Ray runs his business—and his website—just like a regular business. After all, a monster has to make a living too. What I want to do is use the artwork of the characters in the strip to create Ray's company website, wulvs.info.

I'm going to break down what I want for each page and put it into a separate document. OK? I'm looking forward to seeing your work!

Lucky for you, he's happy with the layout that was made from the wireframes in the last chapter. Now you can take the big step of designing the pages the way Chris wants. Well, he isn't sure exactly what he wants quite yet, but that just means you can put on your designer hat and start working on a prototype for this site.

To get started on all the new elements for this design, you'll need to download the files that have been provided and define your Chapter 4 website.

Get Your Files Here

As you did in previous chapters, copy the folder that contains this chapter's files to your computer.

1. Download the project files for this lesson, named `chapter-04.zip`, from the Lesson & Update Files tab on your Account page at *www.peachpit.com*, and store them on your computer in a convenient location.

2. Unzip the files and copy the `chapter-04` folder to the `Learn-Dreamweaver` folder you created in Chapter 1.

Define the Chapter 4 Website

With the files you've been provided for this chapter in the project folder, you're ready to set up the site in Dreamweaver.

1 From the application bar, select Site > New Site.

2 Name the site **Chapter 4**.

3 Browse to the `chapter-04` folder in your `Learn-Dreamweaver` project folder.

4 Click Save.

★ *ACA Objective 2.1*

NOTE

Refer to Video 1.10, "Defining a Site," if you want a quick demo of how the site definition process works.

Image File Formats for the Web

Deciding on the right kind of image to include in a web page goes beyond simply getting the best picture available and sticking it on a page—although making that choice can be a huge chore in itself. You also need to understand which types of files will be displayed properly by the viewer's browser and which type is most appropriate for the kind of image you are adding.

★ *ACA Objective 2.4*

At the most basic level, it's pretty simple. Web browsers can display three file types:

- **GIF** (Graphics Interchange Format) images have filenames that end with the .gif file extension. GIFs can display a limited number of colors, which makes them very efficient. GIFs are a great choice for graphics—such as logos, illustrations, navigation bars, and other design elements—that don't require colors with subtle shades. GIFs can have a transparent background, and of course you can animate GIFs to create miniature movies. How else would we be able to see cats playing pianos?

- **JPEG** (Joint Photographic Experts Group) files use the .jpg or .jpeg extension, and as you can probably guess, this format is best used for photographs and other images with thousands or millions of colors. JPEG images can be compressed by changing quality settings in an image editor to get smaller file sizes. Web designers often compare different quality settings in Photoshop, for instance, until they achieve a good balance between how good the image looks and its file size. JPEGs cannot have transparent areas and cannot be animated.

- **PNG** (Portable Network Graphics) was specifically developed for use on the web. The cartoon character images you've been provided all use the PNG format because images in this format can display transparency, sharp edges, and color changes—like a GIF—but still allow for subtle shades of colors like a JPEG. PNG files are by far the most common file type used by modern web designers.

All these file types are in the family of images known as bitmaps. In a bitmap, every color in the image is defined as a tiny block of data with a color value and other properties. If you've ever zoomed way in on a digital image, you've seen those individual blocks magnified and seen how the image is composed.

Every image in a web page must be downloaded from a remote server somewhere, which makes image file weight—the size of the file as measured by how much data it holds—almost as important as how it looks. Large image files are one of the primary culprits when a page loads slowly—for example, inserting an image that weighs 500 KB versus one that weighs 100 KB.

This process of choosing the right file type and adjusting image properties (to get a small file size that still looks good) is known as optimization. Adobe makes Photoshop for editing and optimizing images. The best method for working with images is to compose and edit the images in a graphics editor and then export a version that has been optimized for viewing on the web.

Whether or not you're optimizing your images or you're working with a graphic designer who will prepare the images while you take on the coding duties, you do need to know the kind of images that are appropriate for different applications. Smart designers *always* work with a source Photoshop file and *never* work directly on an image file or photograph without having a backup.

Prototyping and Designing with Background Images

★ ACA Objective 1.1

★ ACA Objective 1.2

★ ACA Objective 1.5

★ ACA Objective 2.4

★ ACA Objective 4.3

▶ **Video 4.1** *Client Feedback*

▶ **Video 4.2** *Prototyping and Faux Column Layout*

▶ **Video 4.3** *Designing with Background Images*

Chris has been hard at work and has provided all sorts of new information to work with. In the project files for Chapter 4, Chris has supplied a bunch of images and specific feedback on how things should look going forward. Based on the instructions and the materials he has provided, you can start getting content into place.

Examining Client Feedback and Requirements

Take a few moments to familiarize yourself with the new files and folders that Chris provided.

1   Open Dreamweaver and review the structure of the site and the new folders and images.

    The folders and files you created in Chapter 3 are still in place, but new images and documents have been supplied by the client (**Figure 4.2**). The `images` folder contains lots of new cartoon characters, and the `source` folder contains Photoshop files. Also included are two client feedback files.

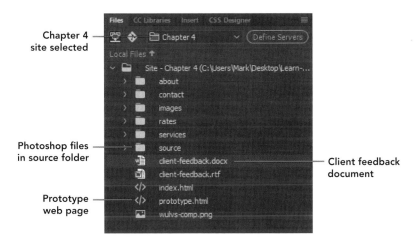

Figure 4.2 The files and folders for the Chapter 4 website

2   Open `client-feedback.docx` by double-clicking the file in Dreamweaver.

    The file opens in Microsoft Word (if that application is installed on your computer). If you don't have Word installed on your computer, you can open the `client-feedback.rtf` file in almost any word processor.

3   Read through the client feedback from the client.

Deciphering information from a client frequently involves a lot of detective work. What specific guidance does the client provide? What things are being left up to you as the designer? And most importantly at this stage, can you determine enough information to get a feel for how things should look?

4   Open the client's design comp by double-clicking `wulvs-comp.png`.

This file opens in the default graphics editor on your computer (**Figure 4.3**).

The design comp includes the major design elements that the client is requesting. The page is centered in the viewport and has a header, sidebar, footer, and main content area. You'll also see design clues as to how the client wants images to be used. This is another good time to jot down some notes on what you discover in this document.

Header with character collage   Character inserted into the page

Figure 4.3 Major design elements in the design comp provided by the client

Sidebar and navigation area

Page background with textured image

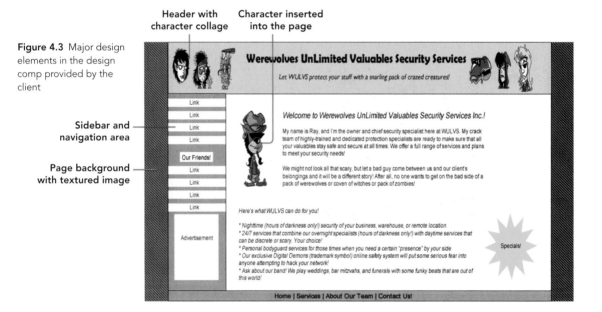

5   Now open `index.html`.

This is the same file that you finished at the end of Chapter 3. Compare this file to the client's composition and you will see many differences (for example, the background colors differ and there are no images).

6   Open `prototype.html`.

This is a file that you might have developed based on your detective work of the information your client provided. In the interest of time, the following tasks have been done for you:

- The document includes the content that will appear in several pages of the website. You'll find new Heading 1 tag sections for the Team, Services, Rates, and Contact pages.
- The Team section has character descriptions, the Services and Rates sections have tables of information, and the Contact section has a spot for a form.
- The sidebar area has text for two navigation sections and placeholder text for where advertising might go.
- New CSS styling rules have been created to assign background colors and borders to the header and footer areas of the page.

7 Open the CSS Designer panel. Select the Show Set check box in the upper-right corner of the panel, and examine the properties that have been applied to the #header and #footer rules in this document.

Once you've thoroughly reviewed all the changes that have been made and compared those changes to the index.html file, you are ready to move on to more styling. You can even close index.html. All the work you do from this point forward will be done in prototype.html.

Prototyping in Web Design

Working with a technical prototype is a very common method used by designers as they reach this stage in designing a website. By using a single document like the one you'll work on in this chapter, all the individual images, text, tables, and other elements can be placed and styled into a single page. The CSS styling rules remain in the <head> of the page while this work is going on, making it easier to keep track of the rules as you create, troubleshoot, and modify styles. When the styling is complete and the client has given final approval to move forward, the CSS file will be converted into a separate, external file, and the contents of each section can be copied to the pages where they'll ultimately reside.

This kind of workflow also allows you as the designer to take advantage of Dreamweaver's automation features as final designs are converted to templates and library items. These templates and library items make it easier to generate new pages and update an entire site full of web pages when a revision takes place.

Using the Faux Column Technique to Style the Sidebar

The client's design calls for a sidebar to extend down the left side of the page. That's a very common arrangement, but it presents a challenge: How does a web designer style this area of the page in such a way that it appears correctly no matter how long the web page is? Let's understand the problem, then see a common solution.

1   With `prototype.html` open, place Dreamweaver in Design view. From the application bar, choose View > Design View Options > Visual Aids > CSS Layout Backgrounds. You can enable and disable this view as you examine the page.

Dreamweaver will apply color coding to help you visualize the `<div>` elements of the page (**Figure 4.4**).

Figure 4.4 The Design window with CSS Layout Backgrounds enabled

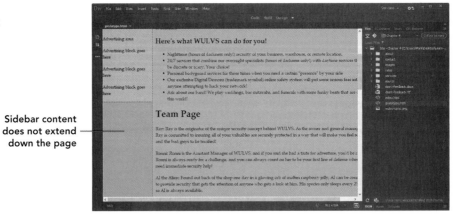

Sidebar content does not extend down the page

Notice that the main area content is longer than the sidebar content. You could insert your cursor into the sidebar and press Enter/Return to add a bunch of empty paragraphs until the sidebar is as full as the content area, but that's a very sloppy way to deal with the issue. It will also generate many problems when you view the page on different devices (such as smartphones and tablets). Instead, you will use a time-tested method of styling with a background image. This method is known as the *faux column* technique.

2 Double-click the `container-bg-gold.png` file inside the `images` folder to open it.

The faux column technique is perfect for a fixed-width page like the one you're working on. Alternative approaches are needed when working with responsive designs for mobile devices. To create the illusion that the left column is filled up, a background image that matches the width of the container is used for the background. In this case, the `#container <div>` is set at 960 pixels wide.

The `#sidebar <div>` is 180 pixels wide. The area of the image that will provide the background color or pattern needs to be set to a matching width. **Figure 4.5** details how this image is laid out.

Image matches the width of the container div: 960 pixels

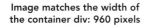

Figure 4.5 An image for use as a faux column

The "column" area of the image is set to 180 pixels wide to match the sidebar width.

Notice that the image is only 20 pixels high. A background image like this one doesn't need to be any larger, because it will repeat vertically inside its container.

3 Open the CSS Designer panel, and select the `#container` selector.

4 In the Background section, locate the `background-image` property and click the Browse for File icon to locate the image.

5 Browse to the `chapter-04/images` folder and select `container-bg-gold.png`. Click OK/Open to set the image as the background.

6 To control how the image repeats, or tiles, down the container, set the `background-repeat` property to **repeat-y**. This will restrict the image to repeating only down the page and not across.

NOTE

You'll actually have to click the folder icon beside the URL field twice in many cases. This might be intentional or just one of those little quirks that software programs sometimes have.

Figure 4.6 The CSS Designer panel set to the Background category

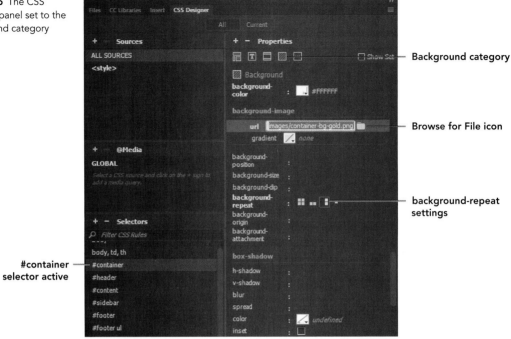

Files
CC Libraries
Insert
CSS Designer
All
Current
Sources
ALL SOURCES
<style>
Properties
Show Set
Background
background-color
#FFFFFF
background-image
url
images/container-bg-gold.png
gradient
none
@Media
GLOBAL
Select a CSS source and click on the + sign to add a media query.
background-position
background-size
background-clip
background-repeat
background-origin
background-attachment
Selectors
Filter CSS Rules
body, td, th
#container
#header
#content
#sidebar
#footer
#footer ul
box-shadow
h-shadow
v-shadow
blur
spread
color
undefined
inset
Background category
Browse for File icon
background-repeat settings
#container selector active

7 Compare your settings to **Figure 4.6**.

If everything looks good, it's time to preview your work in your favorite web browser. Your `prototype.html` page should look similar to **Figure 4.7** after you scroll down to the "Here's what Wulvs can do for you!" heading.

Figure 4.7 `Prototype.html` page viewed in browser (note that the sidebar appears throughout the left side of the web page).

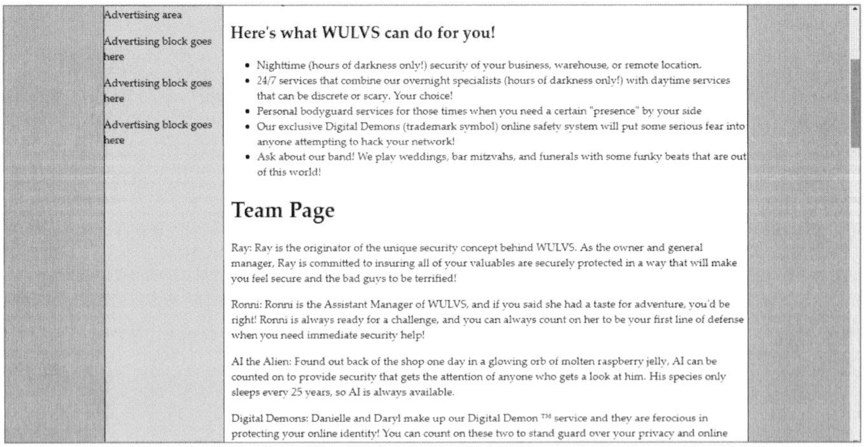

Advertising area
Advertising block goes here
Advertising block goes here
Advertising block goes here
Here's what WULVS can do for you!
Nighttime (hours of darkness only!) security of your business, warehouse, or remote location.
24/7 services that combine our overnight specialists (hours of darkness only!) with daytime services that can be discrete or scary. Your choice!
Personal bodyguard services for those times when you need a certain "presence" by your side
Our exclusive Digital Demons (trademark symbol) online safety system will put some serious fear into anyone attempting to hack your network!
Ask about our band! We play weddings, bar mitzvahs, and funerals with some funky beats that are out of this world!
Team Page
Ray: Ray is the originator of the unique security concept behind WULVS. As the owner and general manager, Ray is committed to insuring all of your valuables are securely protected in a way that will make you feel secure and the bad guys to be terrified!
Ronni: Ronni is the Assistant Manager of WULVS, and if you said she had a taste for adventure, you'd be right! Ronni is always ready for a challenge, and you can always count on her to be your first line of defense when you need immediate security help!
Al the Alien: Found out back of the shop one day in a glowing orb of molten raspberry jelly, Al can be counted on to provide security that gets the attention of anyone who gets a look at him. His species only sleeps every 25 years, so Al is always available.
Digital Demons: Danielle and Daryl make up our Digital Demon ™ service and they are ferocious in protecting your online identity! You can count on these two to stand guard over your privacy and online

Using Images in Page Backgrounds

The second client request is for an image that displays on either side of the content area of the web page. Chris has provided several different images for you to try. You might not actually use these in the final design, but it's a good opportunity to see the different background-repeat settings that CSS provides and to see how images may be used to style the entire visible window in a web browser display.

This process uses the same tools and techniques you just used on the `#container` selector, except this time you'll work with the body selector.

1   Open the CSS Designer panel, and select the body selector. This selector was created previously to "zero out" the page margins and to set a temporary background color.

2   Click the Background category, and move your cursor over the background color setting, as you see in **Figure 4.8**.

You'll see two buttons appear to the right: a button that allows you to disable a setting temporarily and a trash can icon for deleting a property.

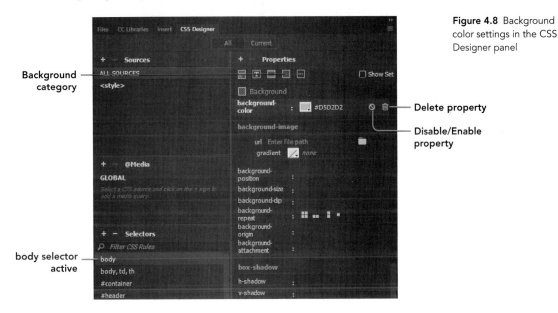

Figure 4.8 Background color settings in the CSS Designer panel

3   Click the trash can icon to delete the background color setting.

Web designers frequently use tiny images set to repeat across and down the page to create a wallpaper effect.

4   Click the Browse icon next to the background-image url field.

5   Browse to the chevron_bg.png file in the images folder. Select the file and
    click OK/Open.

    The background-image setting will appear (**Figure 4.9**).

6   Set the background-repeat option to tile across and down.

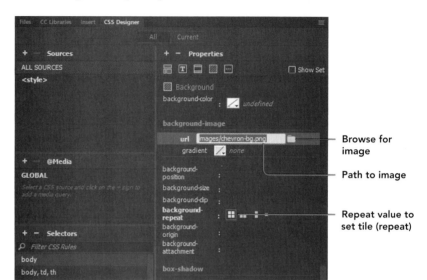

7   Click the Real-time Preview button (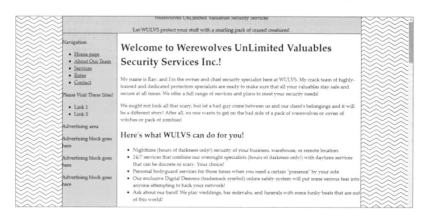) in the lower-right corner of the
    document window. When prompted, choose to save and view the file in your
    favorite browser.

    You'll see this one small image tile across and down the page (**Figure 4.10**).

8 Click the Browse icon in the background-image settings area, and switch the file to `diamond-bg.png`. Again, preview your page in a browser to see tiled background images in action.

The design in **Figure 4.11** might not make the final cut, but you should have a good idea of how this kind of image can be incorporated into a design.

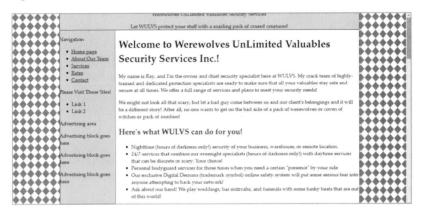

Figure 4.11 The single diamond image repeats horizontally and vertically as the background for the body selector.

Another common background image design technique is to use a wide image with gradients or other visual properties set on either side of a blank area of the canvas.

9 Return to the Files panel. From the `source` folder, open `gradient-bg.psd` (a Photoshop file) (**Figure 4.12**).

Note that this image is quite wide—2200 pixels—but only 20 pixels high. You'll also see that the center portion of the canvas has been filled with a white rectangle that matches the width of the #container `<div>`.

TIP

This approach will work only with static-sized web pages (and may not display properly on mobile devices). You will learn about alternative approaches in a future chapter.

Rectangle matches
container width

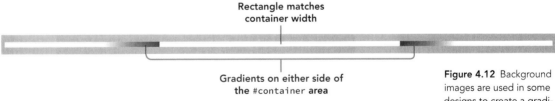

Gradients on either side of
the #container area

Figure 4.12 Background images are used in some designs to create a gradient border effect.

10 Return to Dreamweaver and the CSS Designer panel, and use the Browse for File icon in the background-image setting to switch the background image to `gradient-bg.png`.

11 The background-position setting should be set to 50% and 0% to place this image in the center of the viewport. You can drag your mouse to apply this setting, or click inside the value field and type the value.

12 Click the repeat-y icon in the background-repeat area, and compare your settings to those in **Figure 4.13**.

Figure 4.13 Centering a background image that repeats vertically down the page

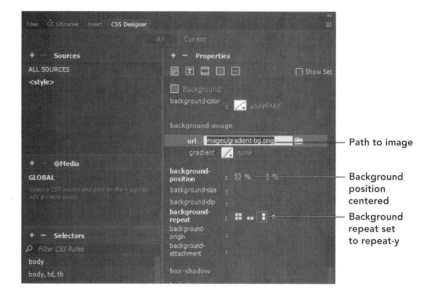

Path to image

Background position centered

Background repeat set to repeat-y

When you preview the page in a browser or switch to Live view, you'll see that the area on either side of the page contents has a gradient background that fades to white. This is another way the client's requirements might be met using background images. Be aware that this may cause significant issues when working with responsive layouts, but it can be a quick approach to develop a prototype for a client (**Figure 4.14**).

Figure 4.14 The effect of using a background image that repeats vertically down the page

Using CSS Gradients in Page Backgrounds

In the past, it was standard practice to include background gradient images in web pages. Many sites you encounter today will still use these approaches. That is why it is important to know how to incorporate background images using Dreamweaver. With the advent of CSS3 support in modern browsers, CSS gradients are now widely used.

Let's return to the **body** selector once again.

1 Open the CSS Designer panel and select the **body** selector.

2 Click the Background category and move your cursor over the background color setting, as you saw previously in Figure 4.8.

3 Click the trash can icon to delete the background image setting.

4 Set Dreamweaver to Split view and scroll to the top of the CSS definitions (just below the **<style>** tag). Locate the **body** selector.

5 Modify the CSS code for the **body** selector so that it appears as shown here:

```
body {
margin-left: 0px;
margin-top: 0px;
margin-right: 0px;
margin-bottom: 0px;
background:linear-gradient(to right, black, grey);
}
```

NOTE

You can also use the CSS Designer panel background tab to create gradients.

6 Save your work and preview it in a browser of your choosing. You result should be similar to what you see in **Figure 4.15**.

Figure 4.15 The effect of using a CSS gradient as a background

In this project, you've learned how you can use background images as a layout technique where a column on the page is visually defined using a background image. You have also seen how the entire viewable area around the page contents can be styled by applying a background to the <body> tag.

LEVEL UP: YOUR OWN BACKGROUND IMAGES

Now that you know how to use background image settings, you can modify the properties of the CSS styling rule that is applied to the header area with the ID #header.

Select the #header rule in the CSS Designer panel, and apply one of the background header images the client has provided.

Looks like Chris is still going with sort of a hipster vibe. The files named argyle-bg.png and diamond-bg.png are two examples you might use. Or you can work a background image into your own design comp and use your own file.

Or you can employ a CSS gradient of your choosing. You can learn more about CSS gradients by searching for additional examples using your preferred search engine. You will discover many additional interesting effects you can employ with CSS gradients.

Inserting and Editing Images

You accomplished a lot in the first project. You've gotten some important page elements all set using background images and CSS styling rules to style the content areas of the page. Did you take the Level Up challenge? If you did, your header should also have a nice background image applied to it.

Now it's time to turn your attention to inserting images into the body of the page. Luckily for you, Chris has provided many images for you, and he's even optimized them and set the file types of the images properly so you can jump right into inserting the images. In this project, you'll use the tools that Dreamweaver provides for working with images in a website, try the editing options that are available, and follow some recommended practices for modifying images.

From your review of the design comp and the instructions the client provided, you know you have a lot of images to insert into the page.

★ *ACA Objective 1.2*

★ *ACA Objective 1.5*

★ *ACA Objective 2.4*

★ *ACA Objective 4.1*

▶ **Video 4.4** *Image Preferences*

▶ **Video 4.5** *Inserting Images Using the Assets Panel*

▶ **Video 4.6** *Inserting Photoshop Source Files*

LEVEL UP: DREAMWEAVER PREFERENCES

Dreamweaver allows you to set numerous individual preference settings that determine how the software works for you. You can determine which browsers you want to have available for previewing web pages, change the colors of your Code window, and set the font size used in the Code window, to name a few.

You can also set your preference for which image editor will open when you are using the image editing tools while working on a document.

1 Open Dreamweaver preferences by choosing Edit > Preferences (Windows) or Dreamweaver CC > Preferences (macOS).

2 Select the File Types/Editors category in the left column. You'll see the three image file types available for use in web pages (GIF, JPEG, PNG), and you can select which editor to use.

3 Choose the editor you wish to use in the right column and click Close.

Photoshop is by far the most popular editor to use and is the one most likely to appear on your computer if you have the Creative Cloud suite installed.

Insert an Image Using the Assets Panel

The Assets panel is a great tool for situations in which you have many available images and want to identify which ones to use.

1   If the Assets panel is not already open, select Window > Assets. By default, the panel appears in the same panel group as the DOM and Snippets panels.

The Assets panel makes it easy to sort through all the images in your site and displays a preview of the images at the top of the panel. You can slide the divider up or down between the preview area and the alphabetical list of files to see a smaller or larger preview. **Figure 4.16** shows the functional areas of this panel.

2   Scroll through the images to locate ray.png and select it.

3   Place your cursor in front of Ray's introduction to the site (*My name is Ray…*) and click the Insert button in the Assets panel to place ray.png onto the page.

Figure 4.16 The Assets panel with the Images category selected

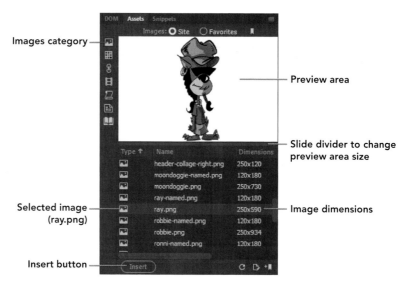

Images category

Preview area

Slide divider to change preview area size

Image dimensions

Selected image (ray.png)

Insert button

Scale and Size an Image

As soon as the image displays on the page (**Figure 4.17**), you can tell that you have a big problem. This image is way too large.

When an image is selected, you'll see a small, square resize handle appear in the image's lower-right corner. You can scale the image by holding down the Shift key while dragging this handle. Or you can click the lock icon in the Property inspector to lock the aspect ratio and keep the image set to the proper width and height dimensions as you drag.

1   Click the image, and drag the image's resize handle to what you think will be the proper dimensions for this image.

As you resize the image, dimensions will change in the Property inspector. Make note of those dimensions. We will need to change the size of the image in a photo editing program (such as Photoshop).

When you resize or scale an image in this manner, you are changing the width and height that the browser will use to *display* the image. The image itself is not changed in any way, and most importantly, the file size of the image is the same as always. Placing a large image onto the page and then setting a smaller width and height is a waste of bandwidth (the very large image must download entirely in order to display the very small resized image). A smaller version of this image works much better in this case.

Figure 4.17 The Property inspector tools for setting image dimensions

Resize handles

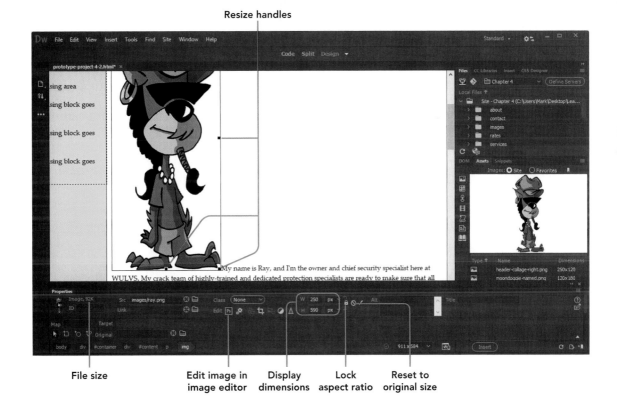

File size   Edit image in   Display   Lock   Reset to
            image editor   dimensions   aspect ratio   original size

2   Undo your changes to the image so that it returns to its original size, or click the Reset to Original Size button in the Property inspector.

In the next steps, you'll use a better method for editing an image that is too large for the page.

Duplicate and Edit an Image

Remember that smart designers never (ever!) destroy an original image. You might be tempted to open `ray.png` in Photoshop, change the image dimensions, save the file, and plunk the smaller version onto the page. But that kind of destructive process changes the file forever. You could never make the image larger again, and because you never really know how you might want to use this image in the future, it's always better to keep the original file as it is and work from a duplicate of the file. The Adobe toolset makes this an easy process.

1   Select the `ray.png` image (in the web page), and press the Delete key to remove it from the page. You will not be using this file for this location.

2   Click the Files panel, and expand the `images` folder.

3   Select `ray.png`. Right-click, and choose Edit > Duplicate from the context menu (**Figure 4.18**).

Figure 4.18 The Files panel allows you to duplicate files and perform other basic file operations.

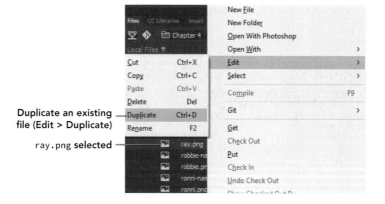

Notice the other basic file operations you can perform from the Edit menu.

Anytime you duplicate a file in this way, Dreamweaver automatically appends the name with – Copy. In this case, Dreamweaver will create a file named `ray – Copy.png`, which you'll see listed in the Files panel.

4 Click twice—but not too fast—on the file named `ray – Copy.png`. The file-name is highlighted in blue. Change the name of the file to **ray-smaller.png**.

This is the file you will use in your design, leaving the original image of Ray as it is, safe and sound.

5 Drag the `ray-smaller.png` file from the Files panel, and drop it onto the page in front of the first sentence ("My name is Ray…").

The image is at its original size, but now you can safely edit this image without harming the original.

6 With the image still selected in the page, click the Edit button in the Property inspector to open Photoshop (or the default image editor you set in Preferences). If the Property inspector is not open, from the menu select Window > Properties.

7 Resize the image and save the changes you make in your image editor. In Photoshop, you can resize the image by choosing Image > Image Size. Set the image width to **90** pixels and save the file.

8 Return to Dreamweaver and note the appearance of the image. It's still too big (and it also now looks grainy). The Property inspector still shows the original dimensions. To set the dimensions to the new, correct dimensions, click the Reset to Original Size button in the Property inspector (**Figure 4.19**). Don't forget to save your work.

New file size measurement   **Reset image to its original size**

Figure 4.19 Resizing an image in a graphics editor, such as Photoshop, reduces the file size of the image and saves on bandwidth.

Notice that the image is displayed at the dimensions you set when working in your image editor. Also note the new file size of this image as shown in the Property inspector: only 34 Kb. You saved almost 60 Kb of unnecessary data that doesn't have to be downloaded by a site visitor. You also saved bandwidth and made a backup of the original client artwork all at the same time. Good job!

Dreamweaver's Image Editing Tools

Dreamweaver includes tools in the Property inspector for editing images and performing small adjustments directly in Dreamweaver. But be warned! These tools make permanent changes to the image once you save the Dreamweaver page you're working on.

Figure 4.20 shows the location of these tools in the Property inspector. You can try these out for yourself, but be sure to choose Edit > Undo after you make each change so that the file you are using isn't permanently altered.

A **Crop Image** displays a crop area. Use the crop area handles to set the size of the area to be cropped. Double-click to crop the image.

B **Resample Image** is used when you have changed the dimensions of an image and you want to improve its picture quality at its new size and shape.

C **Brightness and Contrast** is used to make small changes to how dark or light an image is and how sharply the colors in the image are defined.

D **Sharpen** adjusts the focus of an image by changing the contrast of pixel edges in the image.

Figure 4.20 Image editing tools in Dreamweaver as seen in Design view

LEVEL UP: SMART FILE MANAGEMENT

You're probably beginning to get a feel for just how complex a website can become and just how many files and folders there are to deal with. Remember that this is a very small website.

One file management method that most web designers use is to keep a separate folder within their site where they store all their original Photoshop source files. This might also be the location where files used in other creative tools, such as Adobe Animate CC, might be stored. These source files aren't used in the actual HTML documents you create until a version of the source is published from the editor to a format that web browsers can display. But even though these files aren't part of the final web page product, having them stored inside the main (root) folder for each site you create makes it easier to find them when it's time to make edits and export for the web.

Round-Trip Editing with Photoshop

Recall that at the beginning of this project you were told that smart designers always work from an original source file from Photoshop and never take actions that will destroy an original. However, web designers in particular never know where their artwork might come from or in what format. You might, for example, have the freedom to work from an original composition that you create in Photoshop, using all your own art and photos to compose something entirely new. Photoshop has awesome tools that let you compose an entire page layout and design in one PSD file and export the images and CSS values for use in a web design project.

Web designers *also* have to work in a setting like the one you see here, where the client has provided artwork and instructions on how they should be used. Once you find that you need to modify an image in any way—changing its size, adding text, or even making color corrections to a photograph—you should create a source file so you can have a backup on hand in a format that lets you go back and make additional changes.

Dreamweaver provides a way to do this by allowing you to make **round-trip** edits from a source Photoshop file. Let's see how that works.

1 From the Files panel, expand the `source` folder and locate the file named `ronni-original.psd`.

2 Drag the `ronni-original.psd` file onto the page at the end of the last bulleted sentence (just above the header "Team Page").

   Dreamweaver will display the Image Optimization window, where you'll choose the appropriate image format for the file. For this file, you'll continue to use PNG24 as the format to be saved.

3 Click the dropdown arrow in the Preset field, and select the PNG24 option (**Figure 4.21**).

4 Click OK to set the format, and Dreamweaver will open an Explorer or Finder window so you can save the image into its web-ready format. Browse to the `images` folder inside the Chapter 4 site, and save the file as **ronni-edited.png**.

Choose the PNG24 file format from the available options

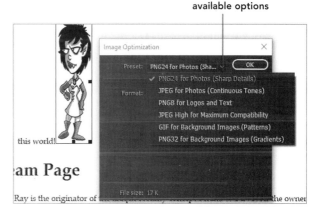

Figure 4.21 The Image Optimization window appears when you insert a PSD file in a page.

In the Property inspector, you'll see that Dreamweaver is now tracking the path and filename of the source image used to create this version (in the area marked original) (**Figure 4.22**). The next time you click the Edit button, the PSD file, and not the version that is on the page, will open in Photoshop.

Now look at the image itself. You'll see a small icon in the upper-left corner of the image that indicates this is a version of an image that came from a Photoshop source file and is available for round-trip editing.

Figure 4.22 Source Photoshop files are tracked by Dreamweaver.

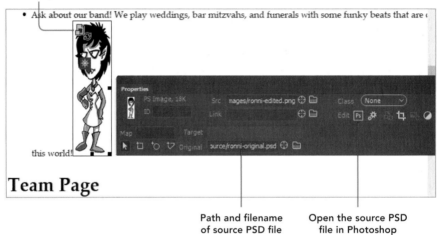

Round-trip icon

Path and filename of source PSD file

Open the source PSD file in Photoshop

5   Click the Edit button in the Property inspector. The PSD file will open in Photoshop.

Let's look at a quick demonstration of how round-trip editing works.

6   In Photoshop, choose Image > Image Rotation > Flip Canvas Horizontal. The cartoon character will rotate to face right instead of left.

7   Save the PSD file. Return to Dreamweaver.

Everything looks the same. No worries. To see the change you made in Photoshop, you have to tell Dreamweaver to update the image.

8   Click the Update from Original button in the Property inspector (**Figure 4.23**). Alternatively, you can right-click the image and choose Update from Original.

The character is now looking to the right, just as she is in the source file.

9   Save the `prototype.html` file you've been working on. This project is complete.

Alternatively, right-click the image,
and choose Update from Original

Update from
original source

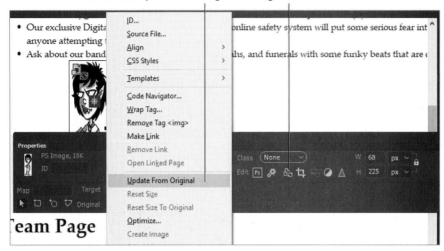

Figure 4.23 The Property inspector when working with a round-trip image

You've just learned a lot about how images are inserted into web pages using Dreamweaver's toolset. You've also seen how you can use Dreamweaver's built-in image editing tools for making minor corrections to an image and how Dreamweaver and Photoshop can be used together in the recommended workflow, where the designer makes edits to a source PSD file that can be easily updated in Dreamweaver. Don't forget to always back up your originals!

★ ACA Objective 1.5

★ ACA Objective 2.3

★ ACA Objective 2.4

★ ACA Objective 4.1

★ ACA Objective 4.3

▶ **Video 4.7**
*Floating Images
into Position*

▶ **Video 4.8**
Accessible Images

PROJECT 4.3

Floating Images into Position

You have inserted the images for the home page into your prototype page, but they still don't look like the design comp. The two images are currently resting on the baseline of the paragraph that contains them. But you can nudge them to the location you want using the CSS `float` property.

In this project, you'll float the two images into place. You'll also learn some of the principles of floating images, learn how to set the `clear` property so that your floats behave themselves, and use some Dreamweaver tools that make this type of work go more quickly.

Create and Apply a CSS Class Selector

By default, images that are inserted into a web page rest on the baseline of the element on which they've been placed. When images are inserted into a paragraph, the image will set along this invisible line along the same line of text that is adjacent to them. The CSS `float` property is used to disengage the image from the baseline and allow the text to flow around the image.

1 Open `prototype.html` in Dreamweaver. Make sure the two final versions of the cartoon characters—Ray and Ronni—that you inserted in the last project are positioned where you want them on the page.

2 Open the CSS Designer panel. Click the + at the top of the Selectors section, as you see in **Figure 4.24**. Dreamweaver will create a new blank Selector field where you can name the selector.

3 Name the new selector **.float-right** and press Enter/Return to accept the name.

4 In the Layout Properties category, click the `float-right` property button.

   You have now created and named a new class selector that can be used over and over again within the document.

   It's a good idea to apply a bit of padding to an image so that text doesn't jam up against the side of the image, making the text harder to read.

5 Click the symbol in the middle of the padding properties section. Set a padding value of **5 px** in one location. Dreamweaver will duplicate the setting to the other three sides all at once—slick!

   Now you can assign the `.float-right` property to one of your images.

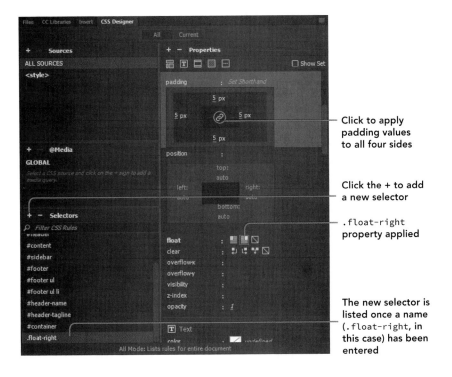

Click to apply padding values to all four sides

Click the + to add a new selector

.float-right property applied

The new selector is listed once a name (.float-right, in this case) has been entered

TIP

Class selector names always begin with a dot (.). One way to remember this is that your classes at school are usually divided into periods as well—just remember that school classes have periods and so do CSS class selectors.

6   Select the ronni-edited.png image on the web page.

7   From the Class dropdown menu in the Property inspector (**Figure 4.25**), select .float-right.

The image floats to the right of its container, and the text flows around the image. You can drag the image into different areas of the page, but the image will always float to the right of its container no matter where you drop it.

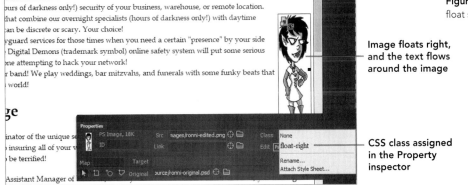

Figure 4.25 Applying a float selector to an image

Image floats right, and the text flows around the image

CSS class assigned in the Property inspector

Duplicate and Apply a CSS Class Selector

You still need a class selector to float an image to the left, but Dreamweaver has a nice way to make this process quick and easy. You can duplicate the existing selector, modify the name, and change the values for the new selector.

1   Right-click the `.float-right` selector (in the CSS Designer panel). Select Duplicate from the context menu. Dreamweaver makes a copy of the selector, and your cursor will be positioned inside the name of the new rule.

2   Change the name of the new selector to **.float-left** and press Enter/Return to accept the new name.

3   In the Properties section of the panel, change the float setting to `left`.

4   Use the Classes setting in the Property inspector to apply the `.float-left` class to the Ray the Werewolf image. The image floats to the left side of the content container.

Modify CSS Float Properties and Apply Clear Values

The design is looking good, but the image of Ronni floated to the right is smashed up against the right border of the container. You could have an issue with overlapping images when you begin floating more images into place. In the next steps, you'll adjust the padding on the `.float-right` class and set the `clear` properties that will prevent the floated images from overlapping other elements that have been floated.

1   In the CSS Designer, select the `.float-right` selector.

2   In the Properties panel, click the center of the Padding section to unlock the settings, and change the right padding setting to **15 px**, as in **Figure 4.26**.

   The other settings will remain the same as you change this one value. Setting the `clear` values for each float class is just as easy.

3   With the `.float-right` selector still selected, click the **both** value for the `clear` setting.

4   Select the `.float-left` selector, and repeat the process of setting the `clear` value to **both**.

   With both float classes properly set to `clear: both`, the next image you float will position correctly without any overlap.

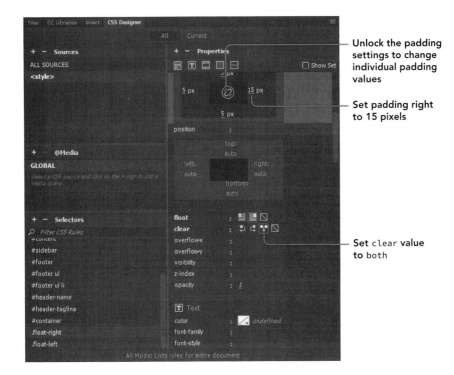

Figure 4.26 Modifying the `.float-right` class selector and setting the `clear` value

Unlock the padding settings to change individual padding values

Set padding right to 15 pixels

Set `clear` value to `both`

Add Alternative Text to Images

For web pages to be accessible to individuals with vision and other disabilities, web page images must always include alternative text. Most US government agencies require web pages to meet accessibility standards (it is also the law in other countries, such as Australia, and in the European Union). It's also just a good practice to follow because the description will display in the event the image doesn't display for some reason. Assistive devices, such as screen readers, will read the alt text to an individual who might not be able to see the image clearly. It's also helpful when your site is indexed by search engines. If the image adds meaning to the web page, include descriptive alternative text. For example, instead of using "my photo" as alternative text, use "photo of me sitting at the beach watching the waves." One gains a much greater understanding of the image contents from the latter text than from the former. Adding alt text is usually handled in the Property inspector.

1   Select the image of Ray.

2   In the Alt field in the Property inspector (**Figure 4.27**), type **Ray the Werewolf in his relaxed pose**. Click anywhere on the page to accept the value.

3 In the Title field of the Property Inspector, type **Ray the Werewolf**. Click anywhere on the page to accept this value.

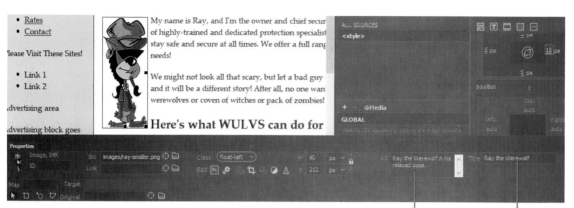

Figure 4.27 The Alt text field and Title field in the Property inspector

Type a meaningful description of the image into this field

Type a descriptive title into this field

4 Select the image of Ronni.

5 In the Alt field, type **Ronni the Vampire in her relaxed pose**. Click outside the field to accept the value.

6 In the Title field of the Property inspector, type **Ronnie the Vampire**. Click outside the field to accept the value.

See how easy it is to make your pages more accessible?

This project introduced you to the concept of floating images—the process by which a CSS rule is applied to an image so that text can flow around the image. You now know how to use Dreamweaver to create a new class selector, how to assign the properties and values you want to the selector, and even how to duplicate a selector to make the design process go a little faster. You've also learned about how to assign alt text and titles to images so that your work meets accessibility standards. Another nice piece of work!

PROJECT 4.4

Creating Structured Layouts with Images

In the last two projects, you worked a bit with client-provided artwork to float images onto the page. Where there are single images like the ones you've used so far, inserting images and applying a float to move the graphic into position is relatively easy.

The About Our Staff page features blocks of text with the name and description of each character in the comic strip. In the olden days, layouts like this—in which an image is aligned and positioned next to a paragraph of text—would have been done using tables. Unfortunately, this approach renders such pages inaccessible to those using assistive devices (and to many search engine bots). Therefore, this practice has not been employed by practicing professionals in many years. In the modern world of web design, designers use more efficient methods that take advantage of advances in browser support for CSS. Through reliance on CSS for the style of the page, the HTML content remains accessible to those using assistive devices (and search engine bots) as well.

Dreamweaver accommodates the kinds of efficient, CSS-based designs that have become the industry standard and adds some visualization features that allow designers to get things just right.

The Design Challenge

The page that features all the characters from the comic strip should have an image of the character, with their name and "bio" alongside the image. The client helpfully provided all the character images at the same width and height, which will make the design work a bit easier.

The challenge for this layout is to maintain the association between the text and the image. You might consider inserting the image and using the CSS floats that were created in the last project to slide the image into place. The problem with this approach is that floated images don't create a new "break" within the content on the page. You would have to insert a number of empty paragraphs by pressing Enter/Return over and over until each image appeared next to a line of text and had blank areas between each character. Of course, this approach would break as soon as the page is viewed on a mobile device with a different screen resolution.

★ *ACA Objective 1.5*

★ *ACA Objective 2.3*

★ *ACA Objective 4.1*

★ *ACA Objective 4.3*

▶ **Video 4.9** *Creating Structured Layouts with Images*

▶ **Video 4.10** *Rulers and Guides*

Alternatively, you might consider inserting a table and placing the images into the left column and the text into the right column. Both of these approaches are semantically incorrect, difficult to maintain, and just a bad idea.

The better approach is to create a container that holds both the image and the text, and then use the power of CSS classes to define the container and all the content that applies to each character. The result of this project's work will have the image of each character appear next to its information (**Figure 4.28**).

Figure 4.28 When this project is complete, each character will have its own content box in which to display its image and bio.

Team Page

Ray

Ray is the originator of the unique security concept behind WULVS. As the owner and general manager, Ray is committed to insuring all of your valuables are securely protected in a way that will make you feel secure and the bad guys to be terrified!

Ronni

Ronni is the Assistant Manager of WULVS, and if you said she had a taste for adventure, you'd be right! Ronni is always ready for a challenge, and you can always count on her to be your first line of defense when you need immediate security help!

AI the Alien

Found out back of the shop one day in a glowing orb of molten raspberry jelly, AI can be counted on to provide security that gets the attention of anyone who gets a look at him. His species only sleeps every 25 years, so AI is always available.

Preparing Content for the First Character Container

The client provided the name of each character and their bios in the Team Page area of `prototype.html`. With that file open, it's time to begin.

1 Place your cursor after the first character's name (Ray) (after the colon), and press Enter/Return to insert a new paragraph. Clean up any extraneous characters (such as deleting the colon) or spaces until your text appears as follows:

Ray

Ray is the originator of…

2 Place your cursor in front of Ray's name, and use the Property inspector to assign the Heading 3 format to the character's name.

3 In the Assets panel, locate the `ray-named.png` file, and insert it into the page in front of the character's Heading 3–formatted name.

Inserting a <div> for the Character Content

Now you need to create the container that will hold all the contents for each character: their image, their name, and their description.

1 Drag to select the image and all the text associated with Ray (**Figure 4.29**).

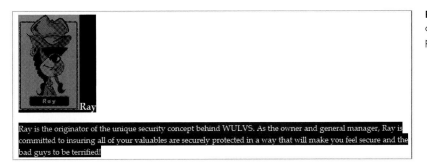

Figure 4.29 The content on the page selected and prepared for styling

2 Choose Insert > Div in the application bar. The Insert Div dialog appears.

3 Leave the Insert field in this window set to Wrap Around Selection, and click the New CSS Rule button at the bottom of the dialog. The New CSS Rule dialog appears.

4 With the Selector type at the top of the window set to Class, name the new rule **.characters**. Click OK. The CSS Rule Definition dialog appears.

5 Select the Box category in the Category column, set the `float` property to `left` and the `clear` property to `both` (**Figure 4.30**), and click OK.

You return to the Insert Div dialog.

Select the Box category

Set the `float` and `clear` properties as shown

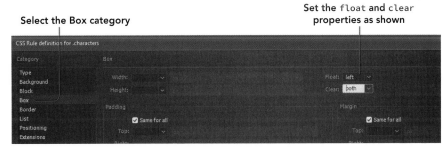

Figure 4.30 The CSS Rule Definition dialog for the new `.characters` rule

6 Click OK in the Insert Div dialog to complete the process of inserting the `<div>`.

The image and all the text are now contained inside their own container with the attribute `class="characters"`. As you recall, when the `<div>` was inserted, the field was set to Wrap Around Selection. Dreamweaver displays this container with a dotted line around it when you are in Design view.

Floating an Image Inside a Container

Now it's time to style the elements that are contained within this new `<div>`. Take note that these styling rules will use descendent selectors to create styling rules that will apply to *any* content found inside a `<div>` with the class name `.characters` applied.

1 Select the image of Ray.

2 In the CSS Designer panel, click the + in the Selectors section to create a new rule based on the item selected on the page.

Dreamweaver will suggest that you name this rule `.characters h3 img`. Do you see how the cascade works? This rule will apply to any image that is inside an `<h3>` tag that is located in a `<div>` with the `.characters` class.

But this is a little more specific than you need in this case.

3 Delete the `h3` descendent so that your rule name is `.characters img`. Don't forget to press Enter/Return.

This rule will now apply to any image found within the `.characters` `<div>`.

4 In the Layout category in the Properties section, set the `float` property to `left` and the `clear` property to `both` (**Figure 4.31**).

The text that's associated with Ray jumps up beside the image, just like you want. Don't be too concerned about the position of other characters on the page. Once all the containers are in place, things will sort themselves out. You can also check in code view to confirm that the image, header, and text are contained in the `<div>` tag.

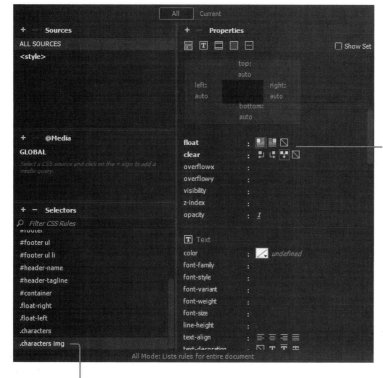

Figure 4.31 Settings for the .characters img rule

Apply float and clear properties

Choose the selector name

Create a Second Character <div>

To see the interplay between two boxes that contain a character, let's repeat the process you just followed for the Ronni character and insert a <div> around that area of the page.

1 Edit the text so that Ronni's name is on a new line, with her description below her name.

2 Format the character's name as an <h3>.

3 Insert the image ronni-named.png to the left of her name.

4 Select all the text and the image, then choose Insert > Div from the application bar or from the Insert panel.

5 In the Insert Div dialog, select the existing CSS `.characters` class from the Class dropdown menu (**Figure 4.32**). Click OK.

The contents of this new `<div>` snap into place. You now have two content boxes that you can use to adjust the styling.

Figure 4.32 You can assign an existing CSS class (`characters`) when you insert a new `<div>`.

Styling the Content Containers

Now that you have two character containers, you can fine-tune the styling properties for their contents. The beauty of using CSS rules is that once you adjust the settings for one container, all the other containers with the same class applied will be automatically updated.

1 In the CSS Designer panel, select the `.characters` selector, and apply a border to the box. Make the border **1** pixel wide, with the style set to solid and the color set to black (#000000).

You can select the Show Set check box to see only those properties assigned to the selector. Your settings should match those in **Figure 4.33**.

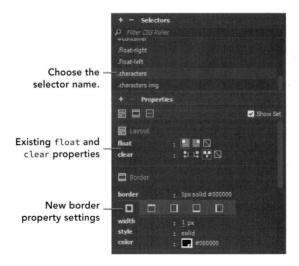

Figure 4.33 Border properties added to the `.characters` selector

Choose the selector name.

Existing `float` and `clear` **properties**

New border property settings

When you switch to Live view, you'll see that the two containers have no space between their respective boxes. Text within the box is too close to the image, and the boxes are jammed up against the right side of the page. You'll adjust these settings using the margin and padding properties.

2   With the `.characters` rule still selected, deselect the Show Set box to see all the properties. In the Layout category of the CSS Designer panel, set the bottom margin of the container to **10 px**. This adds space between the two boxes and separates them from each other.

3   Apply a right margin of **15 px**. This moves the right edge of the container away from the edge of the page.

4   Apply a right padding of **10 px**. This moves the text within the box away from the right border of the box.

The final settings for the `.characters` rule should appear as in **Figure 4.34**.

The final bit of tweaking needs to take place on the image: adding a bit of padding to the image to provide some "air" between the image and the text.

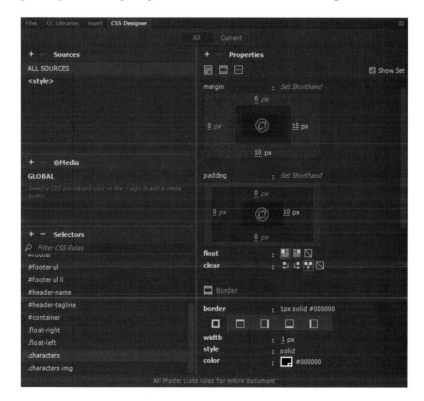

Figure 4.34 Final settings for the `.characters` rule

5   Select the `.characters img` rule.

6   In the Layout category, assign the padding values that you think look best for the right, bottom, and left padding properties. This is a great time to work in Live view so you can clearly see the changes that you make as they are applied.

Aligning Elements with Guides

One of the big advantages to using Dreamweaver to create and style web pages is the ability to put visualization tools into place that let you fine-tune your design. Guides are horizontal and vertical lines that Dreamweaver displays as you're working. You can use these guides to check the alignment of elements on the page.

1   With your document in Design view, choose View > Design View Options > Rulers > Show to display rulers on the top and left side of the document window.

2   Choose View > Design View Options > Guides > Show Guides. With this option selected, you can click one of the rulers and drag a guide onto the page.

3   Click the top ruler, and drag to position a guide directly above the first character's name. If you're having problems getting the guide into just the right place, deselect both View > Design View Options > Guides > Snap to Guides and View > Design View Options > Guides > Guides Snap to Elements.

As you can see in **Figure 4.35**, the image isn't perfectly aligned with the text. But you can fix that easily enough.

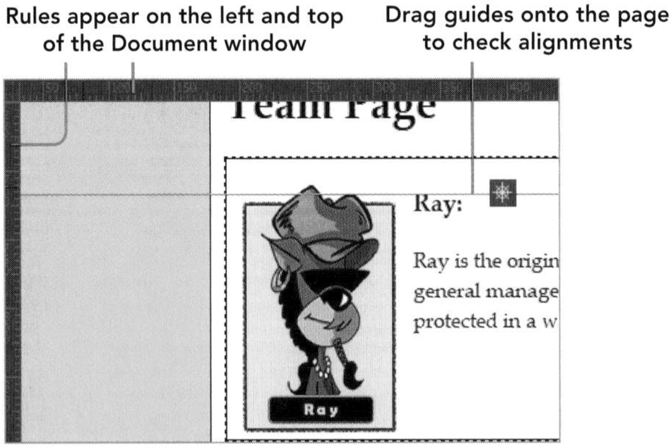

Figure 4.35 Rulers and guides allow you to check alignment of page elements.

Rules appear on the left and top of the Document window

Drag guides onto the page to check alignments

4   In the CSS Designer panel, select the `.characters img` rule, and adjust the top padding property to push the image down until it perfectly aligns with the character's name. Top padding should now be 6 pixels.

5   Drag a guide from the left ruler and position it in line with the right border of the character box.

As you scan up the page, you'll be able to see whether everything falls into alignment with this guide. Everything looks good in your character boxes, but the text in the paragraphs contained in the `#content <div>` are not in line with the borders of the character containers.

6   Click anywhere in the first line of the introductory text on the page, then click the + in the Selectors section of the CSS Designer panel. Dreamweaver will suggest that this rule be named `#container #content p`.

7   Press the Up Arrow key on your keyboard to make this rule a little less specific. The actual name you're after here is `#content p`, which is specific enough for your purposes.

8   Apply a right padding setting to this rule until the text in this paragraph and in others on the page is aligned with the guide. Right padding should now be 12 pixels for this rule.

9   Save your page, and preview it in two of your favorite browsers. Look for alignment issues that need to be addressed and return to Dreamweaver to make adjustments to the styling rules you've just created. Since different browsers use different layout engines, it is important to examine your work in a minimum of two different browsers.

Completing the Character Page Listing

You're almost finished with this project; you have just one more task to complete. Following the same steps you used to get the Ray and Ronni character containers constructed, you need to edit the text, apply a Heading 3 to the character's name, and then insert the character's image next to the name. You'll then wrap the character's contents into a new `<div>` and assign the `.characters` class. As you complete each container, the styling rules you've created will be applied to the contents, and before long all the employees of WULVS will have their own neatly aligned listing on the page.

PROJECT 4.5

Styling the Header Area

From the client feedback document you reviewed, you know that the final design needs to feature some of the characters from the comic strip at the top of the page in the header area. That's going to be a relatively easy task to accomplish since you can use CSS floats and a couple of collage images that the client has provided.

While you're styling this area, you should tend to some other matters as well. In this project, you'll insert and float the images into the header area, add links to the home page of the site, and use a web font to style the name of the company.

LEVEL UP: YOUR DREAMWEAVER SKILLS

Throughout this book, you've seen lots of detailed instructions on how to apply settings and where to find the different working areas of Dreamweaver's user interface. But now it's time for you to build your confidence in using the application by following the steps provided for this project without a great deal of extra instruction. You can follow along with the videos, of course, but at this point I'm confident that you're capable of doing more on your own. *You'll* be more confident too if you endeavor to do more and more on your own as you go forward.

Inserting and Floating the Header Images

Your client has provided new images that he wants to include at the top of the page to the left and right of the company name. In the following steps, you'll insert these images into the header area of the page and then place them into position. Keep in mind these techniques apply only to fixed designs for a desktop or laptop computer. We will learn about making the site responsive for mobile devices in a subsequent chapter. One step at a time, grasshopper.

The header area will need some additional room for the images to fit within the container. So let's do that first.

1   In the CSS Designer panel, choose the #header selector, and set the height in the Layout category to **136** pixels. You're now ready to insert the collage images.

2   Place your cursor in front of the first letter in the first line of text in the header area.

3   Using the Assets panel, insert the images `header-collage-left.png` and `header-collage-right.png`. These images will be floated, so you can just place them side by side. Name the images in the Alt field of the Property inspector. For the `header-collage-left.png` image, I recommend alternative text of "Our team includes: AI the Alien, Robbie, The Twins, Vladimir, and Ronni." For the title, I recommend the text "The first half of our team." You decide on appropriate alternative text and title for the `header-collage-right.png` image.

4   Select `header-collage-left.png`, and assign the `float-left` class to the image in the Property inspector. The image snaps into place on the left side of the header.

5   Select `header-collage-right.png`, and assign the `float-right` class to the image.

    This time the image *isn't* positioned properly; it falls outside the header. That's not good, but more than likely the issue has to do with the `clear: both` property that is assigned to this rule. Since you don't want to change the existing `float-right` class that's in use in other parts of the design, you need a new rule for this image.

6   Right-click the `.float-right` rule in the Selectors area of the CSS Designer panel. Select Duplicate.

7   Change the name of the rule to **.float-right-header**.

8   In the Layout category of the CSS Designer, change the clear value for this rule from `clear: both` to `clear: right`. This change allows the image to properly float into place within the header.

9   Select `header-collage-right.png`, and assign the `float-right-header` class to the image. The image snaps into place.

> **WARNING**
>
> *A word of caution is appropriate at this point. It is easy to duplicate classes and include slight modifications to achieve desired results in a web page. Make certain you understand the underlying CSS rules so that you don't end up creating a large number of classes to accomplish specific styling. This is often called classitis and is to be avoided as much as possible. If you end up with scores of classes on your page with only a few differences in each class, rethink how you are applying your CSS styles.*

Adding Links in the Header

It's common—even expected—for a visitor to a website to be able to click the header at the top of the page and go to the site's home page. You'll add links to the two images and to the company name to make this possible. Later, when this prototype is converted into a template, the links will be in place and ready to go.

1   Click the `header-collage-left.png` image. In the Property inspector Link field, enter the filename of the home page: **index.html**.

2   Click the `header-collage-right.png` image. Also link this image to the `index.html` home page.

3   Select the name of the company in the center of the header area on the page. Also link the selected text to the `index.html` home page.

Removing Default Styles from Text Links

Text links by default have always been shown in blue, underlined text. This obviously won't work for the design the client is after, so you'll remove those properties from the `<a>` tag with a new CSS styling rule.

1   Place your cursor anywhere within the company name in the header.

2   Click the + in the Selectors area of the CSS Designer panel. Press the Up Arrow key once so that the new selector name is set as **#header-name a**. Press Enter/Return to accept the name.

3   In the Text category, set the text color to black and text-decoration to none. Looking at the CSS you just wrote, you should see the following code block:

```
#header-name a {
  color: #000000;
  text-decoration: none;
}
```

Styling the Company Name with Fonts

The client asked for some "weird- or scary-looking" text for the company name. To get text that goes beyond the common fonts that are standard across browsers, you can use Adobe Edge Web Fonts, which is a free service, to find more interesting fonts to work with. This is a library of fonts that is served by Adobe Typekit and can be freely used on your website. Remember that fonts are covered by copyrights. Only use fonts that you are certain can be freely used on your website. By relying on fonts served from Adobe Edge Web Fonts, you don't have to worry about this issue.

The company name in this document already has a rule applied to which you can easily add additional properties and values to make the name "weird or scary."

1 Select the `header-name` rule in the Selectors area of the CSS Designer panel.

2 Set the text color to black (#000000).

3 Click inside the font-family field. From the menu that appears, select Manage Fonts.

   Adobe Edge Fonts are free font packages that will be loaded into the page with a little snippet of JavaScript that is inserted into the `<head>` of the document. The Manage Fonts dialog you see in **Figure 4.36** allows you to choose one of these fonts to use in your page.

4 Select the font `Amatic-sc` or try out another font that you like. Click Done to load the font into your library.

   Once you load a font into your library, you can assign the font as a property.

5 Click inside the font-family field, and select the `Amatic-sc` font (or whichever font you loaded) for this rule.

6 Switch to Live view to see the appearance of the text. Adobe Edge Web fonts display properly only in Live view.

Figure 4.36 Adobe Edge Fonts can be selected from this window and loaded into a font library on your computer.

7 Return to Design view. Use the font-size and font-weight settings for this rule to make the text appear the way you like. I recommend trying to keep all text on one line, but this will depend on your screen resolution. For this example, your styling rule might appear as follows:

```
#header-name {
    margin-top: 0px;
    color: #000000;
    font-family: amatic-sc;
    font-weight: 700;
    font-size: 36px;
}
```

Styling the Company Tagline

One more job to take care of. You need to style and position the tagline that falls below the company name. Here's the styling rule that was created to get this done in the video demonstration:

```
#header-tagline {
    margin-bottom: 0px;
    color: #1B1B1B;
    font-family: "Gill Sans", "Gill Sans MT", "Myriad Pro",
    →"DejaVu Sans Condensed", Helvetica, Arial, sans-serif;
    font-style: italic;
    font-size: 14px;
    margin-top: -36px;
}
```

Can you figure out where to apply these settings in the CSS Designer panel?

In this project you've taken another step in becoming proficient with Dreamweaver by diving in on your own to insert images and links and apply styling to the header of the page. Another job well done! Do you feel your confidence rising?

Challenge! Create Your Own Design with Photoshop

As you've worked through the material in this chapter you've no doubt thought of lots of ways that this design might be done. The client provided only some general guidance, and the examples you've seen here took off in sort of a hipster-look direction. But you're heartily encouraged to do better by creating your own design.

To help get you started, the project folder for this chapter has two files in the `source` folder that you can use to create your own design comps. You'll find a file for Photoshop (`wulvs-layout.psd`). This file is already organized into layers that match the dimensions used in developing this prototype. It's up to you to open this file and use your own creative ideas to make a totally new design.

Conclusion

Although the title of this chapter is "Getting the Big Picture," it might as well have been named "Working with Backgrounds, Inserted Images, Named CSS Class Rules, and Dreamweaver Visualization Techniques." Well, that's a little long, but that's just what you've accomplished as you've worked through these projects.

Along the way to learning how to use Dreamweaver to include the visual elements that images provide, you've also learned more about the principles of web design, how CSS styling rules are used to position elements on a page, and even how to style text using CSS and fonts that are located on a web service.

And the great news is that your design work is nearly complete. In the next chapter, you'll work to get the final elements of this design wrapped up as you learn how to style navigation bars, tables, and more.

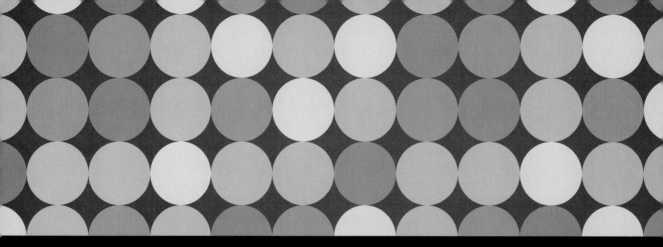

CHAPTER OBJECTIVES

Chapter Learning Objectives

- Respond to new client requirements by modifying an existing design.

- Work with client-provided content to convert Microsoft Word to properly formatted HTML.

- Use CSS to create interactive (and accessible) rollover buttons.

- Learn how to apply special CSS selectors to style links and alternating rows within a table.

- Create and style an interactive (and accessible) HTML form.

- Perform technical tests to check for and correct errors.

- Complete the final steps in the prototype to get the client's okay and prepare to move the site into production.

Chapter ACA Objectives

For full descriptions of objectives, see the table on pages 258–264.

DOMAIN 1.0
WORKING IN THE WEB DESIGN INDUSTRY
1.5

DOMAIN 2.0
PROJECT SETUP AND INTERFACE
2.3, 2.4

DOMAIN 4.0
WORKING WITH CODE TO CREATE AND MODIFY CONTENT
4.1, 4.2, 4.3, 4.4

DOMAIN 5.0
PUBLISHING DIGITAL MEDIA
5.1

CHAPTER 5

Working with Web Page Content

You've gotten more great feedback from your client, Chris the cartoonist. The design for the WULVS website is really coming together. With the work that you did in Chapter 4, the page design is beginning to define itself. Now the client has provided new clues for the remaining design specifications, new images that need to be put into place, and specific information about color values and the appearance of the elements of the design.

In this chapter, you'll take the final steps in preparing this website for production by evaluating a list of additional design and functional requirements that the client has provided. You'll then set out to complete your new to-do list by styling the navigation elements for the site, creating rollover buttons, styling the tables of information that Chris provided, creating a contact form, and cleaning up your code. Along the way, you'll learn even more about using Adobe Dreamweaver CC to create and style your pages using solid coding techniques.

Bring On the Content!

More great news. Your client, Chris the cartoonist (**Figure 5.1**), has provided feedback on the WULVS.info website.

Chris sez:

Really love all the work you've done. Those characters look awesome. Nice and clean. Great job! It looks like there are still a few things to do, so I made you a list.

- *The sidebar navigation area looks pretty plain, and of course we need some buttons over there. I have some ideas about how I want that to look, and I gave you some images to get started.*

- *The tables that I gave you before for the Services and Rates pages still need to be styled, right?*

- *Also, the form for the Contact page. That still needs to be done.*

Overall, I'm really loving the way things are working out! I can't wait to see the final prototype. Chris

Figure 5.1 Chris the cartoonist

Get Your Files Here

As you did in previous chapters, copy the folder that contains this chapter's files to your computer.

1. Download the project files for this lesson, named `chapter-05.zip`, from the Lesson & Update Files tab on your Account page at *www.peachpit.com*, and store them on your computer in a convenient location.

2. Unzip the files and copy the `chapter-05` folder to the `Learn-Dreamweaver` folder you created in Chapter 1.

★ *ACA Objective 2.1*

NOTE

Refer to Video 1.10, "Defining a Site," if you want a quick review of how the site definition process works.

Define the Chapter 5 Website

With the files you've been provided for this chapter in the project folder, you're ready to set up the site in Dreamweaver by giving the site a name and pointing to the project folder for this chapter.

1. From the application bar at the top of Dreamweaver, select Site > New Site.

2. In the Site Setup dialog, in the Site Name field, name the site **Chapter 5**.

3. Use the folder icon to the right of the Local Site Folder field to browse to the `chapter-05` folder in your `Learn-Dreamweaver` project folder.

4. Click Save to finish defining this new site.

Styling the Navigation Sidebar

In this project and in Project 5.2, you'll work "outside in" to complete the styling of the sidebar and make some slick, rounded buttons from the existing list items in the document. First let's take a look at the client's requirements. Review where you should be in your own design work, then finish this project by inserting images into the sidebar and setting the stage for the rollover buttons you'll make from the list of links.

Examining the Client Requirements

Take a few moments to review the list of things to do that Chris provided.

1 If you have Microsoft Word installed on your computer, double-click `WULVS-Things-To-Do.docx` in Dreamweaver. Otherwise, double-click `WULVS-Things-To-Do.rtf` to open the rich text format document in your preferred word processor.

2 Read through the list of requirements and analyze them.

What specific guidance does the client provide? What is being left up to you as the designer? Has the client given you more information about the *feel* for how the website elements should look? You might want to jot down a list of what you want to do, but the really clever ones among you will see that the things to do match up with the projects in this chapter: styling work, images to insert, and some specific ideas from the client.

Checking Your Work

Take a few moments to inspect the current status of the prototype.

1 Open Dreamweaver, and review the structure of the site and the new folders and images provided in this chapter. You'll find that the folders and files that were created in Chapter 4 are still in place. New images and documents have been provided by the client.

2 Open `prototype.html` from the Chapter 5 site. Switch to Live view and enable Inspect mode to examine the containers on the page and the way that padding and margins have been defined in your style sheet (**Figure 5.2**). This is a really useful method for examining the layout blocks of your design.

★ ACA Objective 1.5

★ ACA Objective 2.3

★ ACA Objective 2.4

★ ACA Objective 4.2

★ ACA Objective 4.3

★ ACA Objective 4.4

★ ACA Objective 5.1

▶ **Video 5.1** *Styling the Navigation Sidebar*

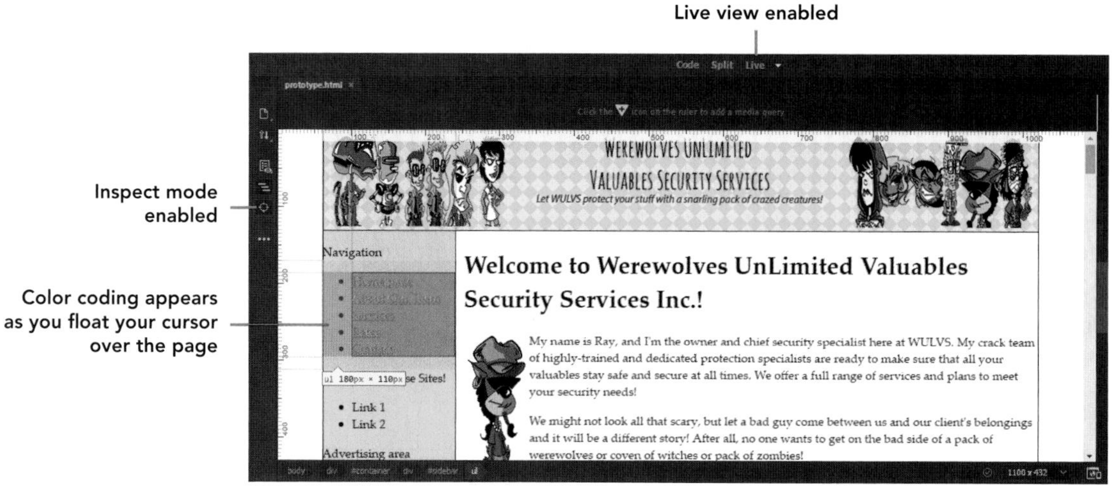

Live view enabled

Inspect mode enabled

Color coding appears as you float your cursor over the page

Figure 5.2 Inspect mode in Live view allows you to visualize the different containers that make up the page.

3 Review the styling rules that you've written into the `<head>` of the document. Take note of the relationship between the named containers in the document and how the styling rules have been "hooked" to the tags using IDs and classes.

Now you're ready to get to work.

Styling the Sidebar: Work from the Outside In

A useful technique when styling elements with HTML and CSS is to work from the "outside in." This means that you start with the outermost container within an area of the page and work your way inside to get all the individual styling rules set for the items *inside* the container. You'll use this technique to style the sidebar of the design and the navigation elements that will be placed in this area of the page.

The client has stated that the solid color of the sidebar is too plain and has supplied a replacement image. Your first task is to replace the image that provides the sidebar background.

1 Open the CSS Designer panel, and select the `#container` selector.

In the `background-image` setting, an image was previously set here to create the faux column look for this design. You'll change this to one that the client provided.

2   Click the folder icon next to the URL field for the `background-image` setting (**Figure 5.3**). Browse to the `container-bg-gold-lines.png` image (in the `images` folder), and set that as the background image for the `#container` selector.

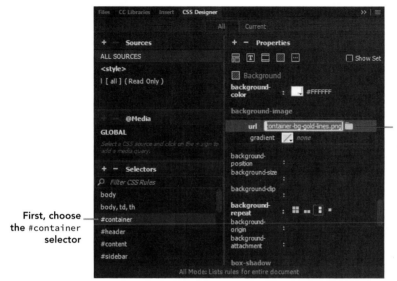

First, choose the `#container` selector

Next, browse and select the `container-bg-gold-lines.png` image in the `images` folder

You'll now see the new image in the sidebar. You also understand more about the design the client is looking for.

Modifying the Sidebar Margins and Adjusting Widths

Now the text in the sidebar area of the page is too crowded and pushes up against the borders of the container (especially on the left). You'll address this by setting new margin properties for the `#sidebar` selector.

Switch to Design view for these operations.

1   In the CSS Designer panel, select the `#sidebar` selector, and go to the margin settings in the Layout category. Apply margins of **10 px** to the left and right of the `#sidebar` selector (**Figure 5.4**). Remember that margins affect the white space outside the border of the HTML tag in the box model.

Content `<div>` slips below the sidebar `<div>`

Margin settings in the CSS Designer panel

Figure 5.4 Applying margins to the `#sidebar` selector

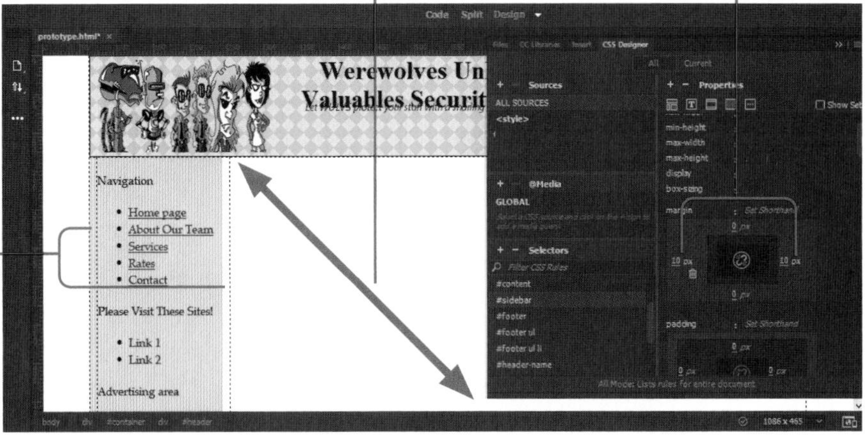

Left and right margins applied

When you apply this setting to the sidebar, the `#content <div>` no longer has room to sit side by side with the sidebar and it slips down under the element that comes before it. To adjust this you'll turn to the `#content` selector.

2 Select the `#content` selector in the CSS Designer panel. In the Layout category, adjust the container's width until the `#content <div>` snaps back into position. A layout width of 745px should do that.

3 Select the `#sidebar` selector. In the Layout category, change the width to **160 px**.

ARE FIXED-WIDTH DESIGNS EVIL?

Throughout this project, you'll be using a fixed-width design as you learn how to use CSS layout principles and the tools that Dreamweaver provides to visualize your design. This isn't the way that modern web pages are designed, where a page needs to have flexible design that scales based on the size of the viewport.

You'll learn about flexible and responsive designs in Chapter 7, but while you're learning about CSS, layouts with a fixed-width design, like the one used in these projects, make it easier for you to see and understand how positioning is done with pure CSS designs. That's not evil, but it probably isn't the choice you'd make for a site that is intended for publication. Remember that you are presently learning many features, and this design helps reinforce your learning without complicating the process. Many modern websites are created with an emphasis on mobile browsers first.

Inserting the Sidebar Images

Chris the cartoonist has provided some nifty images that he wants to use above each of the navigation sections in the sidebar. Not only do these images provide another clue to the design that Chris is after, but he has also asked that the color values used in the images be repeated within the site. Once the images are in place, you'll be able to "pick up" those color values for use in border, text, and other values you'll use as you complete the prototype design.

1 If it's not already visible, choose Window > Assets from the application menu to open the Assets panel. Make certain you remain in Design view of the document.

2 Place your cursor to the left of the text *Navigation* at the top of the sidebar.

3 In the Assets panel, select the us-banner.png file (**Figure 5.5**), and click the Insert button to insert the image.

4 Delete the *Navigation* placeholder text.

5 Place your cursor to the left of the placeholder text *Please visit these sites!*

Figure 5.5 Use the Assets panel to locate images to be inserted onto the page.

Image inserted into the sidebar

Insert the image at the cursor position

Image selected

6   In the Assets panel, select the `them-banner.png` file, and click Insert to insert the image.

7   Delete the placeholder text.

8   In the Property inspector, set the alt text and title for each image as follows:

    `us-banner.png`: alt text **WULVS Navigation**; title **WULVS Pages**
    `them-banner.png`: alt text **Sites of Our Friends**; title **Friends Sites**

Positioning the Sidebar Images

To position these two images inside the `#sidebar` container, you need a new CSS selector. The CSS Designer panel makes this a breeze (**Figure 5.6**).

1   Select the `us-banner.png` image and check the Tag selector to be certain the `<img>` tag is selected.

2   Click the + in the Selectors area of the CSS Designer panel. Refine the selector name until it reads `#sidebar p img`. Press Enter/Return to accept the selector name. Remember that this rule will apply to any `<img>` tag contained within any `<p>` tag in the `#sidebar` container.

Figure 5.6 Create a new CSS Selector to position the images in the sidebar.

Add a new selector

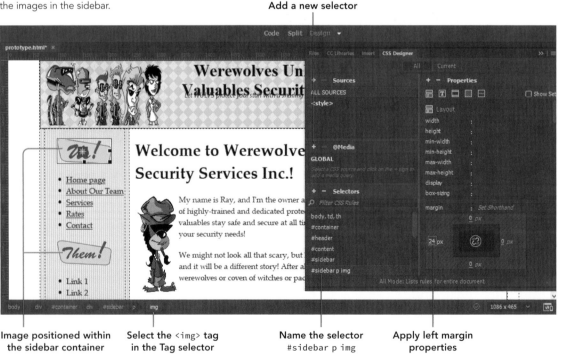

Image positioned within the sidebar container

Select the `<img>` tag in the Tag selector

Name the selector `#sidebar p img`

Apply left margin properties

3   In the Layout category of the CSS Designer panel, apply a left margin property of **24** pixels.

4   Check the position of the images, and when you're satisfied with the result, save your file and preview the results in a browser.

You can fine-tune the left margin setting later, but the goal here is to get the image mostly centered inside the `#sidebar` container.

This first project provided you with a good review of the principles of web design as you evaluated the client's requirements and compared that with the layout of the page. Based on client feedback, you revised the sidebar using the new background image that was provided and put some new images into position. As you completed these steps, the look and feel that the client is after came into focus. In the next project, you'll convert the list of links into interactive rollover navigation buttons.

★ ACA Objective 4.1

★ ACA Objective 4.2

★ ACA Objective 4.3

★ ACA Objective 5.1

▶ **Video 5.2** Part 1:
Styling Navigation
Elements

▶ **Video 5.3** Part 2:
Styling Navigation
Elements

PROJECT 5.2

Styling Navigation Elements

In the last project, you began the process of styling the left sidebar for the pages in this site, and the client's vision started to come into clearer focus. The hipster vibe that Ray the Werewolf seems to be going for is starting to show up, with lighter colors, the striped background for the sidebar, and those groovy shapes for the two images that were inserted.

One of the more essential elements of any web design is the user experience created by the navigation. Literally millions of ways to design navigation bars and buttons are possible. In this project, you'll learn the fundamental methods for creating site navigation. These methods involve unordered lists, the list items that are within them, and the CSS selector known as the pseudo-class. Let's get started.

LEVEL UP: ALTERNATIVE DESIGNS!

You have to wonder if the other employees at WULVS had a different idea of how this design should be done. The vampires probably would have wanted something darker and more gothic, Robbie the Robot might have argued for more metallic elements, and the Twins might have preferred a more preppy look. But that's the beauty of web design. Because the contents of the prototype stay the same, you only have to define a new CSS style sheet and swap out a few images to change *everything* about the look of this design.

As you work through the design choices in this chapter, you might want to imagine that one of the other characters in the comic was put in charge and how that might affect the final design. How would you go about designing a dark and scary theme or a design that another character would approve of?

Adding Links to Other Pages

The client has provided the names of the websites that he'd like to link under the `us-banner.png` file. You'll use these values to replace the placeholder links that are currently in that area of the page. Remember that you are still working on the `prototype.html` document. Remain in Design view as you complete these tasks.

1 Open `WULVS-Things-To-Do.docx` from the Files panel, or open `WULVS-Things-To-Do.rtf` if you want to use a text editor other than Microsoft Word.

2 Locate the sites within `WULVS-Things-To-Do.docx` that the client wants his site to link to:

- Capes & Babes: *http://www.capesnbabes.com*
- Webcomic Alliance: *http://webcomicalliance.com*
- Scott McCloud: *http://scottmccloud.com*
- Dawn Griffin Studios: *http://dawngriffinstudios.com*

3 Change the first item in the sidebar list from Link1 to **Capes & Babes**.

4 With the text still selected, in the Link field in the Property inspector (**Figure 5.7**), type the text **http://www.capesnbabes.com**.

5 Set the target for the link to `_blank` so that the page opens in a new browser window or browser tab when it is selected.

6 Repeat steps 3 through 5 for the Link2 placeholder link, using the URL for the Webcomic Alliance.

7 Press Enter/Return to create a new list item. Repeat the process of adding new list items and linking to the other pages until all four links have been set (Figure 5.7).

TIP

Be aware that setting a link to open in a new browser window may cause issues for those with cognitive (short-term memory) disabilities. They may forget that a new browser tab has opened.

New link listings   **Link field with page URL**   **Target field set to _blank**

Figure 5.7 Adding the new list of links in the sidebar

Inserting a Navigation Tag

The navigation elements in this page will use a new tag that you haven't encountered yet. You can designate a navigation area using a `<nav>` tag, which is read by assistive devices in such a way that it's clear the links are for site navigation. The `<nav>` tag is also used in responsive design and HTML5 layouts because it can use properties that a regular `<div>` tag cannot. Next, you'll use that `<nav>` tag to wrap the existing list of links.

1 With Design view active, click anywhere within the first list of links, and then click the **ul** indicator in the Tag selector. The entire unordered list will be selected.

2 Open the Insert panel with the HTML category selected, and then click the Navigation button located near the middle of the list of items.

The Insert Navigation dialog appears.

3 Click the New CSS Rule button.

The New CSS Rule dialog displays (**Figure 5.8**).

Figure 5.8 You can create new named selectors using the New CSS Rule dialog.

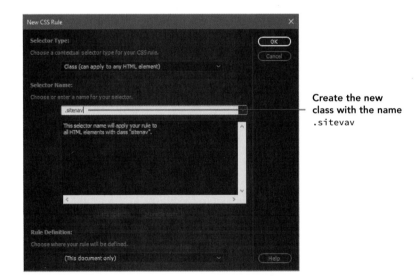

Create the new class with the name `.sitevav`

4 Assign the name `.sitenav` to the new class rule, and click OK. Make certain that this document is selected only in the lower dropdown.

The CSS Rule Definition dialog appears. You'll define the properties of this element in the CSS Designer panel. You don't need to set any properties here.

5 Click OK.

You are returned to the Insert Navigation dialog.

6 Click OK to accept this new selector name.

The list of links is now contained within a new <nav> tag with a class attribute of .sitenav.

7 Repeat steps 1 through 6 to wrap the second unordered list in the sidebar with a <nav> tag. This time when the Insert Navigation dialog appears, you only need to assign the .sitenav class to the new tag using the class menu and click OK. Your second set of links is now contained in a navigation container.

Removing Default List Properties

In the next few steps, you'll remove the default styling properties that are assigned to HTML list items. You need to change the appearance of the items in the list to turn them into interactive buttons.

The first order of business is to remove the bullets next to the items in the list.

1 Click anywhere within a sidebar list, and select the ul indicator in the Tag selector.

2 Click the + in the Selectors section of the CSS Designer panel. Set the name of the new rule to .sitenav ul.

3 With the new rule selected, go to the Text category of the CSS Designer panel, locate the list-style-type property, and set the value to none.

The bullet symbols next to each list item in the sidebar disappear. How cool is that?

Assigning Width and Margin Properties to the List Items

Now, you need to move the list of links a little closer to the left edge of the navigation area by removing the default margins that HTML applies to items in a list. You'll also work on the position and spacing of the individual items in the list.

1 Click anywhere in the list of links and use the Tag selector to choose the li tag indicator.

2 Click the + in the Selectors section of the CSS Designer panel. Set the name of the new rule to .sitenav ul li.

3 With the new rule selected, set the width to **160** pixels in the Layout category.

4 Set the left margin to **–40** pixels.

This removes the default margin that list items contain.

Choosing a Background Color from an Image

The client asked that you use the colors in the sidebar area within other areas of the design. You can use the Eyedropper tool to pick up a color value for the background of the list items. Having a color in place will make it easier to see how other properties are set as you style the buttons.

1 With `.sitenav ul li` still selected, go to the Background category of the CSS Designer panel. Click the color chip to choose the `background-color` setting.

2 In the lower-right corner of the color chooser is a tiny Eyedropper icon. Click the Eyedropper and position your cursor over the yellow-gold area of the image in the sidebar (**Figure 5.9**).

3 When you see the color in the preview area of the color chooser, click the desired color, then press Enter/Return. The sampled color value will be applied to the `background-color` setting and perfectly match the color in the image.

With the background color set, you can more clearly see the spacing between the individual list items.

4 Apply a little top and bottom padding to the list items to spread them apart. I set them to 2px top and 2px bottom.

Figure 5.9 The Eyedropper tool allows you to "pick up" a color from any visible element on the page.

Position the Eyedropper over the image at the top of the sidebar

The selected color is displayed in the color chooser

Select the Eyedropper tool

Setting the Link Values Using Pseudo-Class Selectors

A pseudo-class is a special kind of CSS selector that is triggered by an action that takes place on the screen. In the case of navigation elements, you can use these special selectors to create a rollover effect that changes the appearance of the link when the viewer's mouse moves over the top of it. You'll use these selectors with the `<a>` tag, which is the rule you'll define next—with just a little twist. Pseudo-class selectors must be written in a specific order.

TIP

You can quickly jump to any CSS rule by right-clicking the selector name and choosing Go to Code. Dreamweaver will move you to the last line of the selected rule, and you can get to work on the code.

1 Click anywhere in the list of links and use the Tag selector to choose the `<a>` tag indicator.

2 Click the + in the CSS Designer panel to create a new selector, name it `.sitenav ul li a`, and press Enter/Return.

 The syntax of pseudo-class rules is very specific and best done in Code view for the page.

3 Locate the `sitenav ul li a` rule that you just created. It is in the `<head>` of the document. Just right-click the `.sitenav ul li a` selector and choose Go to Code.

4 Change the name of the selector to **`.sitenav ul li a:link, a:visited`** by typing directly in the code.

 Your first set of pseudo-class selectors is now in place.

> **TIP**
>
> *You can remember the order of these pseudo-classes using the mnemonic "LoVe HAte" (for link, visited, hover, and active). In this case, we focus only on the first two pseudo-classes.*

5 Select the `.sitenav ul li a:link, a:visited` selector in the CSS Designer panel.

6 In the Layout category, set `display` to `block`.

 This makes the entire container that contains the link active and clickable, rather than just the text itself. Now, you need to remove the underlines.

7 Set `text-decoration` to `none` and the underlines disappear.

 Now you have some styling work to do.

8 Set the following properties to create rounded buttons with a red border that matches the red in the image the client provided. Can you locate the parts of the CSS Designer panel where you would set these properties and values?

Figure 5.10 The result of styling the links in the navigation area of the sidebar

```
font-family: "Gill Sans", "Gill Sans MT", "Myriad Pro",
⟶"DejaVu Sans Condensed", Helvetica, Arial, sans-serif;
color: #000000;
font-size: 18px;
border: 1px solid #AC1307;
border-radius: 10px;
padding-left: 7px;
padding-bottom: 3px;
padding-top: 2px;
background-color: #FCD04C;
```

9 Once your buttons are set, you can remove the background color that was applied to the list items themselves. Click the `.sitenav ul li` rule in the CSS Designer panel and click the trashcan icon next to the `background-color` property to remove it.

Switch to Live view, and you'll see that the result of all this work is beautifully styled rounded buttons (**Figure 5.10**). Do yours look like these? If they do, it's time to create the hover effect. If you're not happy with your results, return to the CSS Designer panel and make adjustments until you are.

Setting the Hover Values Using Pseudo-Class Selectors

The selector you just finished provides the styling of the buttons when they are in their "up" state, where the mouse has not rolled over the link. To make the rollover effect work, you'll use a second set of pseudo-class selectors to control the hover and active states of the link. Again, the mnemonic LoVe HAte makes it easier to recall the order of these pseudo-classes.

1 Duplicate the existing rule named `.sitenav ul li a:link, a:visited`. Just locate the code in Split view, then select (including the curly braces), copy, and paste beneath the current rule.

2 In the code, change the selector name to **.sitenav ul li a:hover, a:active**. Make sure this new selector is listed after the first set of pseudo-class selectors so that it falls into the correct order (again, LoVe HAte).

You don't need the full list of values repeated for the hover state—only those that you want to change when the mouse encounters the button.

3　Delete all the extra properties so that only the background color remains. Since these properties have already been defined, they will be inherited by this pseudo-class. There is no need to include duplicate code (it just makes the size of your web page unnecessarily larger). Change the background color to a lighter shade than the original color value. Your final rule for this selector should appear similar to the following:

```
.sitenav ul li a:hover, a:active {
    display: block;
    background-color: #FEF4D5;
}
```

4　Save your file and preview the page in a browser.

Cool, right? The buttons change colors as you roll over them, adding a whole new level of interest to this design.

In this project, you've learned how to use pure CSS styling rules to create interactive, highly attractive navigation buttons that respond to the position of the mouse on the page. No additional programming was required—no JavaScript or any other technology besides CSS pseudo-classes and the <a> tag on the page. This is a powerful method for designing navigation elements and is used on countless websites to create all sorts of visual effects.

PROJECT 5.3

Styling Structured Data

Human beings respond well to information that is organized. Every day, we see data presented in rows and columns. From a listing of the high and low temperatures on any given date, to a teacher's grade book, to financial statements and personal budgets found in spreadsheets, we all are accustomed to seeing ordered and structured data.

In HTML, structured data is presented using the `<table>` tag, the `<tr>` tag (which creates rows), and the `<td>` tag (which defines each individual cell inside the table).

In this project, you'll work with tables that the client has provided and see how to provide spacing and borders using CSS. You'll also create a new CSS selector to style the alternate rows in a table. You will also learn how to add a bit of code to make your tables accessible.

Cleaning Up a Table from Microsoft Word

The client supplied a table in a Microsoft Word document. You need to do a bit of cleanup before you can use the table in your web page.

1   Open `prototype.html` and scroll to the bottom of the page, where you'll find two tables.

The Services table was inserted using the Dreamweaver Insert Table command, but the Rates table was copied and pasted from the client's Word document.

Even though these tables came into being in different ways, the structure is the same. The `<table>` tag defines the table, the `<tr>` tag defines each row of the table, and the `<td>` tag is used for each cell within the table. A fourth tag, the `<th>` tag, is used to define the table heading and appears within the first row of the table.

Your first task is to clean up the HTML in the Rates table. This involves removing any markup that Word included when the table was copied into place. Clients often supply information formatted with tools like Microsoft Word. One common task is to remove this unwanted formatting. Dreamweaver has tools to help with this process.

2   Click anywhere within the Rates table and click the table tag indicator in the Tag selector (**Figure 5.11**) to select the entire table.

Select the table indicator

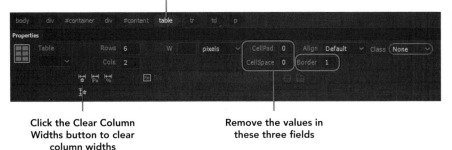

Figure 5.11 The Property inspector for the Rates table

Click the Clear Column
Widths button to clear
column widths

Remove the values in
these three fields

3   Click the Clear Column Widths button to remove the `width="312"` attribute from all the `<td>` tags.

4   Delete the values in the `CellPad`, `CellSpace`, and `Border` properties in the Property inspector.

When your settings match those in Figure 5.11, you have cleared the table widths and collapsed the space between the table cells.

Next you'll use the Find and Replace feature to remove the `valign="top"` attribute from all the `<td>` tags within the tables.

5   Directly in the code, highlight one of the complete `<td valign="top">` tags within any of the tables, and copy the selection.

6   Select the `table` indicator in the Tag selector, and press Ctrl+F (Command+F) to open the Find and Replace dialog (**Figure 5.12**).

7   Verify you see multiple rows in the dialog panel. If not, click the leftmost icon to expand the panel (see Figure 5.12). The code you selected is highlighted. All other instances of this code are also highlighted (in a different color).

Figure 5.12 You can use the Find and Replace dialog when you need to replace specific tags within a document.

The code you selected
is highlighted

All other instances of this code
are highlighted in another color

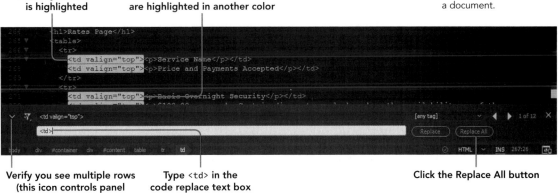

Verify you see multiple rows
(this icon controls panel
expansion/collapse)

Type <td> in the
code replace text box

Click the Replace All button

8 Enter **`<td>`** in the code replace text box.

9 Click the Replace All button and the vertical align attribute will be removed from all the `<td>` tags.

To convert this Word table into a semantically correct HTML table, change the `<td>` tags for each column of data to `<th>` tags.

10 Change the `<td>` tags that are at the top of each of the columns (Service Name and Price and Payments Accepted columns) into `<th>` tags by typing directly in Code view, making sure that you have both tags closed (make certain you also code the `</td>` tags with `</th>` tags).

11 The final step to get this table ready for styling is to remove the paragraph tags that were inserted by Word. Click inside the top-left cell in the table (Service Name), then drag to the lower-right corner of the table until all the individual cells are selected.

12 In the Property inspector, set the format for the selected cells to None.

This table can now be styled right along with the other table in the page without any conflicts from properties that Word created.

Setting Table and Table Cell Properties

Next, you'll set the table width and apply border and padding properties for the table's contents. Time to flex your coding muscles!

1 In the CSS Designer panel, create a new selector named **`#content table`**.

2 Set the width property of `#content table` to **750 px**.

3 Create another new selector named **`#content table, td, th`**.

4 Set the properties for this selector to apply the borders, to collapse the borders, and to add a little padding around the contents of the containers within the table. Your final code block should be similar to the following:

```
#content table, td, th {
    border: 1px solid #000000;
    border-collapse: collapse;
    padding-left: 13px;
    padding-right: 9px;
    padding-top: 3px;
    padding-bottom: 3px;
}
```

Setting Column Widths and Heading Properties

You can control the width of the columns in an HTML table by setting a width value for the divisions within the first row of the table. In these steps, you'll create two new classes to apply to the `<th>` tags at the top of each table.

1 Create a new selector named **#content table .column1**.

2 Select the first `<th>` tag in each table, and use the Property inspector to assign the `column1` class to the tag.

3 In the Layout category of the CSS Designer panel, set the width for the class selector to **250 px**.

   The left column snaps to this dimension, and the other column takes up the remaining space.

4 In the Text category, use the Eyedropper tool to set the text color to match the red color in the images at the top of the sidebar.

5 Modify the size of the text to **120%**.

   This setting makes the text 120 percent larger than the default text size used in the document.

6 Duplicate the rule you just created, and name it **#content table .column2**.

7 Remove the selector's width value.

8 Select the second `<th>` tag in each table, and assign the `column2` class to the tag in the Property inspector.

Your tables now have a nicely labeled heading at the top of each column.

Styling Alternate Rows in a Table

The client requested that the table rows have alternating background colors to make the tables more readable. Luckily you can do this easily because the browser automatically counts each row within a table. This allows you to use a CSS selector type—the child selector—to assign a specific property based on whether the row is an odd or even number. This is an easy styling trick to perform because the computer does all the work for you.

The syntax of this selector is quite specific, so it's best to go directly to the `<head>` of the document and create the new selector in the style sheet code.

1   In Code view in the `<head>` section of the document, create a new selector named **#content table tr:nth-child(odd)** directly below the #content table.column2 selector. Don't forget to include opening and closing curly braces { } after the selector.

2   Return to the CSS Designer panel, and apply a medium gray background color to this selector (#C0C0C0 works nicely).

The odd-numbered rows in the table, starting with the table header, have the background color applied when seen in Live view.

3   Return to Design view and the CSS Designer panel to work with the #content table.column1 and #content table .column2 selectors. Assign a background color to the table headings. The gold color in the sidebar makes an excellent choice, allowing the headings to really stand out while remaining consistent with the rest of the design (**Figure 5.13**). Setting font-weight to bold will also make the text pop.

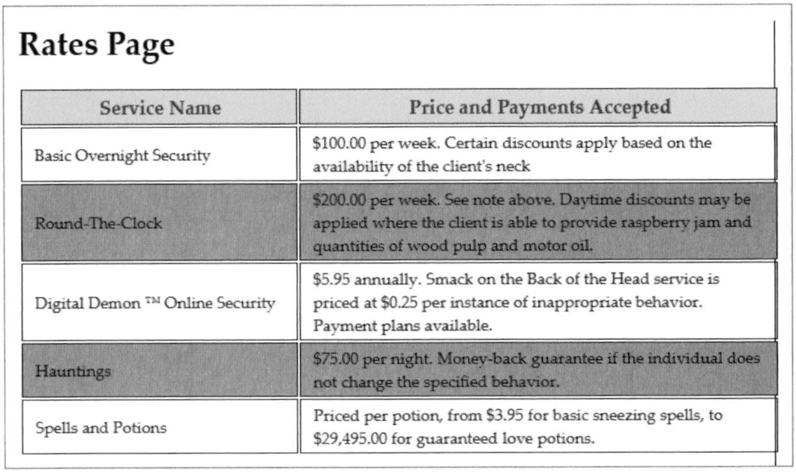

Figure 5.13 The result of your work in Project 5.3 so far

Rates Page

Service Name	Price and Payments Accepted
Basic Overnight Security	$100.00 per week. Certain discounts apply based on the availability of the client's neck
Round-The-Clock	$200.00 per week. See note above. Daytime discounts may be applied where the client is able to provide raspberry jam and quantities of wood pulp and motor oil.
Digital Demon ™ Online Security	$5.95 annually. Smack on the Back of the Head service is priced at $0.25 per instance of inappropriate behavior. Payment plans available.
Hauntings	$75.00 per night. Money-back guarantee if the individual does not change the specified behavior.
Spells and Potions	Priced per potion, from $3.95 for basic sneezing spells, to $29,495.00 for guaranteed love potions.

Making Your Tables Accessible

Although the client did not specifically ask you to make the tables accessible, you know this is an industry best practice. If you had created the tables using the Insert panel, you would have been prompted to include base accessibility information when you first added the table (**Figure 5.14**).

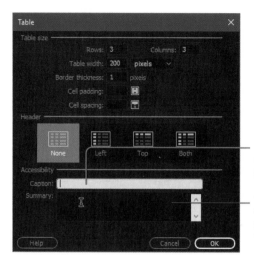

Figure 5.14 When you insert a table using Dreamweaver, you are prompted to include a summary (for assistive devices).

Many assistive devices are not using the table caption presently.

The table summary provides visitors with a general understanding of data contained in the table. It is "viewable" only by assistive devices.

To add these capabilities, we need to return to Code view.

1   In Code view locate the `<table>` tag beneath the `<h1>Rates Page</h1>` tag.

2   Insert the following code within the `<table>` tag so the end result looks like the following.

```
<table summary="We offer numerous services at competitive
→ rates. These are detailed in this table.">
```

Next, locate the Services table and insert similar language. You decide what should be included. Remember that the summary attribute should provide a general overview of the data contained in the table.

Because you already coded the `<th>` cells, assistive devices will be able to identify those table cells properly.

You're one step closer to finishing the design work for Chris the cartoonist. In this project, you learned how to take a table created in a Microsoft Word document and remove all the Word-specific markup. You then created the styling rules that established the borders, width, padding, and background colors for the table and the table headings. You even applied a cool little trick that lets you provide alternating row colors to the table—just as the client requested. Lastly, you made your tables more accessible for those using assistive devices.

★ *ACA Objective 4.4*

★ *ACA Objective 4.3*

▶ **Video 5.6** *Building Interactive Forms*

▶ **Video 5.7** *Styling Interactive Forms*

Building and Designing Interactive Forms

It would be pretty unusual for a company or organization in this day and age not to provide a way for potential customers and clients to contact them from their website. Contact forms and other forms that let the customer request more information, report a problem, or even submit answers in an opinion poll are accomplished through HTML forms.

In a regular production setting, an interactive form (**Figure 5.15**) would be submitted to a web server on which the information the customer sends is stored and processed. For live commercial websites, the company that is hosting the website on their servers would provide instructions on how their email processing works, and how to set the form in Dreamweaver to work on their servers.

Figure 5.15 At the end of this project, you will have a nicely styled, functional HTML form.

> ## Contact Page
>
> **Thank you for your interest in WULVS!**
>
> We stand ready to serve your security needs and *we're waiting to hear from you!*
>
> Please complete the form that you see below and someone will get back to you **within 24 hours.**
>
> Fields marked with an * are required
>
> * Your Name: [Your Name]
>
> * E-mail Address: [E-mail]
>
> Phone: [Phone #]
>
> * Subject :   [I am a human seeking protection ▾]
>
> * Your Message: [   ]
>
> [Submit]

Luckily for you—since you don't have a real live server to work with—your client wants this form to point to a web page where the potential visitor would be reminded that this isn't a *real* company and you can't *really* hire werewolves and vampires to guard your home. This page will allow you to work through the process of building the form and setting the form to open a web page.

Oh, and the styling? This time you're on your own. In this project, you'll build the form and learn which tags you can target for styling, but creating and applying the styling rules will be up to you.

Inserting Text from Microsoft Word

The client supplied text that he wants to appear on the Contact page. Let's insert that text now.

1   Open `client-feedback.docx`. (Alternatively, open `client-feedback.rtf` in your preferred text processor.) Locate the following block of text, and copy it. Notice the styling properties the client used:

Thank you for your interest in WULVS!

We stand ready to serve your security needs, and *we're waiting to hear from you!*

Please complete the form that you see below, and someone will get back to you within 24 hours.

2   Open `prototype.html`, and replace the text *The form will go here* with the text you copied from `client-feedback.docx` (or `client-feedback.rtf`).

Depending on the version of Word that you're using, Word may insert extra markup when you paste text into your HTML page.

WHAT'S SO WRONG ABOUT THE MAILTO: LINK?

Once upon a time, it was standard procedure to create links that would open the viewer's default email program so that a visitor could fill out a blank message and send the message to the specified address. This was done by inserting a special link that used mailto: to send the message, like this: mailto:info@wulvs.info.

But this method has all sorts of problems. First, it depends on the visitor having an email program set as the default handler for mail on their computer. Nowadays, with so many people using web mail from Google, Microsoft, Apple, and others, visitors may not have a dedicated email program on their computer.

Second, every moment of every day, special little programs known as spiders are searching web pages looking for that mailto: indicator. These little buggers harvest the email address and that mailbox starts getting all sorts of interesting offers. So unless you really love spam, listing email addresses using a mailto: link isn't a good idea. Modern web pages use forms instead and avoid both of those problems.

3   Check the code carefully to ensure that only the text and the `<strong>` and `<em>` tags are present, bolding the text inside the `<strong>` tags and creating italicized text with the `<em>` tag. Clean up the text as necessary. Remember that if you have access to the Internet, you can choose File > Validate > Current Document (W3C) to verify that there are no HTML errors in the code you just cleaned up.

4   In the Property inspector, format the first line of text as `<h3>`, and make sure the other lines of text are contained in paragraph tags.

5   Add the text **Fields marked with an asterisk (*) are required.** after the last line that was copied into place. Make certain this text is enclosed in paragraph tags also.

Now you're ready to build your form.

Insert the <form> Tag and Text Fields

Just like everything else in HTML, a form is composed of tags that provide specific information to the browser. In the steps that follow, you'll begin building your form by inserting the necessary tags. Set the document to Design view to complete these steps.

1   Position your cursor at the end of the line of text you just entered. In the Insert panel, switch to the Form category using the dropdown menu at the top of the panel.

    HTML forms are always enclosed within the `<form>` tag.

2   Click the Form button at the top of the Insert panel.

3   In the Property inspector, assign the ID **contact-form** to the `<form>` tag.

4   Click inside the red dashed line that marks the boundaries of the `<form>` tag. From the Insert panel, insert a Text object inside the `<form>` tag.

5   In the Property inspector, assign the Text object the ID of **name** in the Name field, mark the object as a required field, and enter **Your Name** in the Place Holder field (**Figure 5.16**).

6   Replace the text that Dreamweaver provides (*Text Field:*) with *** Your Name:**.

7   Create a new blank line by pressing Enter/Return, and insert a second Text object from the Insert panel. Name this object **mail**, make it a required field, and enter **Email** in the Place Holder field.

8   Replace *Text Field:* with *** Email Address**.

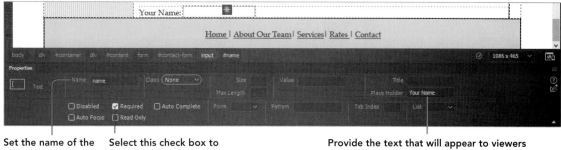

Set the name of the
object to name

Select this check box to
make the field required

Provide the text that will appear to viewers
before they enter their own information

Figure 5.16 Use the Property inspector to assign properties to the Text object in your form.

9 Add a third text field named **phone**. Enter **Phone:** as the replacement text. This field is not required, so leave the Required check box unselected. Replace *Text Field:* with **Phone**.

Insert Additional Form Elements

The next form element you'll insert will provide viewers with a dropdown menu where they can choose from a list of options when they complete the form.

1 In the Insert panel, insert a Select form object in a new paragraph after the phone field.

2 Name this form object **subject** and make it a required field.

3 In the Property inspector, click the List Values button. The List Values dialog displays (**Figure 5.17**).

Add or remove list values   List item labels   List item values

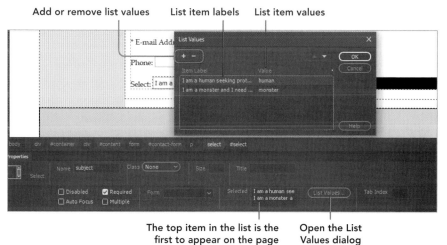

The top item in the list is the
first to appear on the page

Open the List
Values dialog

NOTE

Dreamweaver also adds the appropriate tag (<label>) to make these fields accessible to assistive devices (such as screen readers). You didn't have to write a single line of code to make this happen.

Figure 5.17 The values for a dropdown list are set in the List Values dialog window.

4 Set two list labels and values as follows:

   - Label 1: **I am a human seeking protection**
   - Value 1: **human**
   - Label 2: **I am a monster and I need a job!**
   - Value 2: **monster**

5 Click OK to close the List Values dialog.

6 Change the text label for this field to *** Subject:**.

7 On a new line, insert a Text Area object from the Insert panel. Name this object **message** and make it a required field. Set the Placeholder text to **Your Message**.

8 Change this text label to *** Your Message:**.

9 On a new line, insert a Submit Button item from the Insert panel. In the Property inspector, you will see that this object has the ID **submit** already applied to it.

Adding Function to the Form

The client requested that someone who submits this form be taken to a new web page where they'll see a message reminding them that this isn't a *real* website and you can't *really* hire werewolves and vampires to guard your property. You'll create a new page and then hook the Submit button to the page so that it opens when the form is submitted.

1 In the Files panel, right-click the folder at the top of the panel (the `site` folder) and select New File from the context menu.

2 Name the new file **thankyou.html** and press Enter/Return to accept the filename.

   You'll add content to this page later on, but the filename is needed now to make the form function correctly.

3 Select the Submit button. In the Property inspector, use the Browse for Folder icon next to the Form Action field to browse to `thankyou.html`.

4 Set Form Method to GET. This setting will cause the page to load into the viewer's browser when the button is clicked (**Figure 5.18**).

5   Save your file, and preview the page in a web browser.

Your form is now complete (but not very stylish), and when you click the Submit button you'll be taken to the blank Thank You page.

NOTE

Since you are not actually processing the form data and redirecting to another web page, you may experience issues in some browsers (as they try to protect you from security exposures) or see an "Internal Server Error" message if you preview from Dreamweaver. At the time of this writing, Firefox will properly display the `thankyou.html` *page when you click the Submit button. It is always a good idea to test your web pages in different browsers, as behaviors may vary depending on the layout engine the browser uses.*

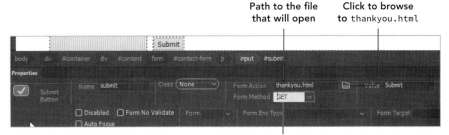

Path to the file that will open

Click to browse to `thankyou.html`

Set Form Method to GET

Figure 5.18 Setting the functional properties of the Submit button

Congratulations, you made a form! In the process, Dreamweaver added the necessary form tags to make your form accessible.

Styling the Form

Your form is now functional, but it certainly needs some styling work. You've become so proficient in this process that you can complete this styling work on your own. Following is a list of things to do and some tips on what selectors you'll need to create to get the job done.

1   Create a new class named `.required`. Set the styling for text on this class so that it has a red color and the font weight is bold.

2   Highlight each of the asterisk symbols in the form area of the page and use the Property inspector to assign the `.required` class to the selection.

This will wrap the symbol in a `<span>` tag, and the symbol will appear with the red, bold text you defined with the class.

3 Create a new selector named **#contact-form** that targets the form itself. Use this selector to style the border of the form, its width, and its margins. If you wish to center the form inside its container, you can set the left and right margins to `auto`.

4 Create a new selector named `#contact-form label` to position all the labels within the form away from the left border. You can use padding properties with this selector to position the left edge of each of the text labels.

5 Create individual selectors for each named field to position the input fields next to their labels. The name field, for instance, will require this selector: `#contact-form p #name`. As you create each new selector, use margin properties to align all the form fields so they're nice and neat, like the example in Figure 5.15.

6 Use margin and padding values on a selector named `#contact-form #submit` to place the Submit button in a location that is consistent with your design.

As you work, be certain to preview your styling choices both in Dreamweaver's Live view and in a web browser. By the time you're finished, you should have a styled, functional, and accessible form.

Finalizing the Prototype for Production

★ ACA Objective 2.3

★ ACA Objective 5.1

▶ **Video 5.8**
Modifying the Advertising Area

▶ **Video 5.9** *Finalizing the Fonts*

▶ **Video 5.10**
Finalizing the Prototype for Production

It might be hard to believe, but you're nearly ready to put the WULVS.info website into production. Do you remember how you started this mission with just a little information from the client and some very basic HTML? You've come a long, long way.

Now you're ready to tend to the final housekeeping that every website production requires. This involves a careful review of the client's requirements and tending to any final details, then doing some technical tests on the prototype to check for errors and finishing up the design. The goal in this final project is to get the prototype file ready to present to the client for final approval. From there your site will be ready to put into production.

This is a good time to carefully check the complete list of requirements that the client provided. Create a checklist of every item the client requested. Work your way down the checklist to make certain every detail has been covered. This checklist will help prevent last-minute changes that might delay your client's final okay. In many design contracts, the final client approval is an important milestone to reach so that you can get paid, and you don't want to delay that!

Adding the Advertisement Block

After running down the checklist, you'll find that an important part of the design was missed in all the design work done to this point. The advertising block where the client wants to place ads is missing. Let's tend to that item.

The client expects to add more advertising as time goes by, so this container needs to have some flexibility but still be consistent with the rest of the design elements.

1 With `prototype.html` open, go to Code or Split view, and locate the placeholder advertising text that is in the sidebar of the page.

2 Delete all the placeholder text and the paragraph tags that contain the text.

3 Working in Code view for the document, place your cursor directly after the closing `</nav>` tag after the list of links in the sidebar, and create a new `<div>` with the class set to `side-advert`. Close the tag, and add the text

placeholder to prop open the `div`. Your completed code block should appear as follows:

```
<div class="side-advert">
    placeholder
</div>
```

4   In the CSS Designer panel, create a selector named **#sidebar .side-advert**.

5   Using this new selector, assign a width of **160 px** to the container, and set the borders so they match the color, width, and radius of the buttons that are above this area. Make the background color white, and set a minimum height to fill out the shape of the container. Once these styling rules are set, you can remove the placeholder text.

The client provided a sample advertising image from the fine folks at BrainBuffet.com. This will allow you to set up a sample ad for the client's review.

6   Click inside the `side-advert` area, and enter **Learn More About Adobe Design Tools at BrainBuffet.com**. Set the formatting for this text to a paragraph format.

7   Highlight all the text, and insert the URL **http://brainbuffet.com** into the Link field of the Property inspector. Set Target to `_blank`.

8   Insert a new paragraph, and from the Assets panel insert the file named `brainbuffet-logo.png`. Don't forget to enter meaningful alt text.

9   Link the image to the same URL you used in step 7, and use the same `_blank` value so the link opens in a new window.

Figure 5.19 The completed advertising block should be consistent with the other design elements of the sidebar.

Now it's time to provide additional styling for the elements within the container. As you review the structure of this content, it should be easy for you to pick out the potential styling hooks. The `<a>` tag, for instance, can be styled against to remove the default underline for the text link and assign a new color for the text. As you complete your own design work, your goal is to have an area in the sidebar where new advertising content can be placed in the future with design properties that are consistent with the rest of the page. **Figure 5.19** shows an example of how this area might be styled, but you are free to come up with ideas of your own.

Fixing Up the Fonts

Readability is a critical quality for web pages, and the client has asked that you experiment with the same font that is used in the header to see if it works in other areas of the page. This is a good time to review the fonts that are in use in your prototype, resolve a potential issue that might come up with the web font you're using in the header, and check that your design is consistent with sound design principles.

NOTE

You may have a slightly different list of fonts than the ones seen here if you are using a Mac.

The **web font** that's used in the header of the page is just what the client is looking for. That's a great thing. But web fonts function correctly only if the page can load the font from the server on which they are stored. If the connection fails, or if someone is viewing the page offline, the web font won't load and the design will fall apart. To address this, you'll need to create a font stack that will allow an alternative font to load when your perfect font is not available.

1   From the application bar, select Tools > Manage Fonts.

The Manage Fonts dialog appears (**Figure 5.20**). You should see a blue check mark next to the font that's in use in the header: amatic sc (you may have to scroll down to see that font).

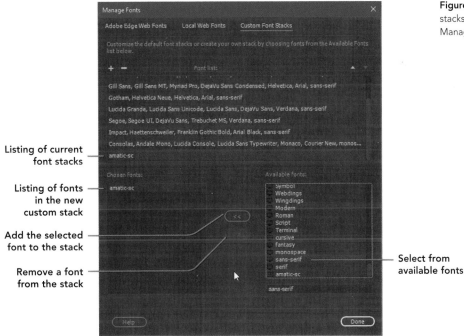

Listing of current font stacks

Listing of fonts in the new custom stack

Add the selected font to the stack

Remove a font from the stack

Select from available fonts

Figure 5.20 Custom font stacks are created in the Manage Fonts dialog.

2 Click the Custom Font Stacks tab. Locate `amatic-sc` in the list of fonts, and add it to the custom stack by clicking the arrow that points to the left.

Now you'll build a list of fallback fonts that will load in case the first font in the stack isn't available on the viewer's computer.

3 In order, add the Gill Sans and generic sans-serif font to the stack. Compare your settings to those you see in Figure 5.20, then click Done to accept the new font stack.

4 Return to the `#header-name` selector that defines the font for the company name, and replace the `amatic-sc` font with this new font stack.

When you view the page in Design view, you'll see the first font in the stack after the web font displayed in the header.

5 Adjust the margin value for the `#header-tagline` selector so that the second line of text is positioned correctly.

The remaining work with your font settings involves some trial and error and a critical eye. You can experiment with setting different font styles for the existing selectors, or you can create new selectors to style the text differently for headings and other elements of the design. Remember that it's considered a good design practice to limit the number of fonts on the page and that you'll have to defend your choices when you meet with the client.

Cleaning Up the Design

Now is the time to be extra critical of the work that you've done. It might even be a good idea to have someone else take a look at your design. Are all the elements of the design neatly aligned? Do the border properties you set previously still look consistent with this design? Do any padding or margin properties need to be adjusted? Does every area of the page present your best work, or do you need to make improvements? The footer, for instance, still has the links displayed as blue underlined text. Shouldn't those <a> tags be styled so that they're consistent with the rest of the design? You now know where to find these settings in your style sheet and how to create new styling rules, if needed, to clean up the design. And even though Chris the cartoonist isn't going to be showing up with a check in his hand, you should be thinking like a designer who wants to get that next important contractual milestone met so you can get paid!

Clean Up Your Code

Whew! Doesn't it feel great to be finished with a job and to be proud of your work? There are just a few more things to do before taking this work to the client, and that involves doing some technical testing to check for errors. We're all human and we all make mistakes, but you have Dreamweaver's tools for catching those errors and fixing them. These operations must be performed while you are in Design view.

- You should tend to the appearance of the code in your page. Dreamweaver has a nifty tool that will clean up the appearance of your code by removing empty lines and setting indents to make the code more readable. The actual contents of your code won't change, but it will appear neater and will be easier to troubleshoot after you run this operation.

  From the application bar, choose Edit > Code > Apply Source Formatting to have Dreamweaver make your code more readable.

- You'll want to check the spelling in the page. Dreamweaver doesn't give you the squiggly red underlines when you misspell a word, like a word processor does, but it does provide a tool to check your spelling. With it, you can replace words, add words to the built-in dictionary, or choose to ignore the spelling of different words. This is a decidedly old-school spell checker, but it does function, and it's always a good idea to check your spelling.

  Choose Tools > Spell Check to open the built-in spell-check dialog.

- An even older old-school tool included with Dreamweaver is the ability to run site reports that will check for errors in the HTML. To be honest, this feature hardly functions any longer, but in the event you decide to take the ACA exam for Dreamweaver you should know that these reports can be run.

  Choose Site > Reports to access the reports.

- The linting technology that is built into the latest versions of Dreamweaver works quite well, and you've probably seen evidence of this in action as you work in two different locations. At the lower-right corner of the Document window is an error indicator ( ) that changes from a green check mark (when everything's good) to a yellow warning symbol (when there's a potential issue with your code) to a red exclamation point (when there is a fatal error in your code). You'll also see the line numbers in Code or Split view display in red when there is an error such as an unclosed tag. Keep an eye on both of those areas as you work to resolve potential problems as they occur.

- Dreamweaver has limited ability to check for accessibility errors. To check for missing alt text on images, from the menu choose Site > Reports and select the type of report desired (missing alt text, in this case), as you see in **Figure 5.21**. You can click each instance where the alt text is missing to go to that image and add the necessary description of the image.

Figure 5.21 Use the Reports dialog to identify images that are missing the required alt text.

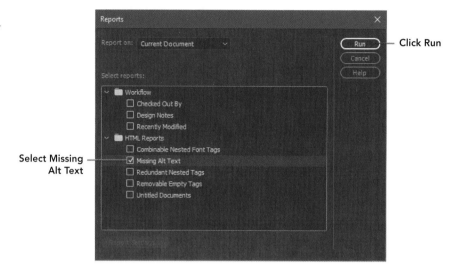

Preview in Multiple Browsers

When you feel as though all your errors are corrected and your design is finalized and perfect, preview the page in multiple browsers. Use the Preview in Browser button to open the page and check for discrepancies in the appearance of the page and as a final check to be sure you haven't missed anything. No matter what platform you're working in, you should preview the page in Google Chrome and Mozilla Firefox. On Windows computers, you should also check your page in Internet Explorer. If your computer has Windows 10 installed, you should also check your page in the Microsoft Edge browser. Macintosh users should check the design in Safari.

Conclusion

To say you've come a long way in understanding how to design web pages with HTML and CSS and the tools that Dreamweaver provides would be a serious understatement. In this chapter, you've taken all the steps required to get a complete prototype design finished and ready to present to the client for final approval.

With the prototype complete, you're now ready to meet with your client and review your design. Are you ready to defend the design decisions you've made? Does the design represent your very best work? If it does, then you'll be ready to get that final okay from your client and move on to the next step in the website building process: turning the prototype file into Dreamweaver templates that you can use for creating and maintaining all the documents in the site.

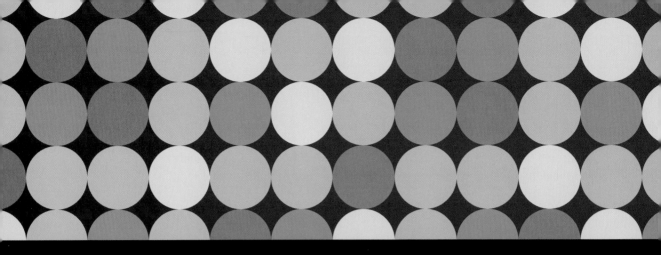

CHAPTER OBJECTIVES

Chapter Learning Objectives

- Prepare web documents for a production environment.

- Use Dreamweaver to modify, edit, and sort Cascading Style Sheets (CSS).

- Create an external CSS file and link the file to the pages in a site.

- Create Dreamweaver templates and apply templates to existing web pages.

- Use Dreamweaver templates and library items to maintain and update a website.

- Publish a website to a live web server and update the pages on the site when changes are made to documents.

Chapter ACA Objectives

For full descriptions of objectives, see the table on pages 258–264.

DOMAIN 1.0
WORKING IN THE WEB INDUSTRY
1.2, 1.5

DOMAIN 2.0
PROJECT SETUP AND INTERFACE
2.1, 2.2, 2.4

DOMAIN 4.0
WORKING WITH CODE TO CREATE AND MODIFY CONTENT
4.1, 4.2, 4.3

DOMAIN 5.0
PUBLISHING DIGITAL MEDIA
5.1, 5.2

CHAPTER 6

Moving from Prototype to Production

As you move from the prototype to the production phase, a number of things need to be done. The site must be ready to have the content moved from the prototype page to all the individual pages in the site. There is a "dirty little secret" when it comes to working with clients: Change is constant. Your client has already asked how easy it will be to update the site in the future. Making changes is an inevitable part of maintaining a website. Luckily for you, you're using Dreamweaver, so you can use the tools that the software provides to publish all the files that make up your client's site to a web server *and* easily revise the documents in the site when your client wants something changed.

In this chapter, you'll learn how to prepare the final master style sheet document that will be used in all the pages of the site. Then you'll prepare Dreamweaver templates and library items to create and update the pages. You will also learn how to publish and update all the assets in the site to a web server. By the time you finish this chapter, you'll be ready to go live with an entire website. How cool is that?

Let's Go Live!

Figure 6.1 Chris the cartoonist

Chris the cartoonist (**Figure 6.1**) certainly is pleased with the final prototype you finished in the last chapter, and he's given you the go-ahead to move on to the production phase of the *wulvs.info* website. This is an exciting time!

Chris sez:

Wow! You've really nailed the look I was going for. I can't wait to see all of this come together.

Okay, so you can consider this my formal approval of the design you created. Now what? I guess you have to make a bunch of copies of the web pages and hook them all together, right? Will I be able to make changes after the pages are all built? I might add some new characters or want to put in some new links to some of my other cartoonist friends' websites. How hard will that be to do in the future?

Oh yeah, and don't forget that I might have some new advertisers lined up real soon. Can I put different ads on different pages? Will it be easy to change the ads in the future?

I'm really excited to see all the pages filled up with all the content you worked out. Thanks again for doing such an awesome job!

Chris

Get Your Files Here

As you did in previous chapters, copy the folder that contains this chapter's files to your computer.

1 Download the project files for this chapter, named `chapter-06.zip`, from the Lesson & Update Files tab on your Account page at *www.peachpit.com.*

2 Unzip the files and copy the `chapter-06` folder to the `Learn-Dreamweaver` folder you created in Chapter 1.

Define the Chapter 6 Website

★ ACA Objective 2.1

With the files you've been provided for this chapter in the project folder, you're ready to set up the site in Dreamweaver.

1 From the application bar, choose Site > New Site.

2 Name the site **Chapter 6**.

3 Browse to the `chapter-06` folder in your `Learn-Dreamweaver` project folder.

4 Click Save to complete the site definition.

> **NOTE**
>
> *Refer to Video 1.10, "Defining a Site," if you want a quick demo of how the site definition process works.*

Reviewing CSS Syntax

★ ACA Objective 4.3

You've spent a lot of time in the CSS Designer panel. It's important that you have a thorough understanding of the kinds of rules that are in the style sheet and the different ways they are used. The syntax that selectors are written in is important to the browser and to your future work as a web designer. There are likely to be questions about it if you decide to sit for the Adobe Certified Associates exam for Dreamweaver. Let's review.

Types of Style Sheets

You can write CSS styling rules in three ways:

- **Internal style sheets** are contained in the head of a document and are enclosed by the `<style> </style>` tags.

- **External style sheets** are separate files that have the .css file extension. These style sheets are linked to an HTML document by using a `<link>` tag in the document.

- **Inline styles** are written directly within HTML tags and should be used sparingly, if at all, as in this example: `<h1 style="font-size: 150%">`.

Selector Types

Let's take a look at the different types of selectors, most of which you have already used in the `prototype.html` document.

- **Element selectors** define the properties of an entire HTML tag. An example of this kind of selector is the `<body>` selector in this document, where the margins are set to zero for the entire page.

- **ID selectors** are used to assign styling properties to tags by their ID attribute. IDs must be unique within an HTML document. You see an ID selector in the styling rules for this document for the `#container` selector. ID selectors begin with the # symbol.

- **Class selectors** are applied as needed and are targeted at tags that include a class attribute. The `.float-right` selector in this document is a class selector. Class selector names are preceded by a dot (period) symbol.

- **Descendant selectors** combine more than one selector with a space between the individual selectors. The browser reads the order of the selectors and applies the styling rules to the last item in the list. The `#sidebar p img` selector is an example of a descendant selector.

- **Group selectors** allow you to apply the same declarations to multiple selectors. If you want to apply the same rules to the `body` tag, the `td` tag, and the `th` tag, you simply group these together and separate them with a comma, as in `body, td, th`.

- **Pseudo-class selectors** evaluate a condition that exists and apply the style when a condition is met. The pseudo-classes you used in this design create the rollover effect and use the link, visited, hover, and active states. The selector is followed by a colon and the appropriate pseudo-class (such as `link` or `visited`). For example, both link and visited states are set for the navigation buttons using the selector `.sitenav ul li a:link, a:visited`.

- **Child selectors** are used where a selector is immediately followed by a specific rule that gets applied to the "parent" element that precedes it. You saw an example of a child selector when you created the styling rule that set a background color for alternate rows using the `#content table tr:nth-child(odd)` styling rule.

Putting the Style Sheet into Production

The first task in taking the site to production is the style sheet that defines the site's appearance. First you should make a backup copy of the file the client has approved. Then you'll take all that beautiful code you created in your earlier exercises, do some cleanup and organizing, and move the styling instructions written into the CSS into a separate external file that will be the master styling document for all your pages.

Setting Shorthand Notations in CSS

Dreamweaver does a great job of writing CSS rules when you use the CSS Designer panel, but sometimes the code isn't as efficient as it might be. In this exercise you'll optimize your styling rules by replacing some of the lengthy styling rules with more compact shorthand versions.

1 Select `prototype.html` in the Files panel, then right-click and select Edit > Duplicate. Dreamweaver will automatically create a file named `prototype-Copy.html`. Change the filename to **prototype-client-approved.html**.

   This file serves as a backup in the event there is a problem with the production phase you're about to enter. Do not open this file unless you need to refer to the original.

2 Open `prototype.html` from the Chapter 6 site files.

   As you review this page, you'll see that it's fundamentally the same file that you finished at the end of the last chapter. A few new styling rules have been added to get the final design elements in place, and the placement of the content on the page has been tightened up. This was the work you were tasked with at the end of Chapter 5.

3 Switch to Code view, and scroll to the top of the page. As you review all the styling rules you've created, be on the lookout for any problems, errors, empty styling rules, or other issues that need to be adjusted.

   Two issues immediately come into view. First, the styling rules include some properties that could be combined into a shorthand version to reduce the amount of the code in the page. Second, the styling rules are not listed in a logical order. You can deal with both problems in the CSS Designer panel.

★ *ACA Objective 2.4*

★ *ACA Objective 4.1*

★ *ACA Objective 4.2*

★ *ACA Objective 4.3*

★ *ACA Objective 5.1*

★ *ACA Objective 5.2*

▶ **Video 6.1**
CSS Review

▶ **Video 6.2** *Putting the Style Sheet into Production*

4   Select the **body** selector in the CSS Designer panel. This rule can be trimmed down with a shorthand notation.

5   Locate the Set Shorthand field directly above the margin properties for this selector, and type **0px** (**Figure 6.2**).

Figure 6.2 You can set CSS shorthand notations in the CSS Designer panel.

Set the margin
shorthand to 0px

6   View the code for the **body** selector; the four lines that were being used to define the margins have been reduced to a single notation: `margin: 0 px;`.

7   Set shorthand padding values for the `.float-left` and `.float-right` styling rules.

When working on your own design, examine your code carefully to find any opportunities to reduce the amount of code in your style sheet.

8   Save your work.

Arranging the Source Order of the Style Sheet

In these next steps, you put your styling rules into a logical order that makes it easier for you to find the styling rules you want to work on in the future. The CSS Designer panel makes this easy to do, since it allows you to drag and drop selectors that are listed in the "stack" of rules in your style sheet.

1 Examine the listing of the CSS selectors in `prototype.html`.

The document has higher-level rules that were applied using ID selectors, such as `#content`, and a number of styling rules that are descendant selectors of the upper-level rule, such as `#content p`. Your goal is to group these selectors in order, with the highest-level selector at the top of the grouping and with longer, more specific selectors underneath.

LEVEL UP: SMART RULE CREATION

When you create a new styling rule, Dreamweaver writes the code for the new rule directly after whatever rule is selected in the CSS Designer panel. When you create new styling rules, it's a good practice to select carefully so that the selectors are grouped together.

Figure 6.3 You can choose multiple selectors in the CSS Designer panel by holding down Shift while you select the rules.

2 In the CSS Designer panel, drag the `#container #content h1` selector up until it falls below the `#container` rule.

3 Select the list of rules that begin with the `#content` ID, as you see in **Figure 6.3**. (Shift-click to select a contiguous group.) Drag this group up until the rules fall below the `#content` selector.

As you examine the source order of the style sheet, be sure that you maintain the proper order for any pseudo-classes that are in the document. Remember that these rules must always follow the correct order of link, visited, hover, and active, also known as LVHA.

4 Order the selectors in the style sheet until the selectors are grouped from the shorter, more general rules to longer, more specific rules. I prefer to place all tag selectors at the top, followed by all ID selectors, followed by all classes. I try to alphabetize these where possible. The more organized your CSS is, the easier it is to find a given selector (and related selectors). Try to have mercy on the person maintaining your CSS (it will likely be you).

Figure 6.4 shows a portion of the CSS Designer panel where the tag selectors are placed at the top and the ID selectors grouped next, with `#content table` and `#contact-form` selectors having the more specific rules below them.

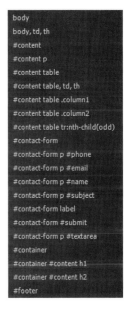

Figure 6.4 Grouping CSS selectors from general to more specific rules

5 Switch to Live view to ensure that none of your reordering work has had an effect on the appearance of the page. Complete the work of ordering and checking the design on your own.

6 Save your work.

Commenting the Style Sheet

You write comments into computer code as a note to your future self, providing a way for you to recall the why and how of the selectors you designed. Comments are also a way that you as a designer can make notations for others to read when you are working in a collaborative environment. Again, have mercy on the poor sap who will have to maintain this code. That is likely you (and you won't remember why you did what you did six months from now).

1 Switch to Code view.

   The Coding toolbar is the icons to the left.

2 Place your cursor at the beginning of the `.characters` selector, and press Enter/Return to create a blank line. Press the Up Arrow key on your keyboard to move the cursor to the blank line (**Figure 6.5**).

Figure 6.5 Comments allow you to make notes that you and your co-workers can use as a reference in the future.

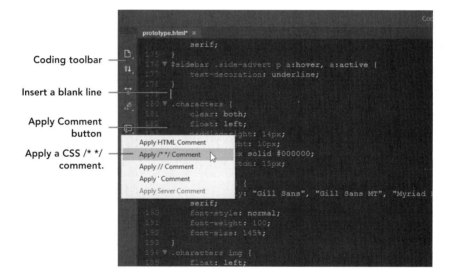

Coding toolbar

Insert a blank line

Apply Comment button

Apply a CSS /* */ comment.

3 Click the Apply Comment button, and choose the /**/ comment type. This inserts CSS comments into your code. Comments that are in between the two asterisks are visible in the code but are not read by the browser.

4 Type the following comment for this block of CSS rules: **/*These rules define the character boxes*/**.

5 Work through the style sheet, adding meaningful comments above each major grouping of selectors.

6 Save your work.

Converting the Style Sheet to an External CSS File

The final step to prepare for production is converting all the styling rules in the `<head>` of the document into a separate CSS file that will be linked to the HTML page. This is a surprisingly quick and easy operation to perform.

1   In Code view, locate the first rule that follows the opening `<style>` tag, and place your cursor in front of the **body** selector.

2   Highlight all the selectors in the document, being sure not to include either the opening or closing `<style>` tags.

3   Choose Tools > CSS > Move CSS Rules.

4   In the Move to External Style Sheet dialog, select the "A new style sheet" option (**Figure 6.6**), and click OK. The Save Style Sheet File As dialog opens.

Figure 6.6 The process of moving selected styling rules to an external CSS file

5   Be sure the file is being saved into the `chapter-06` root folder for the site, and name the file **wulvs-styles**. Click Save when your settings match those in Figure 6.6.

When you save the file, all the selectors are removed from the document and are replaced with a link to the external file. Take note of this line in your code:

```
<link href="wulvs-styles.css" rel="stylesheet"
→  type="text/css">
```

This code directs the browser to retrieve the external CSS file and use the styling rules in that document for this page.

6 Locate the empty opening and closing `<style>` tags, and delete these two lines of code:

```
<style type="text/css"
</style>
```

TIP

Practicing professionals place related documents in an assets folder (with sub-folders for images, CSS, JS, and so forth).

Dreamweaver now displays the name of the CSS file in the Related Files toolbar below the filename, as you see in **Figure 6.7**. You can now switch between the code for the page by selecting the Source Code button, or you can work on the code in the style sheet by selecting the name of the CSS file. You can also open the CSS file in a separate window by right-clicking the name of the file and selecting Open as a Separate File.

7 Save both the HTML file and the CSS file by choosing File > Save All.

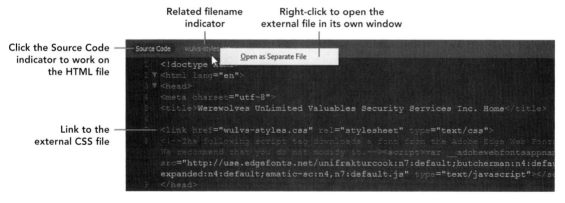

Figure 6.7 Dreamweaver displays a link to the external CSS file in the Related Files toolbar.

You have moved the styles in your prototype file into an external CSS file that can be linked to all the files in the site. This produces a much more efficient way of modifying a styling rule, since you need to make a change only to this single CSS file to make a styling change in all the documents that are linked to the external file.

Building Out the Site with Dreamweaver Templates

★ *ACA Objective 2.1*

★ *ACA Objective 4.1*

★ *ACA Objective 4.2*

★ *ACA Objective 5.1*

▶ **Video 6.3** *Part 1: Building Out the Site with Dreamweaver Templates*

▶ **Video 6.4** *Part 2: Building Out the Site with Dreamweaver Templates*

A Dreamweaver template is a special type of web page used within the Dreamweaver work environment. It locks parts of the page structure in place while allowing the designer to edit other parts of the page that need to change. Templates are how Dreamweaver users give all the pages in a site a consistent design. And the beauty of working with templates is that when one of those inevitable changes takes place, you can update the areas that are shared among all the pages in the site without having to open each file. You don't have to worry about having to modify the content in the page when the template is revised.

You're going to get a lot done in this project. To begin, you'll convert the prototype page to a Dreamweaver template file and then insert some special Dreamweaver markup that will allow you to place the content that goes into each page. At the end of this project, you'll have moved from a single prototype web page to an entire functional website with all the pages designed just the way you want.

Creating the Template File

When you create a template file, you set up a special kind of web page that includes coding specific to Dreamweaver. This markup allows you to lock some areas of the template while allowing changes to other, editable areas of the page.

1   With `prototype.html` open, choose File > Save as Template. The Save as Template dialog opens (**Figure 6.8**).

2   In the Save As field, name the file **wulvs-website** and click Save.

Select the
Chapter 6 site

Set the filename to
wulvs-website

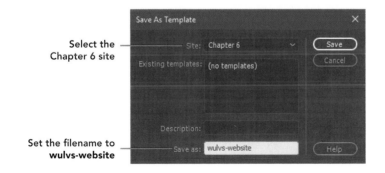

Figure 6.8 When you convert a file to a template, you must designate the site and the filename for the template file.

3 Click Yes when Dreamweaver prompts you to update the links in the document.

Several significant changes occurred. Take note of the new `Templates` folder inside the Files panel. Dreamweaver creates this folder automatically; this is where all template files are located.

Inside the `Templates` folder is a file named `wulvs-website.dwt`. The .dwt file extension designates this file as a Dreamweaver template.

Inserting an Editable Region

When you work on a page that has been constructed from a Dreamweaver template, some areas of the page can be changed and others cannot. The areas that are locked by the template are those that should appear the same on every page. The editable regions—or those areas where changes are allowed—are created in the Dreamweaver template file.

When you're making these changes, the preferred view is Split view. This allows you to see the code that is changed as you work with the file. The area of the template that will be editable is contained within the `<div>` with an ID of `content`.

1 With the `wuvls-website.dwt` file open, click anywhere within the main content area of the page and select the `<div id="content">` in the Tag selector.

2 Choose Insert > Template > Editable Region.

The New Editable Region dialog appears.

3 Name the editable region **Main-Page-Content**. Click OK.

Dreamweaver indicates the editable region with a blue label (**Figure 6.9**) and places special markup in the code.

Now you'll remove all the existing content in this editable region and replace it with placeholder text. This operation is best done in Code view, where you can easily select all the contents in the `<div id="content">` section.

4 Switch to Code view, locate the opening tag for the content section— `<div id="content">`—and click the arrow next to the line number to collapse the entire tag. This makes locating the closing tag easier. Once you have identified where your code begins and ends, click the arrow again to expand this area of your code.

Editable region label

Editable region markup

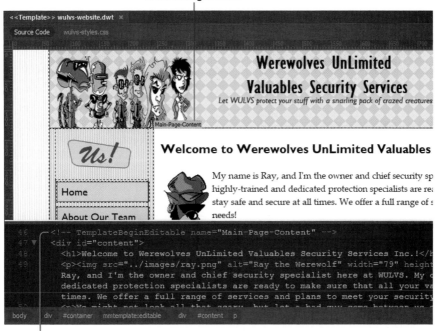

Figure 6.9 Dreamweaver displays a label that indicates the editable region.

5 Highlight all the tags and content inside the `<div id="content">`, and press Delete to remove the code and content from the main area of the page.

6 Insert your cursor inside the empty `<div>` tag, and type **`Content goes here`** as the placeholder text. Your document should look similar to **Figure 6.10**, with the empty `<div>` tag on the page.

7 Save and close your template page. You're now ready to build pages from this template.

```
<!-- TemplateBeginEditable name="Main-Page-Content" -->
<div id="content">
Content goes here
</div>
<!-- TemplateEndEditable -->
<div id="footer">
```

Figure 6.10 The result of replacing all the code in `<div id="content">` with placeholder text

Replacing the Home Page

Now that you have a template to work from, you can start moving content from the prototype page to the individual documents in the site. The home page is a great place to start.

1   Choose File > New to create a new file. You should be in Design view or Split view.

2   From the New Document dialog, select the Site Templates category on the left and Chapter 6 in the list of defined sites in the center of the window (**Figure 6.11**).

A thumbnail version of the template you just created displays on the right.

Figure 6.11 The New Document dialog allows you to create a new page based on a template file.

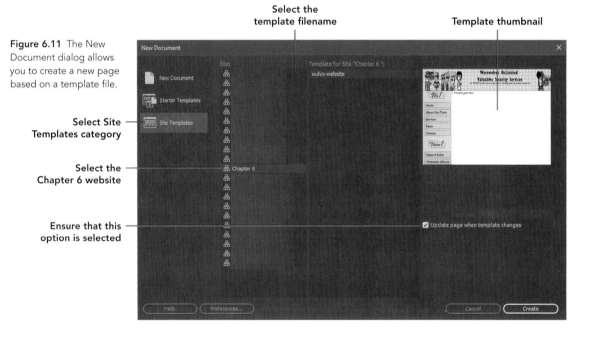

Select the template filename

Template thumbnail

Select Site Templates category

Select the Chapter 6 website

Ensure that this option is selected

3   Select the `wulvs-website` template.

4   Verify that the "Update page when template changes" check box is selected, and click Create.

5   Choose File > Save As, browse to the root folder for the site, and select the `index.html` file. Click Save.

6   Choose Yes/Replace when Dreamweaver asks if you want to replace the existing file.

7   Open `prototype.html`, and copy all the text and images from the top of the page through the bulleted item list just above the Team Page text. Press Ctrl+C/Command+C to copy the selected text and images.

8   Remove the placeholder text in the `index.html` page, and press Ctrl+V/Command+V to paste the copied text and images into the home page. You can close this file after it has been saved.

9   View the contents of the new home page, and save your work.

Congratulations! The home page for your website is finished!

Building the Team Page

The next page in your prototype file is the area marked Team Page. You'll create another new document in these next few steps and replace the existing (empty) page in the site with a new page that uses your template.

1   Choose File > New to create a new file. As you did for the home page, select the Site Templates category, the Chapter 6 site, and the `wulvs-website` template. Click the Create button.

2   Choose File > Save As, and browse to the `about` folder. Select `index.html` as the new filename. Click Save and then Yes/Replace to overwrite the existing file.

    Template files do not overwrite the page title when a new page is created. To change the page title, you edit the title in the Property inspector.

3   Change the Document Title field to **About Werewolves UnLimited** (**Figure 6.12**).

    Now, you need to remove the placeholder text and replace it with the area of the prototype page that includes all the different characters and their descriptions.

Figure 6.12 Page titles may be changed in the Property inspector.

Change the document title to:
About Werewolves UnLimited

4 In `prototype.html`, select the area of the page under the Team Page heading all the way down to the last character box. You might find this easier to do in Code view. Copy the selection.

5 Return to the `index.html` page (making certain you are working with the `index.html` page in the `about` folder), and remove the placeholder text. Paste the copied text and images into the editable region on the page, staying within the `<div id="content">`.

You'll immediately see that the images in the page are not displaying correctly because the path to the image files is no longer correct. If you look at the source for the image in the Property inspector, you'll see that the path to the first image is listed as `images/ray-named.png`. This needs to be corrected to point to the correct location, which is one folder level up in the folder structure for the site. For example, the correct path to the first image needs to be `../images/ray-named.png`.

6 Correct the path using one of the following methods:

- Use Find and Replace to change the source code for the page so that all instances of `images` are replaced with `../images`.

- Browse to the correct file from the Property inspector using the Browse for File icon.

- Type the correct path to the `images` folder in the Property inspector for each image or directly in the code.

7 Save the file.

Your second page is complete!

LEVEL UP: COMPARING CODE

Here's a trick you can use when you run into a situation where you need to determine the correct path to a number of images. In the Property inspector, for the file that isn't showing correctly, browse to the file so that the path is corrected, and then compare the correct code to the code that isn't working. You can then see what changes need to be made to get everything working correctly, and you can more quickly set about making the revisions.

Creating the Additional Pages for the Site

Now that you know how to use a template file to create new pages and replace an existing page, you can set about the task of replacing all the remaining pages in the site. Using the techniques from the previous steps in this project, your task is to replace the three additional remaining index pages in the site. Here are the general steps:

1 Create new pages from the template file, and replace `contact/index.html`, `services/index.html`, and `rates/index.html` with the new pages that you created from your template file. Also create a new page for `thankyou.html` from the template file (replace the existing file).

2 Copy and paste the content from `prototype.html` into the correct pages in the site. Remember that you'll also need to supply a new page title for each page. Each page should also include the heading that leads the section in the prototype file.

3 On the page named `thankyou.html`, insert the `ray.png` image and a short message that thanks visitors for their interest and reminds them that this isn't a *real* company.

4 Remember to save all your work.

PROJECT 6.3

Adding Optional Content with Library Items

It's pretty cool to see the website go from just a single prototype page to an entirely functional site, isn't it? You now have all the contents of the prototype copied into the individual pages within the site. You can click through your navigation to see how the site has come together. Great job!

There's one last thing on the client's list of requirements. The advertising block that sits in the left sidebar needs to have two qualities. First, you need to have the ability to show the advertising area on some pages but hide it on others. Second, the client has indicated that there will be some additional advertisers coming onboard, so the actual ads that show on each page also need to be changed from time to time.

This kind of work—where you show or hide and change one block of content for another—can best be handled with a new template object combined with another tool in your Dreamweaver toolset: the library item.

Adding an Editable Optional Region

An editable optional region in Dreamweaver is created by inserting special markup that allows a certain area of the page to show when its visibility value is set to `true`, and to be hidden when visibility is set to `false`.

1 Open the `wulvs-website.dwt` file from the `Templates` folder.

2 Click anywhere within the advertisement area in the sidebar, and select the `div .side-advert` indicator in the Tag selector.

3 Open the Insert panel, and change the category in the dropdown menu at the top of the panel to Templates (**Figure 6.13**).

4 Click Editable Optional Region.

5 In the New Optional Region dialog, name the region **advertising1** and click OK. Leave Show by Default selected so that this region will continue to be present in this document. You'll hide or show the region in the following steps.

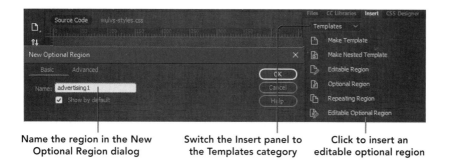

Figure 6.13 Use the Insert panel to insert a new editable optional region.

Name the region in the New Optional Region dialog

Switch the Insert panel to the Templates category

Click to insert an editable optional region

6   Save the file. You will be prompted to update all the pages that use this template. Click Update to modify all the files in the site where this template is in use. Click the Close button when the Update Pages window indicates that the updates are done.

7   Open `contact/index.html`. In the head of the document, locate the following line of code that Dreamweaver has inserted to allow you to show or hide the optional region:

```
<!-- InstanceParam name="advertising1" type="boolean"
→ value="true" -->
```

8   Change `value="true"` to **`value="false"`**.

When you view the page, you'll see that the advertisement still shows.

9   Choose Tools > Templates > Update Current Page to complete the process of hiding the advertising block.

10 Save this file, and close the document.

You now know how to show or hide an optional region by setting the value in the Dreamweaver markup to either `true` or `false`.

Converting Content into a Dreamweaver Library Item

Dreamweaver library items are self-contained chunks of HTML that can be inserted into a document when needed and updated when they need to be changed. The Assets panel is used to add, edit, and manage the library items within a site. In the next steps, you'll create a new library item from the existing advertisement that's in the sidebar.

1 Open **wulvs-website.dwt** from the **Templates** folder.

2 In Code or Split view, highlight the code block that is inside the advertising block in the sidebar. Be sure that you select only the *contents* within the `<div>` tag and not the `<div>` itself.

3 Open the Assets panel. Switch to the Library Item category (**Figure 6.14**). Click the New Library Item button at the bottom of the panel.

   Dreamweaver will provide a warning that styling information does not get included with the library item. Not to worry. Your CSS styling rules will still apply based on the named elements that are within the document. Don't forget to click OK when prompted.

Figure 6.14 Use the Insert panel to insert a new library item.

Select the Library Item category in the Assets panel

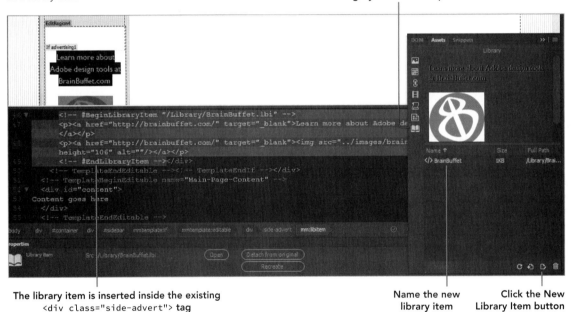

The library item is inserted inside the existing
`<div class="side-advert">` **tag**

Name the new library item

Click the New Library Item button

4 Enter **BrainBuffet** for the new library item name.

5 Press Enter/Return to accept the name. Click Update when Dreamweaver prompts you to update the files in the site.

6 Save the template file. Click Update when prompted to update the pages that use the template file. Click Close when the updates are complete.

7   Open the home page for the site, `index.html`.

Dreamweaver may not automatically replace the code within the advertising block, so the next step in replacing the ad with the library item is to delete the existing content within the `<div>`.

8   In Code or Split view, select the contents that are inside the `.side-advert` `<div>` and delete it.

9   With your cursor inside the `.side-advert` `<div>`, open the Assets panel, select the BrainBuffet library item, and click the Insert button at the bottom of the panel.

The content of the `<div>` now displays the advertisement that belongs on this page.

10 Save your file.

Creating a Library Item from Scratch

So what's the big deal anyway? You already had this content in the advertising block, and all you've done so far is replace what was already there with the same content.

The real value of library items is in your ability to replace content like this easily using the Assets panel. When your client has more advertising content to display, all you'll need to do is replace one library item with another to make the switch. And if you need to edit the contents of a library item, Dreamweaver will allow you to automatically apply the changes everywhere within the site where that item is used.

To see this in action, you'll create a new library item.

1   Open the home page for the site, `index.html`. Make sure that nothing on the page is selected.

2   Open the Assets panel, and click the New Library Item button at the bottom of the panel (**Figure 6.15**).

3   Name the library item **BookAdvertisement**.

4   Click the Edit button at the bottom of the Assets panel. Dreamweaver will open a new Document window for the file named `BookAdvertisement.lbi`. The LBI (.lbi) file type is unique to Dreamweaver and is used for all library items.

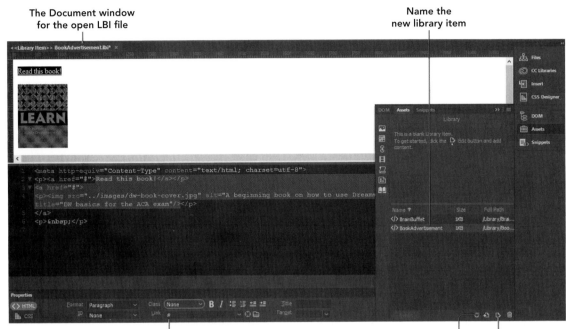

The Document window for the open LBI file

Name the new library item

Figure 6.15 Use the Assets panel to create a new library item and edit its contents.

Links are created and displayed in the Property inspector

Click to create a new library item

Click to open the library item in a Document window for editing

5 In the BookAdvertisement.lbi Document window, type **Read this book!** and press Enter/Return.

6 Insert the dw-book-cover.png image for this book from the images folder. Remember to add the alt text.

7 Select the text and the image, and in the Property inspector's Link field, create a "dummy" link by typing the **#** symbol. Press Enter/Return to accept the link. Verify that your settings match those in Figure 6.15.

8 Save and close the library item.

Your library item is complete!

Inserting and Updating Library Items

With your new library item created, you can open individual pages within the site, swap out the content in the advertising block of a page, and add the new library item. When you change the library item by editing and saving it, Dreamweaver will automatically update the pages where the LBI file is used.

1 Open the `rates/index.html` page.

2 Delete the contents of the advertising block in the sidebar.

3 Open the Assets panel. Select the `BookAdvertisement.lbi` item, and click the Insert button. Save the index page.

4 From the Assets panel, select the `BookAdvertisement.lbi` item, and click Edit.

   The library item opens in a new Document window.

   Now you need to change the link in the Property inspector to the actual link for this book. Don't forget to select the words and image associated with the book.

5 Search Peachpit.com to locate *Learn Adobe Dreamweaver CC for Web Authoring*, and copy the URL. Paste the URL into the Link field.

6 Save the library item.

7 Click Update when Dreamweaver prompts you to update the pages that use the LBI file.

   Dreamweaver automatically changes the link on all the pages that use this library item.

8 Click Done when the update is complete.

Your work is done!

In this project, you've seen how to create an editable region within a template that can be set to either show or hide a region of the page. By combining that option with a Dreamweaver library item, you now know how to quickly change content within a page and update all the pages that use these Dreamweaver content management tools.

PROJECT 6.4

Publishing and Updating a Dreamweaver Site

▶ **Video 6.6** *Part 1: Publishing and Updating a Dreamweaver Site*

▶ **Video 6.7** *Part 2: Publishing and Updating a Dreamweaver Site*

So far in this chapter, you've accomplished a tremendous amount of work, and now it's time to take the next big step and publish your completed work to a live website.

Well, you *could* publish your files to a web server if you owned the *wulvs.info* domain name and hired a web hosting company to provide the services needed for your site to connect to the rest of the World Wide Web. In a real production environment, the web hosting company would provide instructions for how to set up Dreamweaver to connect to the IP address where the live website would be stored. Many companies provide web hosting services and maintain the web servers that make live websites possible.

Given that you may be working in a classroom environment, it may not be practical to work with a live web server. Instead of a live server, you'll create a folder on your computer that you'll use to simulate the process of copying files you've completed on your computer to another location. Fundamentally, this is how web designers interact with the servers where their live files are stored, so this will give you a good idea of how the process of publishing and updating from a local drive to a live server takes place.

Defining the Remote Server

For this project, you'll create a folder on your computer that you can use to simulate the process of publishing to a live web server. Publishing files essentially involves placing a copy of the files on your computer into the folder that a web hosting company has prepared for your site. The following operation mimics that process.

1   Using Windows Explorer (Windows) or the Finder (Mac), create a new folder inside the `Learn-Dreamweaver` folder where all your project sites have been stored. Name this new folder **wulvs-website**.

2   In Dreamweaver, choose Site > Manage Sites. Refer to **Figure 6.16**.

3   Select the Chapter 6 site, and click the pencil icon in the Manage Sites dialog to edit the site. The Site Setup dialog appears.

Select the
Chapter 6 site

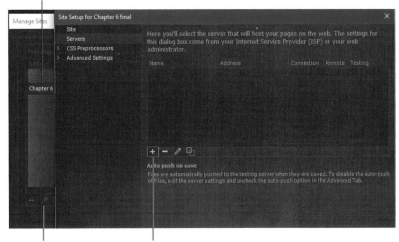

Figure 6.16 Remote
server settings are set in
the Manage Sites window.

Click the pencil icon   Click the + to add
to edit the site settings   a new server

Set the site name to
Simulated Server

Choose Local/Network
from the dropdown menu

Browse to the
`wulvs-website` **folder**

4   Select the Servers category to open the server settings window. Click the
    + sign to add a new server definition.

5   Enter **Simulated Server** as the server name.

6   Change the Connect Using field from the default FTP setting to
    Local/Network.

7   Use the Browse icon to navigate to the folder you created in step 1.

8   Leave the Web URL field blank, and check your settings against the ones in
    Figure 6.16.

9   Click Save to save the server settings. Click Save again to save the site settings.
    Click Done in the Manage Sites dialog to finish defining the remote server.

Publishing to the Remote Server

With the remote server location designated, you're ready to see the process of publishing to a web server in action. You'll use the Files panel for these operations.

1   In the Files panel, select the home page for the website, `index.html`.

2   Click the Put button at the top of the panel (**Figure 6.17**).

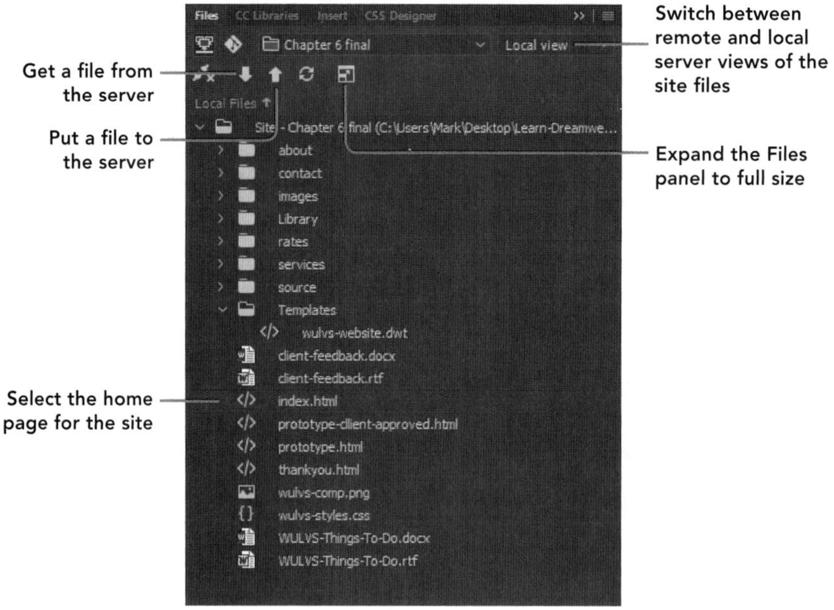

Figure 6.17 File operations for a site are performed in the Files panel.

NOTE

If you select the "Don't show me this message again" check box, Dreamweaver will automatically put dependent files to the server. This setting can be changed by choosing Edit > Preferences (Dreamweaver CC > Preferences on a Mac) and then selecting the Site category. By default, both Prompt on Get/Check Out and Prompt on Put/Check In are selected.

Get a file from the server

Put a file to the server

Switch between remote and local server views of the site files

Expand the Files panel to full size

Select the home page for the site

3   Save the file if prompted, then click Yes when Dreamweaver asks if you want to put the dependent files for this page.

Dependent files are all the files that are linked within a document. Dreamweaver copies the image files and the CSS file that is linked to the document onto the server along with the page itself.

4   Switch the Files panel to the Remote Server view.

Dreamweaver has copied the home page and the images that are on the page along with the CSS file into the folder that you're using as a simulated web server.

You can now put the other pages for the site onto the server with one operation.

5   Switch the Files panel to Local view, and then expand the view of the **about**, **contact**, **rates**, and **services** folders so that the **index.html** file in each folder is visible.

6   While holding down the Ctrl/Command key, click each of the **index.html** files along with the **thankyou.html** file. Click the Put button, and click Yes to including dependent files. Save the files if prompted.

Dreamweaver will copy all the HTML files plus all the image files to the server.

7   Open the expanded view of the Files panel (**Figure 6.18**).

When you compare the files on the server against those on your local computer, you'll see that all the files that make your website functional are present.

The source files and images that have not been used within the site remain on your local computer and have not been placed onto the server. Unless you are working with other people on the site and wish to share those files, they are not needed on the server.

Figure 6.18 You can use the Expanded view of the Files panel to compare the files on your computer with those that are on the server.

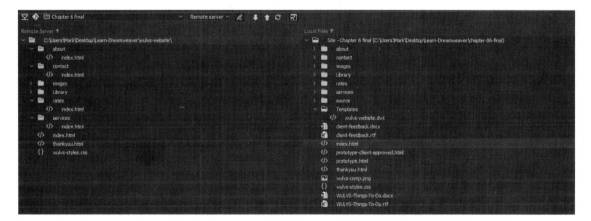

Updating Files on the Server

When you make revisions to documents on your local computer, you will need to upload the revised files to the web server so that the changes become visible.

1   Open the home page of the site, **index.html**.

2   Place your cursor after the last bullet item. Press the Return/Enter key twice to exit the list. From the Assets panel, select the Images icon in the left column, insert **wulvs-comic-sample.jpg** (the sample cartoon the client has provided), and provide alt text in the Property inspector.

3   Create a new class selector in the CSS Designer panel so that this image can be centered in its container. Name the new selector **.centeritem**.

4   Set the properties for the new selector by setting display to **block** and the left and right margins to **auto**.

5   Select the cartoon image, and assign the **.centeritem** class to the image. The cartoon will now be centered in the content container.

6   Choose File > Save All to save both the CSS file and the HTML file.

    The two files that have been changed must be put to the server so that the changes you made can be viewed online.

7   Return to the Files panel and select the **index.html** file and the **wulvs-styles.css** file, and click Put to copy them to the server. Click Yes when prompted for dependent files, and the cartoon image will also be copied to the server.

Synchronizing Local and Remote Files

Dreamweaver allows you to synchronize modified files by comparing the files on your computer with those on the server. This operation is performed when numerous changes have been made and you need to put all the modified files to the server at once.

1   Open **wulvs-website.dwt** from the **Templates** folder.

2   Place your cursor directly after the Contact text in the left sidebar. Press Enter/Return to create a new list item in that location.

3   Type **Learn More**, highlight the text, and provide a dummy link for the text by typing the **#** symbol in the Link field of the Property inspector. The text will take on the appearance of the other buttons once the link is created.

4   Repeat the operation in the footer area of the page to create a new link in that location, using the | symbol to separate the new link from the existing ones. Alternatively, you can copy the Contact Us text and paste it after the | symbol (and change the text to Learn More).

5   Save the template file, and update all the pages that use the template.

    You now have multiple files that have been modified and saved by Dreamweaver.

6   Right-click the site folder in the top of the Files panel, and select Synchronize from the menu that appears.

    Dreamweaver will ask how these files are to be compared and which actions are to be taken (**Figure 6.19**).

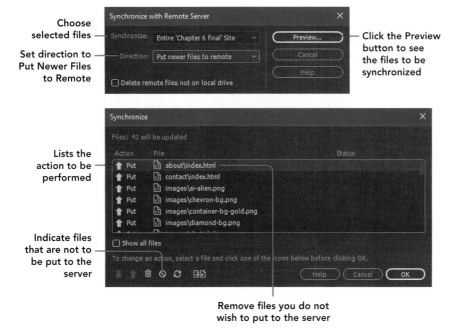

Choose selected files

Set direction to Put Newer Files to Remote

Click the Preview button to see the files to be synchronized

Figure 6.19 Synchronizing files allows you to put multiple modified files to the server in one operation.

Lists the action to be performed

Indicate files that are not to be put to the server

Remove files you do not wish to put to the server

7   Set the Synchronize setting to Entire 'Chapter 6' Site, set the Direction setting to Put Newer Files to Remote, and click Preview.

You will see a report of the files that Dreamweaver has determined need to be copied to the server with the action that is to be performed.

8   Review the list of files. Those files that you do not wish to copy to the server, such as the source files, may be removed from the operation by selecting the file and clicking the Ignore button at the bottom of the window.

9   After you have reviewed your file, click OK and Dreamweaver will perform the requested action. In this case, the files displayed will be put to the server.

Conclusion

You're now ready. With the skills that you've learned, you can develop an entire website in Dreamweaver by carefully structuring the site, creating folders and files that are needed to meet the requirements of your client, and designing the style for the site using modern CSS styling methods. What's more, you can share your work with the entire world by publishing a website to a live web server, and you can modify and maintain the site when those inevitable changes happen.

CHAPTER OBJECTIVES

Chapter Learning Objectives

- Learn how mobile development is driving modern web design work.

- Create new documents in Dreamweaver using the included Responsive and Bootstrap starter files.

- Evaluate the time required to create responsive designs in preparation for giving the client a cost and time estimate.

- Use the Media Queries toolbar and the CSS Designer panel to examine and visualize responsive designs.

- Create and edit the media queries that define a fluid design.

- Understand how jQuery and Bootstrap components are used in responsive design.

- Create styling rules that override the default settings found in Bootstrap components.

- Insert HTML5 video into a web page and understand the methods for preparing video for production.

- Use Dreamweaver to write and edit CSS3 animations and transitions.

Chapter ACA Objectives

For full descriptions of objectives, see the table on pages 258–264.

DOMAIN 1.0
WORKING IN THE WEB INDUSTRY
1.1, 1.2, 1.4, 1.5

DOMAIN 2.0
PROJECT SETUP AND INTERFACE
2.1, 2.4

DOMAIN 3.0
ORGANIZING CONTENT ON A PAGE
3.2

DOMAIN 4.0
WORKING WITH CODE TO CREATE AND MODIFY CONTENT
4.1, 4.2, 4.3, 4.4

DOMAIN 5.0
PUBLISHING DIGITAL MEDIA
5.1

CHAPTER 7

Think Mobile First with Responsive Design

In the projects you've completed up to this point, you've created semantically correct HTML documents that are styled with Cascading Style Sheets (CSS). Bravo for that! You've learned how to do things the right way, but with this one tiny caveat: Your design is not mobile friendly. Yes, the web pages you created were to your client's specifications, and the *wulvs.info* website will look just fine on a desktop browser and on a tablet. But when it comes to phones? Sorry, but the fixed-width design you've created simply won't display properly on a phone.

Not to worry. You can work on some proofs of concept that could be presented as a solution to what the client is asking for in a new development cycle. As it turns out, Adobe Dreamweaver has some excellent resources already built into the program that will allow you to get a jumpstart on designing for mobile devices and for learning about the world of responsive web design.

We have been learning the fundamentals of using Dreamweaver CC to create basic websites. This is why we started with a static page. There is an alternative view (and we recommend it for practicing professionals): Think in terms of mobile first. Develop your page for the small screen and include only the items absolutely necessary to convey your message. Move on to larger screen formats once you have a solid mobile-friendly version. Once you have mastered the fundamentals of working with a tool like Dreamweaver, we recommend thinking in terms of developing for mobile sites first.

Let's Go Mobile!

Figure 7.1 Chris the cartoonist

Chris the cartoonist (**Figure 7.1**) continues to be pleased with the work you have done and is thinking of ways to expand.

Chris sez:

Hey, guess what? Things are really taking off with my web comic, and I have this crazy idea. I know, you think all my ideas are crazy, but hear me out.

The web comic has become so popular that people want to know more about the characters and even collect character profiles, such as baseball cards. Can you believe it?

Can you create a new website that would be viewable on a smartphone and could even be turned into a phone or mobile app? I'm thinking about calling the new website "Wulvs Collectibles." Oh, and I want to work in some video and animations too.

I know that's a tall order and it's a whole new design job for you, so there are two big questions to answer:

Can you do it?

How much would it cost?

Thanks. I look forward to getting your estimate.

Chris

Get Your Files Here

As you did in previous chapters, copy the folder that contains this chapter's files to your computer.

1 Download the project files for this lesson, named `chapter-07.zip`, from the Lesson & Update Files tab on your Account page at *www.peachpit.com*.

2 Unzip the files and copy the `chapter-07` folder to the `Learn-Dreamweaver` folder you created in Chapter 1.

Define the Chapter 7 Website

With the files you've been provided for this chapter in the project folder, you're ready to set up the site in Dreamweaver.

1 From the application bar, select Site > New Site.

2 Name the site **Chapter 7**.

3 Browse to the `chapter-07` folder in your `Learn-Dreamweaver` project folder.

4 Click Save.

★ ACA Objective 2.1

NOTE

Refer to Video 1.10, "Defining a Site," if you want a quick demo of how the site definition process works.

Understanding HTML5, CSS3, and Responsive Design

★ ACA Objective 2.1

★ ACA Objective 3.2

★ ACA Objective 4.1

★ ACA Objective 4.2

▶ **Video 7.1**
Exploring Responsive Design with HTML5

Before we dig into the first project, let's discuss a little about how HTML5 and CSS3 came into being. As it turns out, the project you've been working on is a perfect example of the two big challenges facing web developers as the web matured and new expectations for the delivery of web-based content came into play.

If you look back at the beginning of the journey to create the *wulvs.info* website, you'll recall that the structure of the site was created using five `<div>` tags. Each tag was assigned a name that we made up on our own but that followed the common naming conventions that web designers typically use. Thousands, if not millions, of web pages were built following this kind of structure and using names similar to, or the same as, the ones you used. Common practices were followed, and professional web developers did their best to follow the standards, but the standards themselves were loosely written. That was all fine for humans, but not so great for computer programming, where *naming* things is so very important.

But even as these methods were being refined and revised, many people began to recognize the limitations of this kind of design on two major fronts. First, without a standard naming convention it wasn't possible to efficiently build programming frameworks that could take advantage of what web browsers could do. There were just too many variables in how web pages could be constructed and not enough HTML tags to support standardization.

And then the iPhone arrived.

The release of the iPhone completely changed the landscape of web design and the expectations of consumers. Suddenly, even the web-standard methods that web developers had been using for years became a real problem. The much smaller screen sizes available on iOS, and on the Android and Windows phones that quickly came along after Apple's success, simply couldn't display a web page that was designed for a computer screen in a version that gave a satisfying presentation to the viewer. Apple's decision not to include Adobe Flash Player on its phones also presented tremendous problems for the creators of web video and interactive content.

It's not like any of this came as a surprise and every web developer woke up one morning to a world that was fundamentally different. In fact, the World Wide Web Consortium (W3C) had been working on solving some of these very questions:

- How can web browsers, device manufacturers, and companies such as Apple, Adobe, and Microsoft develop tools that allow web pages to be designed and delivered in a more standard way?

- How can developers leverage a new set of standards so that new methods can be devised that make programming for the web more efficient?

- How can the companies and programmers who make browser software conform to these new standards so that a web page will look the same when seen in the Firefox browser (from Mozilla), the Chrome browser (developed by Google), or the native browsers from Apple (Safari) and Microsoft (Internet Explorer and Edge)? And how do these new standards translate into the browsers available on the iOS, Android, and other mobile platforms?

- How can browsers be programmed so that video and interactive content no longer requires a helper application, such as Adobe Flash, but can function natively within the browser?

After a lot of work by the W3C, new HTML standards were finally released and almost all the standards were accepted for use in the web browsers that were available on desktop computers, tablets, and smartphones. The new HTML standards were to become known as HTML5, and the new CSS standards were given the name CSS3.

These new coding standards addressed the issue of HTML tag compatibility. Instead of leaving things up to individual designers to name a `<div>` with the `id` of `header` and style against those properties, new tags such as `<container>`, `<header>`, `<section>`, and `<article>` and many others were agreed to and became available as new browser versions were released.

These additional HTML tags and CSS specifications made it easier to tackle the other problem of how to scale and reformat a web page so that the experience of viewing on a phone is satisfying to the end user and allows access to the information or entertainment they're after. As of today, two methods of accomplishing this are available, and both are supported by Dreamweaver:

- Responsive design (sometimes called fluid design) lets you write conditional statements known as *media queries* into a document. Media queries are written into the CSS rules for a web page so that when the size of the screen changes, new styling rules are used to position and even hide certain parts of the page. In a responsive design, all the content of the page is loaded into the browser and CSS determines how the content is presented.

- Mobile design also uses HTML5 but takes things a lot further by using a framework of standard CSS rules along with a JavaScript library that actually reformats the content that is visible to the end user on the fly. This allows for much lighter web pages and provides a user experience that is similar to what you would see in a native app built for your device. One accepted framework is the jQuery Mobile JavaScript library and the Bootstrap collection of CSS styling rules. Dreamweaver supports this design environment, as do many other web programming applications.

Dreamweaver provides you with an excellent starting point for learning about these two design methods, with built-in starter pages for both. In the projects you'll tackle in this chapter, you'll see both design methods in action and learn how to provide access to multimedia and animations using the new HTML5 and CSS3 standards. Responsive design and mobile design are two skills that you'll want to develop if you're serious about becoming a web designer, and Dreamweaver provides an entry point into this world.

▶ **Video 7.2**
*Part 1: Exploring
Responsive Design
with Media Queries*

▶ **Video 7.3**
*Part 2: Exploring
Responsive Design
with Media Queries*

PROJECT 7.1

Exploring Responsive Design with Media Queries

In the projects you complete in this chapter, you won't be working toward a final design prototype. In a typical design environment, you would create your design compositions in Photoshop and then translate the design into HTML and CSS. But when your client has only an inkling of an idea of what they want, it's not unusual to dig around and determine what kind of work you'll need to do. Proof-of-concept design exercises let you make a more educated estimate of the time it will take to do the work and of the cost involved in getting the work done.

Examining Client Requirements

In the site files for this chapter, you'll find instructions, in the document named `wulvs-collectibles-concept.rtf`, from Chris the cartoonist on how he wants to get into mobile development. Open that file and review very carefully what your client is asking you to do.

You're really lucky. Chris is a designer too—he understands that new work costs money, and he's not asking you to build something for free. Many clients are likely to add new requirements without taking a look at the cost involved. This kind of project creep—where new work is tacked on with the expectation that the designer will do the job for little or nothing (and have it done immediately!)—is all too common. You should always avoid project creep (also known as scope creep) by discussing with the client the time and resources needed to add new work to a project and be clear with them as to the cost and time involved.

In a situation like this—where no budget has been established and you need to calculate the cost involved in a development project—you'll need to begin by considering what resources you have and the time required to assemble and organize what it will take to meet the client's requirements. Don't make the mistake of thinking of resources as just the client's images and the copy that's been written. *Time* is the single most critical resource you have as a designer, and calculating the time required to complete a job is also central to the project development process.

The most critical requirement you'll find in the client's document is his desire to get into responsive design by developing a prototype that will display on devices at all sizes. To do this (and to learn more about media queries and the Dreamweaver work environment), you'll turn to the starter templates that Dreamweaver provides.

Creating a New Responsive Design Page

To learn about the design interface found in Dreamweaver and the programming methods used in a fluid design, you need to have a page to work with. Dreamweaver provides the resources you need to create this page in the New Document dialog.

1   With the Files panel open in Dreamweaver and Chapter 7 active, right-click the site folder at the top of the panel and select New Folder.

2   Name the folder **responsive** and press Enter/Return.

3   Choose File > New to open the New Document dialog.

4   Select the Starter Templates category, the Responsive Starters sample folder, and the About Page template, as you see in **Figure 7.2**. Click Create.

    Dreamweaver will prompt you to save the file.

Select the Starter Templates category   **Choose Responsive Starters**   **Select the "About page" starter file**

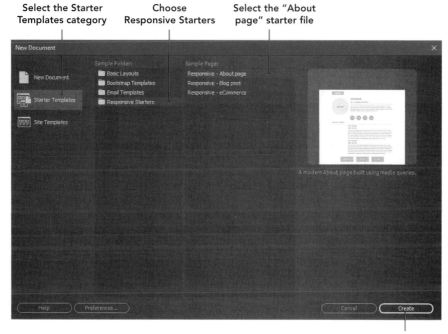

Figure 7.2 The New Document dialog allows you to create new pages from the starter files that Dreamweaver includes.

Click to create the new document

NOTE

There is a known bug on macOS systems in which the system and folder names are the same. If you are not prompted to save the file, choose File > Save As. See the note in the Dreamweaver online forum that discusses this issue: forums.adobe.com/ thread/1921852.pdf.

5 Select the `responsive` folder as the location in which to save the file, and name the file **index.html**. Click Save.

After you save the file, Dreamweaver automatically saves the related files to a folder `AboutPageAssets`. Open the Files panel and drag both the `images` and `styles` folders to the `responsive` folder. You will be prompted to update the links. Click the Update button, as you see in **Figure 7.3**. Make certain you also delete the now empty folder called `AboutPageAssets`.

Figure 7.3 Update the files that Dreamweaver provides and place them in the `responsive` folder you created.

Examining the Live View of a Responsive Design

When you move from a static page (like the one you built previously) to a fluid design (like the one you've just created), the difference between the Live view and the Design view in Dreamweaver becomes very apparent. When you work on a responsive design, you'll use the interface elements that the software provides in Live view to visualize the design.

1 Switch to Live view, verify you have the `index.html` file open, and take note of the different ways that Dreamweaver allows you to view this document.

Figure 7.4 lists the many ways that you can modify your view of the page to see how the media queries that are linked to the `aboutPageStyles.css` file cause the content in the page to flow and resize.

2 Examine each of the interface elements listed here, and become familiar with their use. You can expect to be asked to identify these areas of the Dreamweaver UI if you take the "Web Authoring with Adobe Dreamweaver" ACA exam.

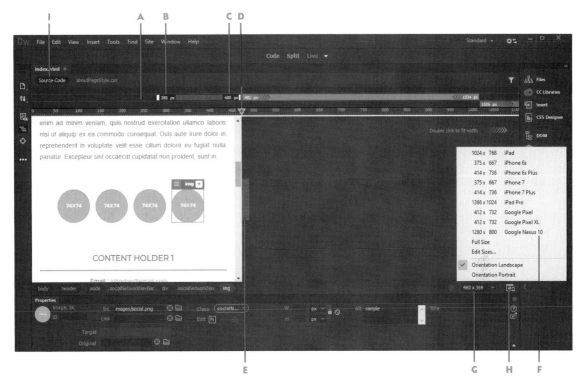

A **Media Query toolbar** displays the media query minimum and maximum widths as color-coded bars.

B **Media query minimum width** shows the smallest screen width supported with the query.

C **Media query maximum width** shows the largest screen width supported with the query.

D **Set new width breakpoint** by selecting the + icon. Dreamweaver will display new media query toolbars when this button is selected so that a new media query can be written to the CSS style sheet.

E **Scrubber handle** is used to manually drag the width of the page to new sizes.

F **Phone display presets** allow you to view the page at the width it would display on popular mobile phones.

G **Document view size** shows the dimensions that are currently being viewed. Click this button to display preset sizes to choose from.

Figure 7.4 You can use Dreamweaver interface elements to examine and visualize responsive page designs.

H **Device preview** allows you to see a live view of a design on a mobile device either by using the QR code reader on a device or through a URL that is provided when you click this button. Note that this feature will not work in many school and training lab settings unless students have an individual (paid) Creative Cloud subscription and their own Adobe ID.

I **Related files toolbar** shows the CSS file and other files linked to this page.

Examining Media Queries and HTML5 Tags

Media queries are conditional statements that are written into the body of a CSS style sheet. Media queries allow a web page to respond to the size of the screen by determining the screen size and using styling rules that are specific to those sizes. Understanding how media queries are written into a style sheet and how Dreamweaver allows you to access those styling rules is central to working in this kind of design environment. Let's examine the media queries that are in the attached style sheet for this page.

1. Right-click the `aboutPageStyles.css` file that is shown in the Related Files toolbar, and select Open as Separate File.

2. Examine the code and note how the different parts of the style sheet have been segmented, with comments starting with the `/* Global Styles */` section.

   The first media query is located after the `/* Media query for Mobile devices */` comment.

3. Take note of the syntax used for writing a media query.

   A media query begins with an @ symbol, followed by the condition that is being evaluated. These conditions can be listed one after the other to build a complete query, as you see in your code—where the first condition is set to check the media and then evaluate the minimum and maximum widths.

   Media queries are written with the same opening and closing curly braces as all CSS styling rules.

   ```
   @media only screen and (min-width : 285px) and
   →  (max-width : 480px) {
   }
   ```

4. Examine the closing tag for the first media query. You'll find the closing tag directly above the next media query comment, `/* Media Query for Tablets */`.

All the rules between the opening and closing media query braces—
color-coded in a green-blue by Dreamweaver—are used to define the properties of elements that should be displayed *differently* when the screen is viewed
at that size.

Dreamweaver displays the different queries that are present in the @Media section
of the CSS Designer panel (**Figure 7.5**). This allows you to select a particular media
query and see what selectors have been defined in those areas of the style sheet.

Add or delete
media queries

Media query
listing

Selectors
defined in the
media query

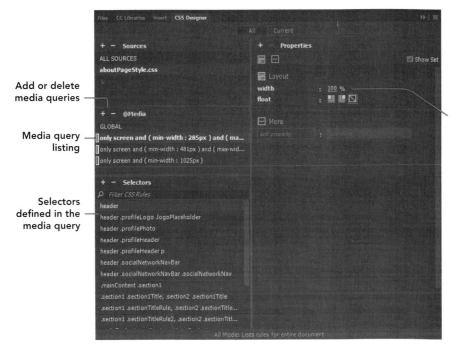

Figure 7.5 Media que-
ries and the styling rules
defined within them are
displayed in the CSS
Designer panel.

Properties of a
styling rule for a
media query

Creating a Responsive Prototype Page

Creating a prototype file from the client's request provides you with a good way to
get comfortable with this kind of design work. In the rest of this project, you'll be
given specific tasks to complete using the design tools that Dreamweaver provides.
With the skills you've developed, you're ready to accomplish these on your own.

With `index.html` open and the information provided for you in the file named
`wulvs-collectibles-concept.rtf`, complete the following tasks on your own:

TIP

Use the Browse for File button in the Property inspector to locate the image of the correct size to replace the ones in the starter page.

1 Change the document title to **Werewolves UnLimited Collectibles: Ray the Werewolf**.

2 Replace the placeholder images in the page with the cartoon characters provided for you in the `images` folder. For example, there are 74 x 74 pixel placeholder images. Replace these with the images that have `-small` in their name. You decide which image belongs where to replace each placeholder image. An example of the result is shown in **Figure 7.6**.

Figure 7.6 Styling the sample About page to show Ray the Werewolf. Note the different hover effect when the cursor moves over the images.

3 Add a page background image to the design by modifying the styling rule for the `<body>` tag.

4 Change the text in the `<h1>` tag at the top of the document to **Werewolves UnLimited Collectibles**. Choose and apply an appropriate font style and size for the text.

5 Style the `<header>`, `<footer>`, and `<section class="mainContent">` tags, and apply a background color that contrasts with the page background.

6 Examine the design as it appears at different widths. Remember that you can always reset your Standard workspace (in the event your tools look a bit different). Just go to Window > Workspace Layout > Reset Standard to see the typical Standard layout. You'll note that the text in the document is crowded against the edges of the container when viewed at a phone-size screen width. Determine the selector and the media query required to modify the padding property to improve the design.

7   Create a new styling rule within the existing media query to modify the prop-
    erties of the containers in which the text requires additional padding.

8   Examine the rollover effect that exists for the four small 74 x 74 pixel images
    that you replaced. Modify the selector that uses the `:hover` pseudo-class to
    create the rollover effect.

9   Replace the sample text that Dreamweaver provided with the text contained
    in the `wulvs-collectibles-concept.rtf` file. Add additional headings
    and other text as necessary to complete your prototype.

    Figure 7.6 depicts an example of how one might modify this page. Obviously,
    your version should differ significantly.

TIP

*Use the search function
in the Selector section
of the CSS Properties
panel to filter the rules
to show those that
include* `:hover` *in the
selector name.*

LEVEL UP: YOUR PERSONAL PORTFOLIO PAGE

This document provides you with a perfect opportunity to create your own
custom profile page. Using the techniques you learned here, you could
define a new Dreamweaver site and then use the New Page dialog to make
a new responsive design just like the one in this project. From there, you can
replace the images with ones of your own and build a personal portfolio that
describes who you are, what you've accomplished in your life, and what your
goals are for the future. That gives you the chance to continue building your
coding skills while reflecting on how you might want to present yourself to a
future employer or client.

★ ACA Objective 1.4

★ ACA Objective 1.5

★ ACA Objective 2.1

★ ACA Objective 2.4

★ ACA Objective 3.2

★ ACA Objective 4.1

★ ACA Objective 4.4

PROJECT 7.2

Exploring Responsive Design with jQuery and Bootstrap

You've now seen the first of the common methods for creating responsive web pages. In the second mobile development environment supported natively by Dreamweaver, the way that the page is coded for mobile viewing is fundamentally different. In a jQuery workflow, a JavaScript file is used to query—or evaluate—the size and orientation of the screen. Using the standard library of functions developed and published as a free and open source resource, jQuery quickly became the world's most popular JavaScript library. Many other JavaScript libraries are available today. We focus on jQuery since it is included with the current release of Dreamweaver. You may want to investigate other libraries once you are comfortable with the fundamentals.

▶ *Video 7.4*
Exploring
Responsive Design
with jQuery and
Bootstrap

The companion library that works right alongside jQuery in Dreamweaver is found in the styling rules created and supported in another open source project, by the good people at Twitter. The Bootstrap CSS file that comes included with Dreamweaver is massive, with over 6000 lines of code. That central Bootstrap style sheet provides access to a set of standardized visual properties but also allows Dreamweaver to provide you with components that can be inserted via the Insert panel or Insert menu.

The cool thing about both of these libraries is the tremendous number of people around the world who now use them and contribute to their future success. Hey, that could be you someday! Many of these phenomenal coding achievements—and many others—were unlocked by people who are your age or just a little older.

The jQuery and Bootstrap development world is supported by thousands of tutorials and other online resources—not to mention entire books and video series—and you can find all sorts of open contributions and ongoing discussions on the best way to take advantage of the power of these tools.

In this project, you'll create a new page using the starter pages that come with Dreamweaver, examine the code that makes jQuery development possible, see how to override Bootstrap styling properties, and determine what resources you'd need to take a proof-of-concept file into production.

Creating a New Bootstrap Design Page

Just as with the responsive starter page you just worked on, Dreamweaver provides all the resources you need to create a new web page that uses jQuery and Bootstrap components in the New File dialog.

1 With the Files panel open in Dreamweaver and Chapter 7 active, right-click the site folder at the top of the panel, and select New Folder.

2 Name the folder **bootstrap** and press Enter/Return.

3 Choose File > New to open the New Document dialog.

4 Select the Starter Templates category, the Bootstrap Templates sample folder, and the Bootstrap-Product page template. Click Create to make the new page, as you see in **Figure 7.7**.

   Dreamweaver will prompt you to save the file.

Select the Starter   Choose Bootstrap   Select the Bootstrap-Product
Templates category   Templates   page starter file

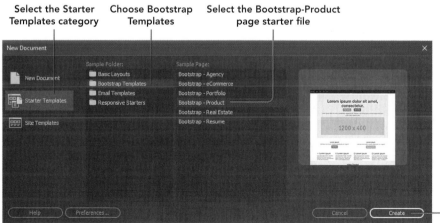

Figure 7.7 The New Document dialog allows you to create new pages from the starter files that Dreamweaver includes.

Click to create the new document

5   Select the **bootstrap** folder as the location in which to save the file, and name the file **index.html**. Click Save.

6   After you save the file, move the `css`, `images`, and `js` folders into the `bootstrap` folder and update the links. If you don't see the folders right away, you can click the Refresh button in the Files panel (lower-left corner of the panel). If you receive a message that the Bootstrap CSS file is locked, you can always leave the files and folders in their current location. We focus on the contents in this project.

Examining Bootstrap and jQuery Components in Dreamweaver

After you save the new document and copy the related files to your local site, you'll be able to examine the page and all the component and related files that Dreamweaver provides. Take a moment to become familiar with how Dreamweaver displays this page and the tools you can use when working in this environment. **Figure 7.8** shows the major elements of the Bootstrap and jQuery toolset that Dreamweaver provides.

1   Switch to Live view, and note the files listed in the Related Files toolbar.

     You will see a link to the single **bootstrap-4.0.0.css** file that Dreamweaver provides as well as links to other JavaScript files linked to this page.

2   Open the **bootstrap-4.0.0.css** file, and note how some elements in this design have been styled using the standard Bootstrap styles. These design properties are intended to provide a standard starting point for styling a page. The **bootstrap-4.0.0.css** file may be locked. We won't be making any changes to this file (it is okay to leave it locked).

3   Click the **jquery-3.2.1.min.js** file listed in the Related Files toolbar. (Your file version number might be slightly different.)

     You'll find a version of this JavaScript file that has been minified by removing all the line breaks and white space in the code to make it as compact as possible.

Although this file is meant only for your computer to read, there's still plenty that you can learn about how jQuery works by visiting the home page for the project at *jquery.com*, where you'll find tutorials, sample files, and a community of developers working to make the most of what jQuery provides.

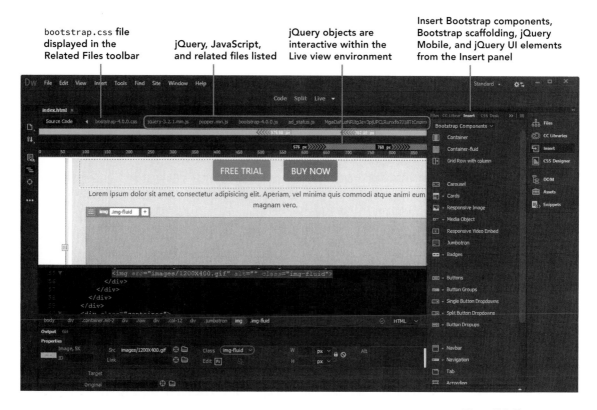

bootstrap.css file displayed in the Related Files toolbar

jQuery, JavaScript, and related files listed

jQuery objects are interactive within the Live view environment

Insert Bootstrap components, Bootstrap scaffolding, jQuery Mobile, and jQuery UI elements from the Insert panel

Figure 7.8 The major user interface controls that you'll use when working with jQuery and Bootstrap in Dreamweaver

jQuery and jQuery Mobile components are fundamentally different from media queries in how they provide a different size and appearance for design elements within a responsive design. Although media queries change the display properties of items that are already in the document, the programming behind jQuery allows those components to change on the fly. As the screen size changes, the conditional variables written into the JavaScript files present the appropriate version of the component. You can enable the Live Code view using the button on the Document toolbar to see how the code is rewritten when jQuery components are activated. You can click different media queries (such as the smartphone view) to see this in action.

Dreamweaver provides numerous jQuery components that can be accessed from two categories in the Insert panel: jQuery Mobile and jQuery UI. From those panels you can insert any number of prebuilt jQuery widgets, including accordion menus, date pickers, password fields, and many more.

Using Live View to Modify Bootstrap Properties

Although the Bootstrap CSS file contains many styled elements, you're certainly not limited to those styles. You can create your own CSS file and override these styles.

Select the button labeled Free Trial just below the banner text. You may find that you need to select the <a> tag in Split view used on this object to select it properly. Your screen should match **Figure 7.9**.

Because a standard set of named classes are in place in the Bootstrap CSS file, you do not have to touch any of the styling properties.

Is the Live view user interface perfect? Well, no, the Live view interface in Dreamweaver is still a little buggy, and you may find that in this version it can be difficult to navigate and select items in a logical way. But Adobe is still actively improving the performance of Dreamweaver and in particular tinkering with Live view. It may be that the next version of Dreamweaver makes things much better.

Figure 7.9 Dreamweaver uses a heads-up display to indicate the classes applied to an object.

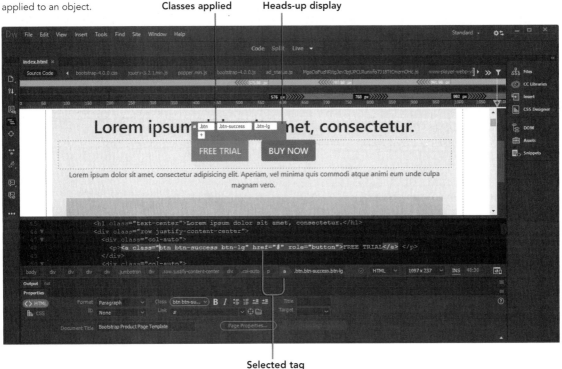

Classes applied   Heads-up display

Selected tag

Creating a Custom CSS File to Override the Bootstrap Settings

It would be a very dull world indeed if all web pages had to look like the default Bootstrap template. To change the design of a page or the components in the page, a custom CSS file is required. This file is used to hold alternate classes and custom CSS selectors that will be displayed in place of the Bootstrap selector properties.

1 You can continue working on the current file.

   To override the Bootstrap styling rules, a new CSS file with new selector settings will need to be created.

2 Position the scrubber so that the + indicator appears in the Media Queries toolbar, as you see in **Figure 7.10**.

Figure 7.10 Dreamweaver allows you to add new media queries and set their width properties in the Media Queries toolbar.

Click to add a new media query

3 Click the + to add a new media query. When you do so, a pop-up window will appear.

4 You will need to choose `min-width` from the dropdown to set the minimum width value to **250 px**. You need to choose `max-width` from the dropdown to set the maximum width value to **767 px**. Leave the setting Create a New CSS File as it is. Click OK when your settings match those in **Figure 7.11**.

   You will now be prompted to create and save the new CSS file.

5 Click the Browse button, set the file location to the same folder where the Bootstrap CSS file is located, and name the file **custom.css**. Click the Save button in your Explorer or Finder window to save the file. Don't forget to click OK to confirm.

Figure 7.11 The minimum and maximum widths of a new media query can be set in the pop-up window that Dreamweaver displays.

6   The CSS Designer panel now displays the two source CSS files linked to this document, as you see in **Figure 7.12**.

It is important that the `custom.css` file follow the `bootstrap-4.0.0.css` file in the source order. Browsers interpret the last setting they encounter. Your custom settings will be applied only if they come after the Bootstrap file. If the `custom.css` file is above the `bootstrap-4.0.0.css` file, drag it beneath.

Figure 7.12 Dream-weaver displays the two CSS files in the Sources section and the new media query dimensions.

`custom.css` **is after** `bootstrap-4.0.0.css`

New media query

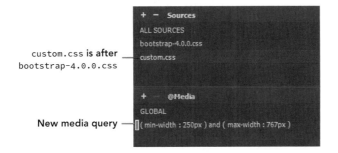

Applying Override Settings in a Custom CSS File

Once your custom CSS file has been created, you can set about creating new selectors that will override the Bootstrap settings. Remember that you aren't changing the Bootstrap source file in any way. You are merely writing new styling rules that the browser will display *instead of* those found in the Bootstrap file.

1   Select the link that defines the Free Trial button. You may need to go into the code to ensure that this tag is selected.

```
<a class="btn btn-success btn-lg" href="#" role="button">
```

2   You can use the CSS Designer panel to evaluate the existing settings by setting the panel to show the Current setting. Then select the Show Set check box and scroll through the list of styling rules. You are only investigating at this point, not writing new styling rules.

3   The rule you are searching for is the one that applies padding to the button container. This rule is contained in the `.btn` selector.

4   Switch the CSS Designer panel to the All setting, then select the `custom.css` file in the Source section and the media query listed in the @Media section, as you see in **Figure 7.13**.

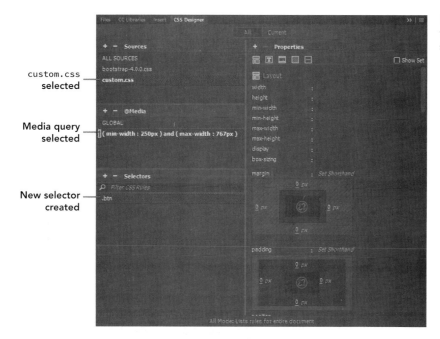

custom.css selected

Media query selected

New selector created

Figure 7.13 Preparing to override a Bootstrap styling rule

5   Click the + in the Selectors section, and filter the results down until you see the `.btn` class listed. Press Enter/Return to create the `.btn` class selector.

6   Apply new padding settings to all four dimensions until the button becomes smaller. Remember that a button on a phone still needs to be selectable by using a finger, so don't make them too small. It is recommended that at least 44 pixels square be available for a button on a phone. The Free Trial and Buy Now buttons should be vertical in phone view.

7   Scrub the page width to phone size, and confirm that the button is sized reasonably.

Once your design looks satisfactory to you and you've checked it at various screen sizes, your work on this exploratory mission is complete.

8   As always, you should save your HTML file and the new `custom.css` file you've been modifying.

In this project, you've had an opportunity to see just how to work in a design environment that includes all three of the modern web design methods that are rapidly gaining ground around the world. In combining HTML5, CSS3, jQuery JavaScript files, and Bootstrap CSS components, much has changed in how responsive web pages are built.

LEVEL UP: BROWSER DEVELOPER TOOLS

Dreamweaver certainly has a wealth of different ways to visualize and edit a design, but even with all the different panels and inspectors and interface widgets that are included, sometimes it's easier to inspect a design using the very cool inspectors that come built into almost all modern browsers. Mozilla Firefox, Google Chrome, Microsoft Edge, and Apple's Safari browser developer tools do a great job of allowing you to see the DOM structure of a page, look at the CSS styling properties that are applied, and view your design at various sizes. You'll likely decide on your own favorite, but in all those browsers, you can start up the page inspector by right-clicking any web page and choosing Inspect, or Inspect Element (depending on the browser).

Inserting HTML5 Video

★ *ACA Objective 1.5*

★ *ACA Objective 4.1*

★ *ACA Objective 4.2*

Our next stop on this exploratory mission into HTML5 is the `<video>` tag that was released as part of this HTML specification.

 **Video 7.5** *Inserting HTML5 Video*

While most modern browsers support the MP4 format, the encoding technologies behind the MP4 file format belong to any number of copyright and patent holders. Big companies currently pay licensing fees to build encoders like the one you'll find in Adobe Premiere Pro, but that runs contrary to the more open nature of the web. So new video formats have been developed to address the openness of web video formats. Google is the leading proponent of the WebM format, and others continue to push for a third format, known as Ogg Vorbis.

Dreamweaver's solution? Use all three files when you insert HTML5. And with a little bit of advance preparation, it's a snap to add HTML5 video to a web page.

Examining the Video Assets

The project files for Chapter 7 include a folder named `video`, where you'll find the resources that are required to insert HTML5 video into this page. Since there are some very specific requirements that you'll need to meet to make the process of placing video onto a page, let's start by taking a look at the files provided.

1   Open the Files panel for Chapter 7, and expand the `video` folder, as you see in **Figure 7.14**.

2   Identify the three video files included for this project.

These files have identical filenames but different file extensions.

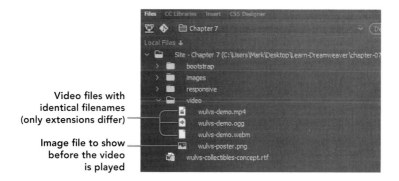

Figure 7.14 Files required for HTML5 videos

Video files with identical filenames (only extensions differ)

Image file to show before the video is played

Some variation still exists in which browsers support different video file types. All three video types are required to be universally compatible with all the web browsers in use.

The MP4 file format is compatible with most web browsers and should be the first one listed so that video displays properly on iOS devices. MP4 files are the first ones to be processed in most productions, and they must use H.264 video encoding. That encoding format option is present in the Adobe Media Encoder that comes included with the Creative Cloud desktop applications.

The two additional videos are created by converting an MP4 source file to the WebM and Ogg file types. There are many online file converter services where you can upload your files for conversion, or you can use a free software program such as VLC Media Player to convert the file to different file types. In a commercial production environment, the individuals who are producing the videos would take on this task and hand the files off to the web team for inclusion in a project.

For this project, that work has been done for you on a short sample video.

3   Identify the image file included for this project, `wulvs-poster.png`.

A poster image will be displayed in the area of the page where the video is inserted before the viewer of the page plays the video. This file has been prepared at the same pixel dimensions as the video itself, allowing for a seamless transition between the static view of the video and how it appears when it begins playing.

Inserting HTML5 Video

The starter page that you're working with already contains a video that was placed into the document by way of an embed code that points to a YouTube video. In many settings, it's preferable to have videos hosted on a dedicated server rather than using the YouTube servers.

1   Open the `index.html` file that is located in the **bootstrap** folder. You can make a new page following the steps at the beginning of Project 7.2 if you need a fresh version of this file.

2   Switch to Design view, and scroll down the page until you locate the Video Tutorial section. Select the video object contained within the `<iframe>` tag. Switch to Split view to ensure that the `<iframe>` tag is selected.

3   Press Delete to remove the embedded video.

4   Directly in the code, add placeholder text inside the `<div>` tag that reads **video here**. This is done simply to make it easier to see the location of the `<div>` where the new video will go. Click the Refresh button in the Property inspector.

5   Highlight the placeholder text, and open the Insert panel. In the HTML category, click the HTML5 Video button near the bottom of the panel.

This action will remove the placeholder text and replace it with the `<video>` tag. The Property inspector displays all the settings for this tag.

6   Click the Browse icon next to the Poster setting, as you see in **Figure 7.15**. Browse to the `wulvs-poster.png` file (in the video folder), and set it as the image source. This will establish a width and height for the video player.

7   Click the Browse for File icon next to the Source setting. Browse to the `wulvs-demo.mp4` file, and set that as the primary source file to be played.

When you perform this action, Dreamweaver will automatically populate the Alt Source fields with the other videos, provided they are in the same location and have the same filename as the primary source.

8   In the Title field, give the video the title **WULVS Collectibles video**.

9   Set the Preload value to `metadata`.

This allows the browser to load a description of the video and other information before the video is ready to play. You can also have the entire video pre-load, but this may cause the page to load slowly and should be tested prior to putting that setting into production.

10 Review the settings, as shown in Figure 7.15, and then save your file. You have now completed this mission.

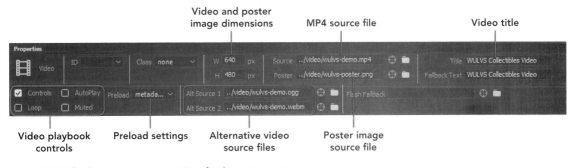

Figure 7.15 The Property inspector settings for the `<video>` tag

The actual process of inserting HTML5 video is quite easy as long as you understand that the majority of the work has to take place before you turn to Dreamweaver. This involves creating, formatting, and converting video files into the three file types in use. At least for now. Web standards and practices are shifting, and in the future you may see that one of the open source video formats will replace the MP4 format as the standard for delivering video on the web. But for now, you can see just how this video will be displayed on different devices by changing your view of the page. In a responsive design, the video and poster image will scale up and down as the page size changes, giving end users exactly the kind of experience they expect.

Exploring CSS3 Animation

★ ACA Objective 1.5

★ ACA Objective 3.2

★ ACA Objective 4.2

★ ACA Objective 4.3

You've likely seen CSS3 animations in action in your daily web surfing, whether you knew it or not. CSS3 animations and transitions are used routinely to display animated flyout menus, rollover effects that reveal more information, and animations that ease images in and out of a container.

▶ **Video 7.6**
*Exploring CSS3
Animation*

Adobe provides Animate CC to enable complex animations and interactions. You can insert an animated composition from the Insert panel.

You should also be able to read and understand CSS styling rules including animations, as you will likely encounter them in sites you are asked to maintain (or create).

You need to have an understanding of how CSS animations are created and the theory behind the code if you want to edit or modify code that's been written by someone else.

In this project, you'll create a very simple animation in Dreamweaver and see how the structure of the HTML comes together with the animation methods available in CSS3.

Creating the Animation Page and Containers

In this project, you'll be working to understand the principles behind CSS3 animation, and you'll need only a simple web page to see animations in action.

1   In the Chapter 7 Files panel, right-click the site folder, and choose New Folder. Name the folder **animation**.

2   Choose File > New to create a new page. In the New Document dialog, set the category to New Document and the document type to HTML. Set the document title to **Ray's Animated Card**.

   With Framework set to None and Doc Type set to HTML5, click the Create button to make the new page.

3   Save the page in the `animation` folder, and name it **index.html**.

4   Set the view of the document to Live/Split, and place your cursor directly after the opening `<body>` tag. Press Enter/Return to create a new line in the code.

The way that the `<div>` tags are nested in this instance is very important, and it's often difficult to get Dreamweaver to nest elements properly in Live view. Working directly in the code is preferable in cases like this.

5   Insert the following code block between the opening and closing `<body>` tags:

```
<div class="card">
<div class="infobox">
<p>Ray the Werewolf</p>
<p>President & CEO</p>
</div>
</div>
```

The classes applied to the `<div>` tags will be used to assign styling properties to the image and to the box that contains the information about the character.

6   In the code, place your cursor after the `<div class="card">` tag.

7   Use the Assets panel to insert the character image by browsing to `images/ray-profile-photo.png`. Note that the size of the image is 212px by 257px. You'll use the width and height values for setting styling properties later.

8   Enter the alt description **Ray the werewolf** for the image, and save your file.

Styling the Card Container

With the structure of the HTML determined, you can now set about styling the elements of this design using the same methods you've used in the past to create new selectors in the CSS Designer panel.

1   In the CSS Designer panel, click the + in the Sources section. Choose Define in Page to insert a `<style>` tag block into the head of the document.

2   Select the `<div class="card">` tag in the code or by using the Tag selector.

3   In the CSS Designer panel, click the + in the Selectors section to create a rule. Dreamweaver will automatically name the selector `.card`.

4   In the Layout category of the CSS Designer panel, set the width and height to match the image dimensions of the image that you noted in step 7 of the previous section: `212px` width and `257px` height.

5   Set the Position property to `relative`.

6   In the More category, click inside the Add Property field, and type **cursor**. Press Enter/Return to assign the property to the class, and then select Pointer from the options provided.

7   Add a second property in the More category by typing **overflow**. Choose Hidden from the options available. Your settings should now match those you see in **Figure 7.16**.

More category selected

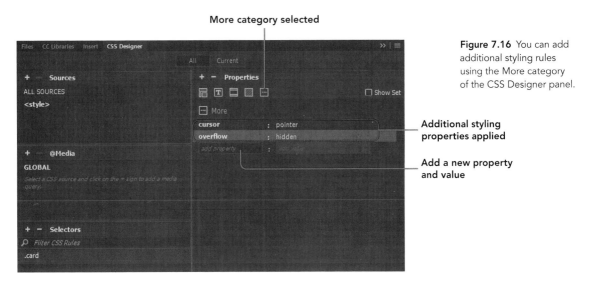

Figure 7.16 You can add additional styling rules using the More category of the CSS Designer panel.

Additional styling properties applied

Add a new property and value

Styling the Image Container

Next, you'll style the <img> tag to fix the size of that container and set a position property that will allow the box with the character's information to appear over the top of it.

1   Select the <img> tag in the Tag selectors or directly in the code.

2   Click the + in the Selectors section of the CSS Designer panel to create a selector. Set the new selector name to .card img, and press Enter/Return.

3   In the Layout category, set the Position property to absolute and the left position to 0px.

Styling the Information Box Container

Now you can turn your attention to the `<div>` that contains the information that will appear when the cursor is placed over the image. In these steps, you'll create a new styling rule to define this container.

1 In the Tag selector or directly in the code, select the `<div class="infobox">` tag.

2 Click the + in the Selectors section of the CSS Designer panel to create a selector with the name `.card .infobox`.

3 Use the Background category of the CSS Designer panel to set a medium gray background color for the selector.

4 Use the Layout category to assign an `absolute` position to the selector and to assign width and height values that match the dimensions of the image.

5 In the More category, add a new property by typing **z-index** into the New Property field. Set the value of this property to **100**. This will set a stacking order that places the contents of this container above the image.

When you've finished adding these properties, the contents of the `<div>` with a class of `.infobox` will cover the image. Just as expected! Refer to Video 7.6 to see the effect.

Styling the Information Box Text

The final styling rules will be used to set properties for the text that is inside the `.infobox` container. The name and title of the character are contained within paragraph tags that you'll now style against.

1 Select either of the paragraph tags in the document.

2 Click the + in the Selectors section of the CSS Designer panel, and accept the suggested selector name of `.card .infobox p`.

3 In the Text category, set the color of the text to white and set `text-align` to `center`.

You can assign different styling properties to the text as you choose, using padding and font properties to position and style the text. Note that the text is under the image, so you won't see it yet.

4 Save your file.

Styling Animations with CSS Transitions

Now that all the containers and their styling properties are in place, you can begin animating the interaction that occurs when the cursor is positioned over the image. First, you'll hide the container with the character's information and then set a CSS hover pseudo-class to reveal the `<div>`.

1   In the CSS Designer panel, select the `.card .infobox` selector.

2   Using the Layout category, add an opacity setting of **0** to the selector.

The container will disappear from view as it becomes transparent. All the code and information inside the container is still present, but using CSS you've just hidden it from view.

In Dreamweaver, animations can be added and edited in the CSS Transitions panel.

3   Choose Window > CSS Transitions to open the CSS Transitions panel.

4   Click the + at the top of the panel to open the New Transition dialog that you see in **Figure 7.17**.

5   From the Target Rule drop-down menu, select the `.card .infobox` selector.

6   Set the Transition On setting to `hover`.

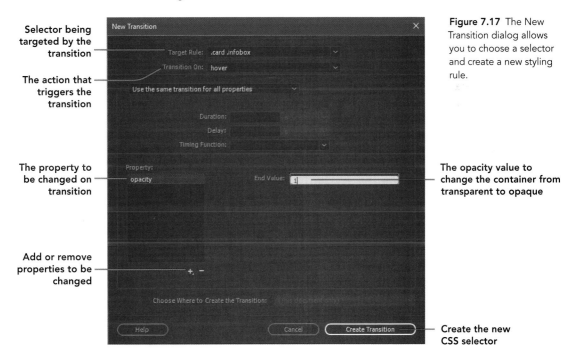

Selector being targeted by the transition ⎯

The action that triggers the transition ⎯

The property to be changed on transition ⎯

Add or remove properties to be changed ⎯

Figure 7.17 The New Transition dialog allows you to choose a selector and create a new styling rule.

The opacity value to change the container from transparent to opaque

Create the new CSS selector

7 Click the + in the Property section, and choose opacity. Set the End Value to **1**, and then click Create Transition.

When you place your cursor over the image in Live view, you'll see the information in the `.infobox` `<div>` tag come leaping into view. Move your mouse away and the box instantly disappears. That's all a little too abrupt, but you can add additional transition properties to smooth things out.

In the event your animation does not appear correctly, the likely culprit is the nesting order in your HTML. Be sure your code matches the block you see here:

```
<div class="card"><img src="../images/
⟶ ray-profile-photo.png" width="212" height="257"
⟶ alt="Ray"/>
<div class="infobox">
<p>Ray the Werewolf</p>
<p>President and CEO</p>
</div>
</div>
```

8 In the CSS Transition panel, click the `hover` property, and click the Pencil icon to reopen the Edit Transition dialog, as you see in **Figure 7.18**.

Open the Edit
Transition dialog

Select the property
to be edited

Set the amount
of time that the
transition will occur

Set the time the
animation should wait
until the transition
occurs

Preset easing
functions

Save the new CSS
selector settings

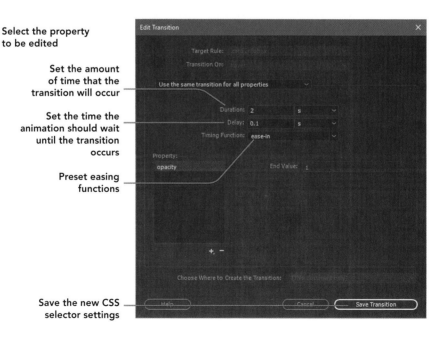

Figure 7.18 Applying timing, delay, and easing functions in the Edit Transition dialog

9 Set the Duration value to 2 s, Delay to .1 s, and Timing Function to ease-in. When your settings match those in Figure 7.18, click Save Transition.

Now when you place your mouse over the image, the animation will appear over the course of 2 seconds instead of immediately. You'll also see that the animation is delayed slightly and that as the box appears it gently speeds up.

10 Save your file now, and turn back to the CSS that Dreamweaver has created for you.

In the style sheet, you'll find the following code block that defines the transition that is to take place. Because of differences in how browsers implement CSS transitions, Dreamweaver has inserted three separate sets of properties and values to cover all three.

```
.card .infobox {
    background-color: #B9B8B8;
    position: absolute;
    width: 212px;
    height: 257px;
    z-index: 100;
    opacity: 0;
    -webkit-transition: all 2s ease-in .1s;
    -o-transition: all 2s ease-in .1s;
    transition: all 2s ease-in .1s;
}
```

11 Now locate the trigger that has been created using the hover pseudo-class. For this new selector that Dreamweaver created, only two sets of properties and values are required.

```
.card .infobox:hover {
    -webkit-opacity: 1;
    opacity: 1;
}
```

You've now created a very simple animation using nothing but CSS transitions, and you should have a good understanding of how these kinds of effects are achieved. Obviously, there is much more that could be done with this animation. You could, for instance, modify the position of an object by setting transitioning from one position value to another. But fundamentally this is how CSS animations are created. You define the containers that hold the elements on the page, apply the initial values that they should have, and then animate against those settings by setting a new value to take effect when something happens on the page. Although you may not use Dreamweaver for creating animations, turning instead to another application, you now know the theory behind CSS3 animations and how the programming is written to take advantage of these functions.

LEVEL UP: MOBILE APP DEVELOPMENT

One question that hasn't been answered is whether you could build a phone app using Dreamweaver. And the answer is yes. Dreamweaver can be used along with a free service from Adobe, PhoneGap (*phonegap.com/developer*), to turn an entire website into a native application for iPhones, Android phones, and the tablets that use those operating systems.

There are some things you'll need if you want to investigate how the PhoneGap service works. First, you'll need an Adobe ID. (You don't need a paid subscription to Creative Cloud to upload files to create an app.) You'll also need the desktop application for Windows and Macintosh, and you'll need to get the free PhoneGap app for your device on the Apple App Store, Google Play, or Windows Phone Store. With all of those things, you can read through the documentation and discover how you can create simulated phone apps on your computer and then instantly view them on your phone.

Of course, there's much more that would have to be done to package and send a completed app from your computer for distribution. But Adobe has done a great deal to promote the workflow that allows developers to use their design tools, like Dreamweaver, to publish mobile apps of all kinds.

Your Final Challenge (a New Client)

As you close your look at Dreamweaver and prepare to dig further into the creative process and workflow in the coming chapters, you should be keeping an eye on ways that you can use your new skills to develop websites of your own. Whether you design something purely for yourself, such as a digital portfolio or résumé site, or you volunteer to build a website for a nonprofit or religious organization, or you decide to start up your own company and take on real clients, at this point in your transition from web design student to web design professional you should be working with the software as much as you possibly can. As with any skill, it will take hours of practice before you become proficient, and your challenge now is to spend as much time as you can coding, designing, and building websites in Dreamweaver.

When you are ready to test your skills, visit *hideous.design*. Phineas Hideous has a landscaping business and is in need of serious help with his website. Review the site and begin developing a document outlining what changes need to be made to the site. If you were to meet with this client, what questions might you ask of him? What changes would you recommend be completed as soon as possible? What changes can wait, but will eventually need to be made? Use the knowledge you have learned in working with Chris the cartoonist to level up your skills in working with this new client.

Conclusion

In this chapter, you've dipped your toes into the world of responsive design and learned a great deal about how the interface in Dreamweaver is used to work on sites that feature media queries, jQuery and Bootstrap components, HTML5 video, and CSS3 animations. You've seen how to create documents in Dreamweaver that already include many of the components required for a responsive design environment, and you should have a better understanding of the work required to design with these new methods.

And even though it seemed at times that you were just noodling around and discovering what you need to do to meet a client's mobile design requirements, you've actually gathered a lot of valuable information that could be used to prepare a time and cost estimate for your client.

You now have the fundamental knowledge and skills to use Dreamweaver as a tool to develop and modify websites. You are on your way to becoming a web professional.

ACA Objectives Covered

DOMAIN OBJECTIVES	CHAPTER	VIDEO
DOMAIN 1.0 Working in the Web Industry		
1.1 Identify the purpose, audience, and audience needs for a website.	**Ch 3** Project 3.1, Translating Client Project Requirements, 72 **Ch 7** Project 7.1, Exploring Responsive Design with Media Queries, 228 **Ch 9** Who You're Talking For and Who You're Talking To, 9-3 **Ch 9** Ideal Ivan and Danielle Demographic, 9-6 **Ch 9** The Language of Web Project Management, 9-28	**3.1** Translating Requirements into Structure **7.2** Part 1: Exploring Responsive Design with Media Queries **7.3** Part 2: Exploring Responsive Design with Media Queries
1.1a Determine whether content is relevant to the purpose, audience, and audience needs.	**Ch 3** Project 3.1, Translating Client Project Requirements, 72	**3.1** Translating Requirements into Structure
1.2 Communicate with colleagues and clients throughout the project.	**Ch 3** Project 3.2, Modifying Page Properties, 77	**3.2** Modifying Page Properties
1.2a Demonstrate knowledge of techniques for communicating ideas about expected outcomes with peers and clients.	**Ch 3** Project 3.4, Adding Content Containers and Attributes, 91	**3.4** Adding Content Containers and Attributes
1.2b Demonstrate knowledge of basic project management concepts.	**Ch 3** Project 3.2, Modifying Page Properties, 77	**3.2** Modifying Page Properties
1.3 Determine an understanding of the type of permissions required to use specific content.	**Ch 4** Project 4.1, Prototyping and Designing with Background Images, 113 **Ch 4** Project 4.2, Inserting and Editing Images, 125 **Ch 9** Copyrights and Wrongs, 9-9 **Ch 9** The Language of Web Project Management, 9-28	**4.1** Client Feedback **4.2** Prototyping and Faux Column Layout **4.3** Designing with Background Images **4.4** Image Preferences **4.5** Inserting Images Using the Assets Panel **4.6** Inserting Photoshop Source File
1.3a Identify legal and ethical considerations for using third-party assets such as copywritten, trademarked, and licensed content.	**Ch 9** Copyrights and Wrongs, 9-9	

DOMAIN OBJECTIVES	CHAPTER	VIDEO
1.3b Identify when and how to obtain permissions in order to use code and content.	**Ch 9** Copyrights and Wrongs, 9-9	
1.4 Demonstrate an understanding of key terminology related to web design and development.	**Ch 1** Project 1.1, Create Your First Dreamweaver Website, 21 **Ch 9** Feedback Loop, 9-26	
1.4a Demonstrate fundamental knowledge of internet technology.	**Ch 1** Project 1.2, Under the Hood—Examining Code in a Web Page, 26	**1.2** How the Internet Works **1.5** Understanding the Structure of Websites **1.11** Under the Hood—Examining Code in a Web Page **1.12** Challenge! Customize the Starter Page and Make It Your Own
1.4b Demonstrate fundamental knowledge of search engines and search engine optimization.	**Ch 4** Project 4.3, Floating Images into Position, 134 **Ch4** Project 4.4, Creating Structured Layouts with Images, 139	**4.8** Accessible Images **4.9** Creating Structured Layouts with Images
1.4c Demonstrate fundamental knowledge of web security concepts.	**Ch 5** Project 5.4, Building and Designing Interactive Forms, 178	**5.6** Building Interactive Forms
1.4d Demonstrate knowledge of key web development concepts.	**Ch 1** World Wide What, 4	**1.2** How the Internet Works
1.5 Demonstrate knowledge of basic design principles and best practices employed in the industry.	**Ch 4** Project 4.1, Prototyping and Designing with Background Images, 113 **Ch 4** Project 4.4, Creating Structured Layouts with Images, 139 **Ch 4** Project 4.5, Styling the Header Area, 148 **Ch 7** Project 7.1, Exploring Responsive Design with Media Queries, 228	**4.1** Client Feedback **4.2** Prototyping and Faux Column Layout **4.3** Designing with Background Images **4.9** Creating Structured Layouts with Images **4.10** Rules and Guides **4.11** Part 1: Styling the Header Area **4.12** Part 2: Styling the Header Area **7.2** Part 1: Exploring Responsive Design with Media Queries **7.3** Part 2: Exploring Responsive Design with Media Queries

continues on next page

continued from previous page

DOMAIN OBJECTIVES	CHAPTER	VIDEO
1.5 Demonstrate knowledge of basic design principles and best practices employed in the industry. *(continued)*	**Ch 8** The Design Hierarchy, 8-5 **Ch 8** The Elements of Art, 8-10 **Ch 8** The Element of Color, 8-24 **Ch 8** The Element of Type, 8-29 **Ch 8** The Principles of Design, 8-37	**8.1** Design School: Introduction **8.3** Design School: The Design Hierarchy **8.4** Design School: The Elements of Art **8.11** Design School: The Element of Color **8.13** Design School: The Principles of Design **8.12** Design School: The Element of Type
DOMAIN 2.0 Project Setup and Interface		
2.1 Create a new site with the appropriate settings.	**Ch 1** Project 1.1, Create Your First Dreamweaver Website, 21 **Ch 2** Define the Chapter 2 Website, 45	**2.1** A Quick Tour of the Dreamweaver Workspace **2.2** The Dreamweaver Document Window **2.3** The Property Inspector
2.1a Set appropriate options for defining a new site.	**Ch 2** Define the Chapter 2 Website, 45	**2.1** A Quick Tour of the Dreamweaver Workspace
2.1b Create a new page for specific project needs.	**Ch 6** Project 6.2, Building Out the Site with Dreamweaver Templates, 203	**6.3, 6.4** Building Out the Site with Dreamweaver Templates
2.2 Navigate, organize, and customize the application workspace.	**Ch 2** Project 3.3, Setting Font Formats and Links, 84	**2.1** A Quick Tour of the Dreamweaver Workspace **2.3** The Property Inspector **2.4** Panel Groups in Dreamweaver **3.3** Setting Font Formats and Links
2.2a Identify and manipulate elements of the Dreamweaver interface.	**Ch 2** Dreamweaver Workspace Overview, 46	**2.3** The Property Inspector
2.2b Organize and customize the workspace.	**Ch 2** Dreamweaver Workspace Overview, 46	**2.4** Panel Groups in Dreamweaver
2.2c Configure application preferences.	**Ch 4** Level Up: Dreamweaver Preferences, 125	

DOMAIN OBJECTIVES	CHAPTER	VIDEO
2.3 Use non-visible design tools in the interface to aid in project workflow.	**Ch 4** Using images in page backgrounds, 119 **Ch 7** Project 7.1, Exploring Responsive Design with Media Queries, 228 **Ch 7** Project 7.2, Exploring Responsive Design with jQuery and Bootstrap, 236	**4.3** Designing with background images **7.2** Part 1: Exploring Responsive Design with Media Queries **7.3** Part 2: Exploring Responsive Design with Media Queries **7.4** Exploring Responsive Design with jQuery and Bootstrap
2.3a Configure content viewing options.	**Ch 4** Using Images in Page Backgrounds, 119	**4.3** Designing with Background Images
2.3b Navigate a site.	**Ch 3** Follow That File, 90	
2.4 Manage assets in a project.	**Ch 3** Project 3.2, Modifying Page Properties, 77 **Ch 4** Project 4.1, Prototyping and Designing with Background Images, 113 **Ch 4** Project 4.2, Inserting and Editing Images, 125 **Ch 5** Project 5.1, Styling the Navigation Sidebar, 157 **Ch 5** Project 5.4, Building and Designing Interactive Forms, 178 **Ch 6** Project 6.1, Putting the Style Sheet into Production, 197 **Ch 6** Project 6.2, Building Out the Site with Dreamweaver Templates, 203 **Ch 6** Project 6.3, Adding Optional Content with Library items, 210	**3.2** Modifying Page Properties **4.1** Client Feedback **4.2** Prototyping and Faux Column Layout **4.3** Designing with Background Images **4.4** Image Preferences **4.5** Inserting Images Using the Assets Panel **4.6** Inserting Photoshop Source Files **5.1** Styling the Navigation Sidebar **5.6** Building Interactive Forms **5.7** Styling Interactive Forms **6.1** CSS Review **6.2** Putting the Style Sheet into Production **6.3** Part 1: Building Out the Site with Dreamweaver Templates **6.4** Part 2: Building Out the Site with Dreamweaver Templates **6.5** Adding Optional Content with Library Items
2.4a Add and organize assets.	**Ch 2** Using the Assets Panel, 64	**2.7** The Assets Panel
2.4b Configure assets in a project.	**Ch 6** Synchronizing Local and Remote Files, 220	**6.6, 6.7** Publishing and Updating a Dreamweaver Site

continues on next page

continued from previous page

DOMAIN OBJECTIVES	CHAPTER	VIDEO
DOMAIN 3.0 Organizing Content on a Page		
3.1 Use the DOM panel to organize page structure.	**Ch 3** Inserting <div> Tags in Dreamweaver, 93	**3.4** Adding Content Containers and Attributes
3.1a View, edit, and manage the structure of a page.	**Ch 3** Project 3.3, Setting Font Formats and Links, 84	**3.3** Setting Font Formats and Links
3.2 Apply responsive and adaptive design concepts.	**Ch 7** Understanding HTML5, CSS3, and Responsive Design, 225	**7.1** Exploring Responsive Design with HTML5
DOMAIN 4.0 Working with Code to Create and Modify Content		
4.1 Organize and display content using HTML.	**Ch 1** Tag: You're It, 8	**1.3** Tag, You're It
4.1a Identify the appropriate use of <html>, <head>, <body>, and <div> tags.	**Ch 1** Tag: You're It, 8	**1.3** Tag, You're It
4.1b Differentiate between block and inline elements.	**Ch 6** Types of Style Sheets, 195	
4.1c Format content using headings, paragraphs, and lists.	**Ch 3** Working With Text and Text Formats, 84	**3.3** Setting Font Formats and Links
4.1d Insert and manipulate images, video, and sound, and animation.	**Ch 3** Project 3.1, Translating Client Project Requirements, 72	**3.1** Translating Client Requirements into Structure
4.1e Create, manage, and edit hyperlinks.	**Ch 3** Creating Hyperlinks, 89	**3.3** Setting Font Formats and Links
4.2 Apply semantic elements to describe content.	**Ch 5** Project 5.3, Styling Structured Data, 172	**5.5** Styling Structured Data
4.2a Display and organize information using tables.	**Ch 5** Project 5.3, Styling Structured Data, 172	**5.5** Styling Structured Data
4.2b Display and organize information using other basic semantic elements.	**Ch 7** Creating a Responsive Prototype Page, 233 **Ch 6** Project 6.2, Building Out the Site with Dreamweaver Templates, 260	**7.3** Exploring Responsive Design with Media Queries **6.3** Part 1: Building Out the Site with Dreamweaver Templates **6.4** Part 2: Building Out the Site with Dreamweaver Templates
4.3 Style a web page using CSS.	**Ch 4** Styling the Content Containers, 144	**4.9** Creating Structured Layouts with Images

DOMAIN OBJECTIVES	CHAPTER	VIDEO
4.3a Configure initial page properties.	**Ch 3** Adding Content to a Web Page and Setting Basic Properties, 79	**3.2** Modifying Page Properties
4.3b Manage fonts.	**Ch 4** Styling the Company Name with Fonts, 150	**4.2** Styling the Header Area
4.3c Create and manage CSS rules using the CSS Designer panel.	**Ch 4** Inserting and Floating the Header Images, 148 **Ch 4** Styling the Company Name with Fonts, 150	**4.12** Styling the Header Area
4.3d Create and use inline styles, internal styles, and external style sheets.	**Ch 6** Reviewing CSS Syntax, 195	**6.1** CSS Review
4.3e Create and modify selectors that reference specific HTML elements.	**Ch 6** Project 6.1, Putting the Style Sheet into Production, 197	**6.2** Putting the Style Sheet into Production
4.3f Apply common CSS declarations.	**Ch 4** Project 4.1, Prototyping and Designing with Background Images, 113	**4.1** Client Feedback **4.2** Prototyping and Faux Column Layout **4.3** Designing with Background Images
4.3g Organize a web page layout with relative and absolutely positioned div tags and CSS styles.	**Ch 7** Styling the Information Box Container, 252	**7.6** Exploring CSS3 Animations
4.4 Add interactivity using JavaScript.	**Ch 7** Project 7.2, Exploring Responsive Design with jQuery and Bootstrap, 236	**7.4** Exploring Responsive Design with jQuery and Bootstrap
4.4a Create and manage forms.	**Ch 5** Project 5.4 Building and Designing Interactive Forms, 178	**5.6** Building Interactive Forms **5.7** Styling Interactive Forms
4.4b Add interactivity to a web page.	**Ch 7** Project 7.2, Exploring Responsive Design with jQuery and Bootstrap, 236	**7.4** Exploring Responsive Design with jQuery and Bootstrap

continues on next page

continued from previous page

DOMAIN OBJECTIVES	CHAPTER	VIDEO
DOMAIN 5.0 Publishing Digital Media		
5.1 Prepare project for publishing.	**Ch 4** Project 4.3, Floating Images into Position, 134 **Ch 7** Project 7.1, Exploring Responsive Design with Media Queries, 228 **Ch 7** Project 7.2, Exploring Responsive Design with jQuery and Bootstrap, 236 **Ch 7** Project 7.3, Inserting HTML5 Video, 245 **Chaper 7** Project 7.4, Exploring CSS3 Animation, 249	**4.7** Floating Images into Position **4.8** Accessible Images **7.2** Part 1: Exploring Responsive Design with Media Queries **7.3** Part 2: Exploring Responsive Design with Media Queries **7.4** Exploring Responsive Design with jQuery and Bootstrap **7.5** Inserting HTML5 Video **7.6** Exploring CSS3 Animation
5.1a Set up for testing and publishing.	**Ch 6** Project 6.4 Publishing and Updating a Dreamweaver Site, 216	**6.6, 6.7** Publishing and Updating a Dreamweaver Site
5.1b Check project for errors and project specifications.	**Ch 5** Clean Up Your Code, 189 **Ch 7** Project 7.2, Exploring Responsive Design with jQuery and Bootstrap, 236 **Ch 9** The Language of Web Project Management, 9-28	**5.10** Finalizing the Prototype for Production **7.4** Exploring Responsive Design with jQuery and Bootstrap
5.2 Publish a website.	**Ch 6** Project 6.4 Publishing and Updating a Dreamweaver Site, 216	**6.6, 6.7** Publishing and Updating a Dreamweaver Site
5.2a Save web pages.	**Ch 1** Project 1.2 Under the Hood—Examining Code in a Web Page, 26	**1.11** Under the Hood—Examining Code in a Web Page
5.2b Publish a live site.	**Ch 6** Project 6.4 Publishing and Updating a Dreamweaver Site, 216	**6.6** Part 1: Publishing and Updating a Dreamweaver Site **6.7** Part 2: Publishing and Updating a Dreamweaver Site

Glossary

absolute links Links to a website outside the current site. For example, *http://adobe.com.*

absolute positioning Used to place objects on the page at precise X and Y coordinates. The X coordinates measure an element's position from the left side of the page, whereas Y coordinates measure an element's location from the top of the page.

accessibility The practice of removing barriers that prevent access to website interaction and information by people with disabilities.

action A response triggered by an event initiated by the viewer of a web page, such as rolling the mouse pointer across an image.

active A hyperlink that is currently selected by a viewer of a web page.

additive color Created by combining light.

address The unique location of an individual web page on the Internet. *See* Universal Resource Locator (URL).

alignment Indicates how the lines are aligned on the right and left edges, such as left, centered, and right.

all caps Uses only uppercase letterforms for each letter.

alternative text Additional information that is displayed when an image is loading or when the viewer is using a screen-reading device.

anchors Navigational elements of a web page that allow the viewer to jump to a particular point on the page.

animated GIF An image file that plays a series of frames, creating the illusion of movement.

analogous Colors that are side by side on the color wheel. They create gentle and relaxing color schemes.

analytics The process of collecting and analyzing data about a website's visitors for the purposes of improving site performance.

aspect ratio The proportional relationship between the width and height of an image. Written as 16:9, 4:3, and so on.

asymmetrical Achieves balance with different elements with different weights on each side (or the top and bottom) of an image.

attribute Named properties that assign additional information to an HTML tag.

attribution Written acknowledgment provided with the name of the original copyright holder of the work. Creative Commons and other licenses feature different kinds of attribution requirements.

balance Evenly distributed, but not necessarily centered or mirrored.

bandwidth The rate of data transfer, bit rate, or throughput, measured in bits per second (bps).

baseline An imaginary line used to organize text along a horizontal plane.

bitmaps Images created on a computer screen using discrete bits of individual colors.

blackletter fonts Also known as Old English, Gothic, or Textura. Feature an overly ornate style. Convey a feeling of rich and sophisticated gravitas.

Bootstrap A popular open source library of HTML, CSS, and JavaScript used to build web page layouts and components.

box model The CSS box model refers to the box that wraps around individual HTML elements. Each box consists of margins, borders, padding, and the actual content.

browser A computer application used to access and view web pages stored on the World Wide Web.

Cascading Style Sheets (CSS) Coded instructions to a web browser describing how elements of HTML are to be styled or displayed.

cast shadow The shadow cast on the ground and on any objects that are in the shadow of the form. Shadows fade as they get farther from the form casting the shadow.

chaotic lines Look like scribbles and feel unpredictable and frantic. Convey a sense of urgency, fear, or explosive energy.

check in Marking a file as available for others to work on.

check out Locking a file to prevent others from working on it.

child selector A CSS attribute that immediately follows a "parent" selector, as in `tr:nth-child(even)`.

class selectors CSS styling rules targeted at class names assigned to elements in the page. May be used multiple times in a document.

client The software and computer device used to access information on a remote server.

client-side programming Programming that runs on a client computer and that is written in a language, such as JavaScript, that can be executed by the browser.

client survey (interview) The process used at the beginning of project planning to determine the customer's objectives for a website and the requirements and resources available.

Code Navigator The Dreamweaver pop-up display that allows you to view all the styling properties applied to an object on the page.

color The perceived hue, lightness, and saturation of an object or light.

color harmonies Color rules that are named for their relative locations on the color wheel.

complementary Colors that are opposite each other on the color wheel. They are high in contrast and vibrant.

contrast Creates visual interest and a focal point in a composition. It is what draws the eye to the focal point.

Creative Commons Ways that artists can release their works for limited use and still choose the way the works are used and shared: Public Domain, Attribution, ShareAlike, NoDerivs, and NonCommercial.

CSS Designer panel The Dreamweaver panel that displays the source, media queries, selectors, and properties of a CSS style sheet.

CSS box model *See* box model.

curved (line) Expresses fluidity, beauty, and grace.

database Structured data stored on a remote server that allows for dynamic data on a client device.

declaration block The styling properties to be applied to a particular selector as determined by the CSS rule.

decorative fonts Also known as ornamental, novelty, or display fonts. They don't fall into any of the other categories of fonts. Convey a specific feeling.

deliverables A predetermined list of items that will be delivered to the customer.

deprecated A technique or code designated as obsolete.

descendent selectors The descendent selector matches all elements that are descendants of a specified element.

design comp A digital image that shows all the design details of a project. Typically used for client reviews.

design elements The building blocks of art defined by artists to provide a framework for creating art.

design principles The essential rules or assembly instructions for art.

diagonal (lines) Lines traveling on neither a vertical nor a horizontal path. Express growth or decline and imply movement or change.

dingbat fonts Also known as wingdings. They are a collection of objects and shapes instead of letters.

direction A common way to describe lines, such as vertical, horizontal, diagonal.

Document Object Model (DOM) Defines the logical structure of the HTML in a web page.

Document toolbar The Dreamweaver UI element that displays buttons to toggle between Live, Design, and Code views and access other inspectors for visualizing a page.

document tree A method for visualizing the relationship between computer files and folders.

Document type <!doctype> The first element of an HTML document. Used to declare to a web browser the version of HTML the page is written in.

domain name server An Internet service that translates domain names to IP addresses.

domain name The portion of the Internet registered to a particular company, organization, or individual, such as *microsoft.com*, *adobe.com*, and *google.com*.

dynamic website A website that uses a database and web programming, such as PHP, to provide live interactions with client computers.

element selectors CSS rules that target elements of the page by the tag used to define them.

element styles *See* element selectors.

elements of art The building blocks of creative works. They are the "nouns" of design, such as space, line, shape, form, texture, value, color, and type.

emphasis Describes the focal point to which the eye is naturally and initially drawn in a design.

encoding The process of converting a digital file from one format to another. Usually used when referring to the preparation of digital video files.

external CSS file *See* external style sheet.

external style sheet A separate document containing CSS styling rules that is linked to an HTML page.

fair use A set of rules that specify how and when copyrighted material can be used and that make sure copyright protection doesn't come at the cost of creativity and freedom.

feedback loop A system set up to continually encourage and require input and approval on a project's direction.

file extension The three- or four-letter designator that follows a filename and that specifies which program can use the file, such as .png, .jpg, and .html.

File Transfer Protocol (FTP) The networking standard that allows files to be transferred from a client to a remote server.

file weight The amount of data that must be downloaded from a web server in order to display a page. This includes the HTML, images, scripts, and all other assets required for the page to display.

Files panel The Dreamweaver panel that allows you to view, open, edit, and perform server interactions with the folders and files in a website.

flow A category related to the energy conveyed by lines and shapes.

focal point What the design is all about. The call to action or the primary message you are trying to get across.

font family A CSS styling rule that allows you to list a set of fonts to be used when styling text. Allows for a "fallback" if one or more fonts are not present on the client device.

font weight CSS styling property that determines how thick or thin the text characters should be.

fonts The whole collection of a typeface in each of its sizes and styles.

form Describes three-dimensional objects, such as spheres, cubes, and pyramids.

framework A set of computer rules, procedures, and standardized programming methods.

geometric (lines) Tend to be straight and have sharp angles. Look man-made and intentional. Communicate strength, power, and precision.

geometric shapes Predictable and consistent shapes, such as circles, squares, triangles, and stars. They are rarely found in nature and convey mechanical and manufactured impressions.

get The Dreamweaver term for copying a file from a remote server to a local computer.

Git A free and open source version control system—sort of a time machine for data—that allows files to be copied, moved, renamed, and deleted, all while maintaining backups through the entire process.

glyph Each character of a font, whether it is a letter, number, symbol, or swash.

group selectors A CSS selector rule that is written to assign the same properties to more than one tag, as in `h1, p`.

hand-drawn lines Appear as though created using traditional techniques, such as paints, charcoal, or chalk.

handwritten fonts Also known as hand fonts, they simulate handwriting.

head (head of the document) The area of a web page enclosed by the <head></head> tags. Used for storing instructions to the browser that are not visible in the page, such as metadata and links to external files.

hexadecimal The six-digit code used to define colors on a web page, such as #F0F0F0.

highlight The area of a form that is directly facing the light and that appears lightest.

horizontal Moving from left to right; for example, the horizontal line in an "H." Expresses calmness and balance.

horizontal scale Describes the function of stretching letters and distorting the typeface geometry.

HTML5 The current version of the web language used to mark up and display documents on the World Wide Web. HTLM5 contains new specifications for embedding page divisions, graphics, audio, video, and interactive documents.

hyperlink A word or picture in a web page that allows the viewer of the page to go to a different location when it is clicked or tapped.

Hypertext Markup Language (HTML) The web programming language used to mark up and display documents on the World Wide Web.

Hypertext Transfer Protocol (HTTP) The underlying set of communication rules, or protocols, that allow web servers to transfer information to and from client devices on the World Wide Web.

hyphenation Determines if and when words should be split with hyphens when wrapping to the next line.

ID selectors CSS styling rules targeted at an element that has a named identifier (ID).

ideographs (ideograms) Images that represent an idea, such as a heart representing love.

image map An image in which some portion of the graphic contains a hotspot that contains a hyperlink.

implied lines Lines that don't really exist but are implied by shapes, such as dotted or dashed lines, people waiting in lines, or the margins of a block of text.

indent Settings that determine how far an entire paragraph is indented from the rest of the text on each side or in just its first line.

information architecture The methods used to structure and organize computer data.

inline style A type of CSS styling that is contained directly inside a tag, such as `<span style="color: #AC1316">`.

internal style sheet CSS styles that are written inside the `<head>` of a document used for styling on that single page.

Internet Protocol (IP) The coding rules that govern how data is sent over the Internet or other networks.

IP address A unique string of numbers separated by periods (version 4) or colons (version 6) that identifies each computer attached to the Internet.

iterations New versions of a design that successively become closer to the desired result.

iterative work Work that is shared as it is completed, allowing the customer to chime in with comments while it is still easy to make a change.

JavaScript A scripting language for adding interactive elements to a web page. JavaScript is based on ECMAScript (European Computer Manufacturers Association).

JavaScript library A set of preprogrammed JavaScript functions for adding interactions, animations, and other common tasks to a web page.

jQuery Mobile The JavaScript library that uses CSS selectors to access and manipulate HTML elements on a web page.

justified Aligns text to a straight edge on both the right and left edges of a paragraph.

kerning The space between specific letter pairs.

leading The amount of space between the baselines of two lines of text.

library item An element within a site that is available for reuse and automated updating using the Dreamweaver Assets panel.

licensing A way to legally use copyrighted material for a certain time and in a certain way, usually associated with paying a fee established by the copyright holder.

ligatures Special characters used to represent letter combinations such as "fi."

light source The perceived location of the lighting in relation to the form.

line A mark with a beginning and an end point.

linting The program that examines computer code for potential errors as it is being written.

Live view The Dreamweaver view of a document that mimics how the page will display when viewed in a web browser or mobile device.

media queries CSS styling rules that allow a page to adapt to different screen sizes and orientations. Also used for creating print and other versions of web pages.

metadata Information that is included in a document but is hidden, such as copyright, lens information, location via GPS, camera settings, and more.

minified Computer code that has been optimized by removing all unnecessary characters and spacing without changing its functionality.

model release The permission that is required when a person's face is identifiable in a photo and the image will be used to promote something—whether it's a product or an idea.

monochromatic Different shades and tints of the same color. Communicates a relaxed and peaceful feeling.

monospaced fonts Fixed-width or non-proportional fonts that use the same amount of horizontal space for each letter.

movement Visual movement within an image, such as the natural tracking of the eye across an image as the eye moves from focal point to focal point.

negative space Blank areas in a design. Also known as white space.

NoDerivs (ND) Creative Commons licensing. Requires that you not change material when you incorporate it into your own work. It can be used freely, but you must pass it along without change.

NonCommercial (NC) Creative Commons licensing. Means you can use work in your own creative work as long as you don't charge for it.

object shadow The area of the form that is facing away from the light source and appears darkest.

open source Source code that is freely available for modification or enhancement by anyone.

optimization The process of choosing a file type and compression settings to provide the smallest file sizes possible while maintaining quality.

organic lines Lines that are usually irregular and imperfect. Found in nature.

organic shapes Are random or generated by something natural. They are usually asymmetric and convey natural, homemade, or relaxed feelings.

page title The name of the web page that is seen in the title bar of the browser and in web search results.

paragraph settings Affect an entire paragraph rather than selected words. These settings include alignment, hyphenation, and so on.

paragraph spacing Similar to leading, but applies to an entire paragraph instead of lines of type within them. Also includes the spacing above or below paragraphs.

path A sequence of symbols and letters that indicates the name and location of a computer file, as in `C:\My Documents\MyFile.doc`.

pattern A repetitive sequence of different colors, shapes, or values.

pictograph (pictogram) Graphic symbol that represents something in the real world. Computer icons are pictographs that suggest the function they represent, such as a trash can icon to delete a file.

primary colors Red, blue, and green. These can be combined to create every other color in the visible spectrum.

project creep Unplanned changes that increase the amount of work, or scope, that a project requires. When the project loses focus and spins out of control, eating up more and more time and effort.

project deadline Dictates when work needs to be completed.

project scope Outlines the amount and type of work to be completed.

Property inspector The contextual Dreamweaver panel that is located below the Document window; used to display and edit the properties of a selected element on the page.

proportion (scale) Describes the relative size and scale of elements.

protocol Computer programming and communication rules.

pseudo-class selectors Keywords added to selectors; specify a special state of the element to be selected when an action occurs on the page, such as a mouse pointer rolling over a link.

public domain Creative Commons licensing. When copyright is expired or released and no longer applies to the content or when an artist releases their work. It can be used without worrying about infringement.

put The Dreamweaver term for copying a file from a local computer to a remote server.

radial Circular type of balance that radiates from the center of a design.

reflected highlight Area of a form that is lit by reflections from the ground or other objects in a scene.

related files Files that are linked to a document. Displayed in Dreamweaver's Related Files toolbar.

repetition Repeating an element in a design.

representative shapes Shapes used to represent information. They are helpful in communicating with multicultural and multilingual audiences.

RGB Red, green, blue color values used to write color specifications into CSS styling rules.

rhythm Creative and expressive, rather than a consistent pattern or repetition in a design.

root folder The highest folder in the structure of a website. All the files and folders for a site are located in this folder. Also called the site folder.

round trip The process by which an image can be associated with a source application, such as Photoshop, so that it can be opened and edited from within Dreamweaver.

rule of thirds A technique for laying out the space of your page to provide a focal point. Two vertical and two horizontal lines evenly divide the space into nine equal boxes, as in a tic-tac-toe board.

sans serif fonts Text without serifs. Often used for headlines and titles for their strong, stable, modern feel.

scale *See* proportion.

script fonts Mimic handwriting. They convey a feeling of beauty, grace, or feminine dignity.

secondary colors Created when you combine primary colors.

serif fonts Associated with fonts created by typewriters. They convey tradition, intelligence, and class.

server A computer with special software that allows data to be transferred back and forth to a client computer or device.

shape An area enclosed or defined by an outline, such as circles, squares, triangles, or even clouds.

ShareAlike (SA) Creative Commons licensing. Allows you to use an item (design) in any way you want as long as your creation is shared under the same license as the original work.

sitemap A model of a website's content that shows the logical structure of the folders and files within the site. Also used as a navigational guide for viewers as well as a roadmap for search engines to discover and index.

sketches Representative drawings of how to lay out a document or web page. These are sometimes one of the deliverables of a project.

slab serif fonts Squared-off versions of a typical serif font. Also known as Egyptian, block serif, or square serif. Convey a machine-built feel.

small caps Uses only uppercase letterforms for each letter and appears in a smaller size.

space The canvas or working area. Its dimensions are determined by the resolution of the page you are creating.

specifications Detailed written goals and limits for a project. These are sometimes one of the deliverables of a project.

Split view The Dreamweaver view that splits the Document window into two panes in which the design and code for the page may be viewed at the same time.

static website A website that does not have a connection to a database but relies on the manual updating of content by a web designer.

stock photos Images for which the author retains copyright but for which a license for use is available.

storyboard A sketch of the initial design for a web page; includes the basic layout blocks of the page as well as specific information about colors, fonts, and other styling properties.

style (line) An effect applied to a line, such as varying width, hand-drawn, and implied.

subtractive color Created by subtracting light.

swashes Special characters with flowing and elegant endings for the ascenders and descenders.

symmetrical Occurs when you can divide an image along its middle, and the left side of the image is a mirror image of the right (or the top reflects the bottom). Conveys an intentional, formal, and mechanical feeling.

syntax Determines the rules to be followed when writing code. The spelling and grammar of a programming language.

tags The instructions written by the programmer (or generated by Dreamweaver or another web authoring program) that tell the browser what to do.

templates HTML pages that contain special code that allows certain portions of the page to remain the same on every page that uses the template, while other portions are available for editing.

tertiary colors Created by mixing primary and secondary colors.

texture Describes the actual tactile texture in real objects or the appearance of texture in a two-dimensional image.

tracking The overall space between all the letters in a block of text. It allows you to compress or expand the space between the letters as a whole rather than just between specific pairs, as you do with kerning.

type size A font's height from the highest ascender to the lowest descender.

typeface Specific letterform set, such as Helvetica, Arial, Garamond, and so on. It is the "look" of letters.

unity Also known as harmony and sharing similar traits. Low contrast. Things that go together should look like they belong together. The opposite of variety.

Universal Resource Locator (URL) The unique web address of pages and files located on the World Wide Web.

usability Describes how easy it is for users of a website to find information and interact with the site in a positive way.

value Describes the lightness or darkness of an object. Together with color, value represents the visible spectrum, such as a gradient.

variety High contrast. The opposite of unity.

varying width lines Expresses flow and grace.

vertical Moving from top to bottom. Vertical lines tend to express power and elevation.

vertical scale Describes the function of stretching letters and distorting the typeface geometry.

viewport The visible area of a web page when viewed on a computer, tablet, or mobile device.

web font A library of fonts stored on a remote server that may be displayed in a web page by using the `@font-face` rule. Browsers download the font from its hosted location, and then display the font as specified in the CSS styling rules.

website A collection of web pages, files, and links all associated with a unique name.

weight (line) The thickness of a line.

wireframe A schematic sketch of a website that shows how pages are connected and how users are expected to access information on the site.

World Wide Web (web) The portion of the Internet that supports HTML documents that feature links to other documents, as well as graphics, audio, and video files.

World Wide Web Consortium (W3C) The international organization for the World Wide Web. In addition to developing recommendations for web documents, it engages in outreach and education.

workspace layout The arrangement of panels and windows in the Dreamweaver work environment.

Index

C

card container, 250–251
Cascading Style Sheets. *See* CSS
challenge projects
    creating page comps, 106
    customizing the starter page, 37–40
    designing with Photoshop, 153
    testing your new skills, 257
`.characters` rule, 144–146
Check In/Check Out options, 52, 63
child selectors, 175, 196
Chris the Cartoonist project
    client resources, 78–79
    content containers, 91, 93–96
    described, 70, 110, 156
    design process, 77–78
    hyperlinks, 89–90
    page properties, 79–83
    planning process, 72–74
    project files, 71, 110, 156
    setting up, 71, 111, 156
    site structure, 74–76
    text formats, 84–88
    wireframes, 91–93
Chrome browser, 81, 190, 244
`class` attribute, 12
class selectors, 31, 196
    creating and applying, 134–135
    duplicating and applying, 136
    name convention for, 135
classes, 30
    caution on overusing, 149
    IDs distinguished from, 95
cleaning up
    code on web pages, 189–190
    tables from Word, 172–174
    web page designs, 188
Clear Column Widths button, 173
`clear` property, 134, 136–137
client computer, 6
client feedback, 113–115
code
    cleaning up, 189–190
    collapsing, 66, 95

    colored, 32, 33, 64, 65
    comparing, 208
    validating, 35–36
    viewing, 27–28
code font, x–xi
code hints, 65
Code Navigator, 66
Code view, 27, 48
Coding toolbar, 200
coding tools, 65–66
collapsing code, 66, 95
color
    background, 99, 168
    caution on using, 14
    sampling from images, 168
    text, 13
colored code, 32, 33, 64, 65
columns
    faux styling of, 117–118
    indicator for rows and, 53
    table width values for, 175
    See also rows
comments, 200
company name styling, 150–151
company tagline styling, 152
comparing code, 208
comps, design, 91, 92, 106
containers
    card, 250–251
    content, 91–96, 144–146
    floating images inside, 142–143
    image, 251
    information box, 252
Contrast tool, 130
conventions used in book, x
Creative Cloud desktop application, xii
Crop Image tool, 130
CSS (Cascading Style Sheets), 7
    animation styling, 253–256
    class selectors, 134–136
    elemental properties, 81–83
    `float` property, 134–137
    gradients, 123, 124
    media queries, 52

editors
    image, 125
    text, 9
    visual, 16
educator resources, xiv
element selectors, 82, 196
element styles, 30
elemental CSS properties, 81–83
`<em>` tag, 180
encoding, 246
error indicator, 54, 189
external CSS file, 51
external style sheets, 195
Eyedropper tool, 168

F

faux column technique, 116–118
file extensions, 17
file formats
    for images, 111–112
    for video, 245, 246
File Management button, 52
file management method, 130
File Transfer Protocol (FTP), 62
file weight, 112
filenames, 19, 80
files
    backing up, 116
    dependent, 218
    image, 111
    project, 23
    related, 51, 202
    synchronizing, 220–221
Files panel, 25, 62–63, 75, 128, 218–219
Find and Replace dialog, 173
Firefox browser, 81, 190, 244
fixed-width designs, 160
Flash Player, 226
Flick, Chris, 70
`float` property, 134–137
floating images, 32
    header area, 148–149
    inside containers, 142–143
    positioning by, 134–137

fluid design. *See* responsive design
folders
    organizing websites into, 18–19
    rules for naming, 19
    source files stored in, 130
font weight, 56
fonts, 50
    company name styled with, 150–151
    CSS styling properties for, 56
    fixing on web pages, 187–188
    for indicating code, x–xi
    setting formats for, 84
    web, 187
footers
    links in, 104–105
    styling, 102–103
`<form>` tag, 180
forms, 178–184
    adding function to, 182–183
    dropdown menu added to, 181–182
    inserting text from Word into, 179–180
    styling process for, 183–184
    text fields for, 180–181
forums, Adobe, xiii
framework, 227
FTP (File Transfer Protocol), 62

G

gaps, margin, 103–104
GIF image files, 111
Go to Code option, 169
Google Chrome browser, 81, 190, 244
gradients, background, 121, 122, 123–124
graphic design, 76
group selectors, 196
guides, 146–147

H

`<h1>` tag, 10, 30
H.264 video encoding, 246
head, page, 10
`<head>` tag, 10, 29

headers
    adding links in, 150
    inserting and floating images in, 148–149
    styling, 101–102, 148–152
headings, table, 175
Help & Support resources, xiii
hexadecimal code, 64
hints, code, 65
home page creation, 206–207
hover values, 170–171, 255
`href` value, 90
HTML (Hypertext Markup Language), 7, 8–10
    new standards introduced for, 226–227
    Property inspector for, 54–55
HTML5, 11
    inserting video using, 245–248
    new standards introduced with, 226–227
`<html>` tag, 9, 10
HTTP (Hypertext Transfer Protocol), 5
hyperlinks, 4
    adding, 164–165
    changing, 38–39
    creating, 89–90
    footer, 104–105
    header, 150
    mailto:, 179
    setting values for, 169–170
    text, 150
Hypertext Markup Language. *See* HTML
Hypertext Transfer Protocol (HTTP), 5

I

ID attribute, 55, 95
ID selectors, 196
`<iframe>` tag, 246
image container, 251
image editors, 125
image maps, 59
Image Optimization window, 131
images
    alternative text added to, 137–138
    backgrounds using, 119–122
    duplicating, 128–129

editing tools for, 59, 130
file formats for web, 111–112
floating, 134–138, 142–143
header area, 148–149
inserting, 126, 148–149, 161–162
listed in Assets panel, 64
optimization of, 112, 131
Photoshop edits of, 59, 131–133
Property inspector for, 58–59, 127
replacing on web pages, 40, 158–159
sampling colors from, 168
scaling and sizing, 58, 126–128, 129
structured layouts with, 139–147
tiling of background, 120–121
`<img>` tag, 11, 30, 162, 251
incremental backups, 116
Indent settings, 55
`index` home page, 17
information architecture, 74
information box container, 252
inline styles, 57, 195
Insert button, 64
Insert Div dialog, 141, 144
Insert Navigation dialog, 166, 167
Insert panel, 94, 166, 211
inserting
    `<div>` tags, 93–96, 141–142, 143–144
    editable regions, 204–205
    HTML5 video, 246–248
    images, 126, 148–149, 161–162
    library items, 215
    `<nav>` tags, 166–167
    text from Word, 179–180
installing Dreamweaver, xi
interactive forms. *See* forms
internal style sheets, 30, 195
Internet
    diagram of connections on, 6
    World Wide Web distinguished from, 4
Internet Explorer browser, 190
Internet Protocol (IP), 6
IP addresses, 6
iPhone, 53, 225–226, 256
    See also mobile devices

<title> tag, 10, 29
title attribute, 59
titles
    link, 55
    page, 38, 80, 207
tools
    coding, 65–66
    image editing, 59
<tr> tag, 172
transitions, CSS, 253–256

U

<ul> tag, 31, 55, 84–85
unordered lists, 55, 84–85
Update Files dialog, 230
updating
    Adobe software, xii
    files on remote server, 219–220
    library items, 215
URLs, 39, 64
usability, 74
user experience, 78
user interface, 46–66
    Document window, 48–54
    overview of elements in, 46–48
    panels and panel groups, 60–66
    Property inspector, 54–59

V

validating code, 35–36
video
    asset examination, 245–246
    inserting HTML5, 246–248
    See also animations
<video> tag, 245, 247
View menu, 28
view switcher, 48–51
views
    Property inspector, 59
    switching between, 48–51
visual editors, 16
visualization tools, 96
VLC Media Player, 246

W

W3C validator, 35, 36
wallpaper effect, 119
web browsers
    historical origin of, 4
    mobile devices and, 226
    page inspectors included in, 244
    previewing web pages in, 34, 52–53, 118, 190
    rendering engines for, 81
Web Edition of book, ix, xii–xiii
web fonts, 187
web pages
    customizing, 37–40
    design cleanup for, 188
    examining properties of, 29–35
    previewing in browsers, 34, 52–53, 118, 190
    replacing images on, 40, 158–159
    reviewing fonts on, 187–188
    rulers and guides for, 146–147
    templates for creating, 206–209
    viewing code in, 27–28
web server. See remote server
WebM video format, 245, 246
websites, 22
    change as constant for, 193
    site definition for, 23–25, 45–46
    static vs. dynamic, 16–17
    structure of, 16–19, 74–76
Welcome screen, 23
Window size option, 53
Windows computers, xi
wireframes, 91–93
Word documents. See Microsoft Word
workspace, 46–66
    customizing, 60–61
    Document window, 48–54
    overview of elements in, 46–48
    panels and panel groups, 60–66
    Property inspector, 54–59
workspace layout, 25, 60
World Wide Web (web), 4
World Wide Web Consortium (W3C), 10, 226
WYSIWYG web editors, 16